PARADOXES OF LABOUR REFORM

Chinese Worlds

Chinese Worlds publishes high-quality scholarship, research monographs, and source collections on Chinese history and society from 1900 in the 21st century.

'Worlds' signals the ethnic, cultural, and political multiformity and regional diversity of China, the cycles of unity and division through which China's modern history has passed, and recent research trends toward regional studies and local issues. It also signals that Chineseness is not contained within territorial borders – some migrant communities overseas are also 'Chinese Worlds'. Other ethnic Chinese communities throughout the world have evolved new identities that transcend Chineseness in its established senses. They too are covered by this series. The editors see them as part of a political, economic, social, and cultural continuum that spans the Chinese mainland, Taiwan, Hong Kong, Macau, South-East Asia, and the world.

The focus of Chinese Worlds is on modern politics and society and history. It includes both history in its broader sweep and specialist monographs on Chinese politics, anthropology, political economy, sociology, education, and the social-science aspects of culture and religions.

The Literary Field of Twentieth-Century China
Edited by *Michel Hockx*

Chinese Business in Malaysia
Accumulation, Ascendance, Accommodation
Edmund Terence Gomez

Internal and International Migration
Chinese Perspectives
Edited by *Frank N. Pieke* and *Hein Mallee*

Village Inc.
Chinese Rural Society in the 1990s
Edited by *Flemming Christiansen* and *Zhang Junzuo*

Chen Duxiu's Last Articles and Letters, 1937–1942
Edited and translated by *Gregor Benton*

Encyclopedia of the Chinese Overseas
Edited by *Lynn Pan*

New Fourth Army
Communist Resistance along the Yangtze and the Huai, 1938–1941
Gregor Benton

A Road is Made
Communism in Shanghai 1920–1927
Steve Smith

The Bolsheviks and the Chinese Revolution 1919–1927
Alexander Pantsov

Paradoxes of Labour Reform
Chinese Labour Theory and Practice from Socialism to Market
Luigi Tomba

Chinas Unlimited
Gregory Lee

Birth Control in China 1949–2000
Thomas Scharping

Confucian Capitalism
Yao Souchou

PARADOXES OF LABOUR REFORM

Chinese Labour Theory and Practice from Socialism to Market

Luigi Tomba

UNIVERSITY OF HAWAI'I PRESS
HONOLULU

Editorial Matter © 2002 Luigi Tomba

Published in North America by
University of Hawai'i Press
2840 Kolowalu Street
Honolulu, Hawai'i 96822

First published in the United Kingdom
by RoutledgeCurzon
11 New Fetter Lane
London EC4P 4EE
England

Printed in Great Britain

Library of Congress Cataloguing in Publication Data
A catalogue record for this book has been requested

ISBN 0-8248-2658-2

CONTENTS

CONTENTS

ACKNOWLEDGEMENTS

This book would not have been possible without the decisive help of many people and of several institutions. The 'Scuola Superiore di Studi Storici di San Marino' (Higher School of Historical Studies of San Marino) accepted my project and funded my studies in the years between 1993 and 1997, when the research work for this book was undertaken. G.G. Feltrinelli Foundation in Milan also offered some financial support to my research.

My gratitude goes to Tony Saich who accepted to act as my supervisor during the PhD that was the origin of this book and offered meaningful comments during the revision of my thesis for publication. Also, without his practical help (and the hospitality of his wife, Zeng Yinyin) my field visit in Beijing would have been impossible at a time when my 'budget constraints' were particularly difficult.

Some Chinese colleagues were both sources for my research and insightful advisors: Feng Lanrui, who had a great deal of stories to tell and a lot of experiences to share, Dai Yuanchen, Guo Shuqing, Zhao Shukai, Xiang Biao, Zhu Jianfang, Yuan Yue. I am also indebted to Steve McGurk for sharing with me his contacts in Beijing.

Thanks are due to Flemming Christiansen, Anita Chan, Enrica Collotti Pischel and Guido Samarani who offered suggestions on earlier drafts of this study and were always ready to share information on their own research, and to two anonymous readers whose suggestions contributed to this final version.

I am grateful to Nancy Hearst who agreed to spend her time and expertise to refine my English and my quotations.

Mine, of course, remains the responsibility for all mistakes and inaccuracies in the text.

I had the privilege to share this experience with many friends who have been valuable sources of encouragement. They will probably be relieved to know that this book goes to press. The heaviest burden was on Silvia's shoulders: thanks.

Finally, this work is dedicated to my parents.

1

LABOUR THEORY AND PRACTICE AND THE MAKING OF A MARKET

An Introduction

1.1 The Issue

What is labour? To what extent did the continuous yet contradictory evolution of theoretical understanding in this field affect the process of reform of existing socialism in China from the late 1970s to the early 1990s? Why is the theory of labour so intimately intertwined with the Chinese socialist policymaking process, and why did the ability of public policy to intervene as a regulatory tool in the reality of the labour economy diminish with the passing of time and with the emergence of new, different, and contending interpretations of the labour issue? To what extent is the evolution from a full-employment policy and full state-led allocation to labour market theory and practice the result of conscious policy options rather than merely of the 'retreat' of public intervention and the growing importance of 'market forces'? What does the word 'labour' mean at the end of this process and what purpose does this meaning serve?

Questions arise at the beginning of every research study. The questions I have listed above emerge from my difficulties in tackling separately the two streams of economic reform, that is, the political/theoretical debates resulting from political struggles and elite politics on the one hand, and the transformation of economic and social life in Chinese urban centres on the other.

The histories of theory and practice are generally kept separate, as they usually stem from different backgrounds and social circles, opposing or contradictory forces. This is impossible in the context of Chinese socialism. In the case of China, the claim to coordinate theory and praxis, thought and action, has been a challenge in the field of policy ever since the basic assumptions of all-embracing theories proved insufficient to address the social changes after the beginning of reform in 1978. The theoretical debate under socialism is an integral component of policymaking and, in most cases, players in the theoretical arena are involved directly in policy elaboration. It is hardly conceivable that any public theory on labour is not the formal result of political efforts.

The 'theory' I will deal with in this study is therefore a pragmatic (sometimes, however, only in its premises and not in its final outcome), policy-oriented concept, the ground for evaluation of which is – rather than its coherence with ideological frameworks – its ability to lead towards the formation of guiding principles of policymaking and to synthesise different positions into political or economic guidelines. The 'practice' to be investigated, in contrast, is the outcome of policy action, a result both of the implementation of planned guidelines and of general (economic, social, and political) constraints.

China's economic reformist leadership claims that today's labour economy is the achievement of coherent and unaltered policy options taken by the government during the twenty years' experience of *gaige* (reform). Yet many factors beyond the control of the central authorities and many unexpected and indirect outcomes have combined to shape the socialist market economy that is found in China today.

Many works appearing in the 1980s investigated both the nature of labour institutions and the power relations embedded in the traditional industrial labour system, and the evolution of labour institutions in the post-Mao era. These studies benefited from the larger availability of material and eyewitness accounts of the Chinese industrial system, and by the greater facility to investigate Chinese factories directly.

One major focus of research on the transformation of labour relations in the 1980s has been the peculiar nature of the Chinese work-unit. Some studies focus on the resistance met by the leadership in implementing the central directives on labour reform on the shop floor, thus concluding that the steps taken have been largely ineffectual.[1]

While some authors re-evaluate the role of workers' movements and the working class in determining policy options during the entire history of socialist labour organisation,[2] others instead prefer to investigate the way in which the work-unit, taken as the basic element of socialist China's social organisation, has faced the reforms and how the peculiar nature of internal bargaining among workers, management, and the state or Party has been affected by the transformation of the economic meaning of labour;[3] the originality of the social role of the *danwei*, in the context of the organisation of urban life in socialist countries, has also attracted a great deal of interest.[4] More recently a new stream of research has focused on the informal side of the labour issue, on rural-urban migration and on the informalisation process, as a consequence of the crisis of *danwei* employment and of increased mobility and insecurity in the workplace.[5]

The labour reform process portrayed in the international literature is generally one in which the extensive effort in policy formulation has not been matched by a radical transformation of institutions and in which practices have largely remained unchanged. This portrait is probably the result of different factors, the most important of which is a substantial separation between the study of institutions and their roles and that of society. Institutions have undoubtedly maintained a fundamental position in Chinese urban organisation, and their role – now that the initial years of reform have passed – is probably being reinvigorated by the consolidation of urban society and the completion of the reform of state-owned enterprises; nonetheless, many social 'constraints' hinder institutions from having overwhelming power over individual life and over the organisation of the economy. These constraints are the result of policy no less than of the social forces that have been released. This has become much clearer in the 1990s, when the contradictions between labour marketisation and bureaucratic control, though clearly perceived by both Chinese and foreign analysts, are far from being resolved and the attempted 'institutionalisation' of labour market forces seems progressively less likely.

Such phenomena as the informalisation of the economy are viewed today as a positive outcome of the reform policy but nevertheless present themselves as a difficult challenge to the institutional culture.

The present work intends to investigate processes rather than to portray situations, in an attempt to verify whether and to what extent theory and policy options have been the outcome of the other. The process envisaged for labour reform (and this might well apply to other fields of the Chinese reform as well) consists of three steps: decentralisation (that is, an informal release of public power that allows for greater independence), informalisation (market-driven experiments inside and outside institutions and work-units) and *ex-post* institutionalisation (a recognition of important experimental achievements and their transformation into policies).

As noted by Peter Lee

> Chinese policy-makers adopted an incremental approach to policy-making which was closely bound to policy prece-dents and was guided by feedback of each phase. In most cases they adopted a 'sequential decision model,' by making choices of alternatives on the basis of a limited review of existing pilot schemes.[6]

The question arising from this deconstruction of the policymaking process is whether we can assume a certain degree of rationality in the behaviour of the Chinese state or not. My assumption in this respect is that the rationality that drives labour reform is one with limited liability, as it only entered the arena once the real economy had already expressed its judgement and designated the winning strategies for the short term. This is evident from analy-sis of the theoretical efforts *vis à vis* policy formulation, and even clearer if the twenty years are considered as one historical period and the method of historical narration is utilized as I try to do in this book.

I agree with Barry Naughton, that there is no recognizable and rational strategy in China's reform,[7] if not the one emerging as a later acknowledgment by the winners, and from the constraints imposed to restless experiments. Nonetheless, contradictions in the lines and the distance between debate and reality in labour reform define a sort of 'rationale of postponement,' that – while history draws a line between theory, practice and policy – makes clear that decisions were indeed taken with some lucid (albeit contradictory) long term objectives, which might be ex-post recognised as 'stabil-ity' and 'gradualism'.

The historical perspective chosen here (although the proximity of the events described might compromise the use of this method) should therefore help to highlight the far-reaching effects of this process on the one hand, and of its continuous reproduction, with increasing difficulties and growing informalisation on the other.

The investigation has been conducted on a double track: the first is that of the theoretical debate, which has changed drastically from a rarified and ideological discussion in the initial years to an open acknowledgement of the social effects caused by the unrelenting emergence of a market-driven economy after a mere dozen years. The second track takes into account the progressively decreasing importance of policy in the organisation of the urban labour economy, from initial, *danwei*-centred reform steps to the almost uncontrollable dynamics of a labour market and informalisation.

This work represents an attempt to put the historical method at the service of an understanding of the dynamics that determine the process of state-led development. Issues that sociologists and development studies specialists might find relevant are touched upon only marginally, and my work tries to integrate some of their findings within the narration and to use them to discover contradictions.

Since the key I have chosen for my account is to expose the paradoxes of the labour policy during the Chinese reform, I have attempted to summarize the major terms of these contradictions within the framework of conceptual 'pairs', which will weave the fabric of the analysis.

The first pair has a historical taste and is composed of *modernisation* and *continuity*. It is indisputable that the foundation of Chinese reform lies in the idea of 'modernisation,' that is, the rationalisation of economic and social/organisational processes. This is not simply because the slogans of the post-1978 leadership are moulded around Zhou Enlai's earlier idea of 'four modernisations' (agriculture, industry, defence, and science), but more practically because the fast pace of recent Chinese development has been paralleled by a steady rationalisation of production. The reorganisation of labour practices has played a pivotal role in this process, not only because of its central importance as an economic factor – given the critical state of the Chinese economy after the years of leftist radicalism – but also because of the major importance of labour in a socialist theoretical and political background. Labour has therefore been central during Chinese reform: at the beginning, when the egalitarian redistributive policy was finally challenged by productivist views, after the Cultural Revolution had slashed the workers' purchasing power and their 'motivation' to work; and later, when considerations of production growth and the need to drastically reform state-owned enterprises favoured a deregulation of labour relations, mitigated only by the fear of social unrest and disruptive effects on central control of the economy. As much as 'modernisation' was the propelling principle of reform, 'continuity' (of leadership methods, of central control over political and economic factors, of the structure of interest networks) was the condition that allowed it to overcome crises without serious consequences and to learn progressively from different stages and experiences. Therefore, although the initial objectives and the final outcomes of the reform transformation process seem to be strikingly different, evaluation of it in a historical perspective inevitably focuses on continuities rather than on discontinuities.

The coexistence of these two terms in the ideology underlying policy formulation is the basis for the very existence of China's market socialism, and constitutes the ideological reference for what I shall later call 'double orthodoxy'. This is, however, rather the outcome of a slow adaptation and continuous reformulation of policies than of a consciously planned path of development.

The orientation of the policymakers that governed reform introduces a second set of related concepts: *flexibility* and *decentralisation*. This pair simply points to the two paths apparently followed by the reform. The flexibility of the labour reform policies clearly appears in the continuous balance between experimentation and implementation, within the framework that imposed productivity (first) and marketisation (later) as general references for the reform and as counter arguments to the previously dominant idea of central control. 'Decentralisation' meant enterprise autonomy and a reduction in the role of public actors in allocation, management, and regulation of labour relations. Flexible reform steps could be experimented with and later implemented due to the increased autonomy of enterprises and local departments, to greater freedom in the process of interpreting central policies and directives, and to increased interest on the part of the centre to consider changes going on in the localities and to appropriate the most successful cases for national policy.

At the same time it meant greater exposure for enterprises to the instabilities and uncertainties of the market and a transformation of the entrepreneurial behaviour of cadres, who, according to the original intention, were to be transformed from executors of central policy into self-reliant and business-oriented managers.

It is disputable from the point of view of reform politics, that state policy played a largely developmental role in China's rapid economic growth. The fact that the Chinese state managed to foster development by taking a capitalist path but without collapsing or releasing political power, engenders the expectation that centralized policymaking is able to maintain tight control over the gradual implementation of its policy and plans. However, this is not the case. The implementation of labour policy reveals how this process was not a linear, hierarchical, univocal stream beginning with ideological relaxation and leading to market deregulation. Rather – to a certain extent – it was the other way around. The role played by local governments of agencies of the principal's policy allowed for an increasing role for local administrations and enterprises, and central planners often reacted only later to experiments by enforcing regulations. From experiences far away from Zhongnanhai, policymakers came to understand that there were ways for China to become part of the world economy and they gradually adopted policies aimed at maintaining control over the fast moving economy. After the 'market economy' received official blessings from the centre, policymaking was devoted essentially to controlling the dramatic transformations in the economy and in society. At the same time it was the deeply rooted local bureaucracy that took control of economic levers and was able to 'restrain the private sector from becoming an independent economic class.' As noted recently by Jean C. Oi

> local state corporatism managed to channel resources towards development, exhibiting a 'noteworthy flexibility … in adapting to changing political and economic conditions while at the same time keeping at least indirect control of the development process.[8]

The process of decentralisation should not be seen as an outcome only of the reform policy and the subsequent disruption of the totalitarian structure of the 'classic' socialist state and its omnipresent redistributive bureaucracy. Many today tend to exclude the totalitarian pattern and to portray the Chinese socialist state as a 'functionally fragmented bureaucracy which contains tensions, bargaining, and conflicts of interest between different sectors and different levels.'[9] Such a structure is indeed an advantage for the decentralisation boom and the emergence of differences among places and within analogous institutions, without preventing the bureaucratic structures of the socialist state from maintaining control over the key features and ideology of the reformed system. This approach attaches priority and importance to the interaction at the local or shop floor levels and to greater dependence of social organisations such as work-units on personal or group networks and low-level bureaucratic interventions rather than on some distant centre.

Andrew Walder's analysis of the classic period of socialist industry focuses on the high degree of dependency at the *danwei* (work-unit) level, based mainly on the 'foreman's empire,' that is, on the great influence wielded by unit level personal networks and shop floor cadres on industrial relations and worker dependency.[10] The reform, according to the initial analysis of the later period contained in Walder's 1986 book, did not change the situation dramatically: labour relations shifted 'from ascetism to paternalism,' that is, from a focus on politics to a focus on economics and productivism, without fundamentally modifying the levels of dependency.

Through the study of work-unit transformation, later works helped to understand the segmentation of the labour market and the evolution of market behaviour, with the process of labour reform drastically modifying (though not yet completely) the patterns of dependency of Chinese workers and the methods of adaptation to a more hostile environment, throwing them into a 'sea' beyond the shores of the unit-island. Ching-Kwan Lee argues that the increasing social complexity (the consequence of a larger supply and a more articulated demand) in the labour arena fundamentally changed the basic assumption of Walder's *organised dependency*, leading to the emergence in the 1990s of a pattern of *disorganised despotism*, where disorganised reflects the 'lack of coordination among diverse reform measures' and despotism is the outcome of economic pressure on workers, that (as we shall see), is derived from both the labour market and administrative power.[11]

A third conceptual pair (*redistribution* and *market*) embodies the changing and contradictory role of labour institutions. Labour changed from a tool of social redistribution of wealth into a production factor, increasingly exposed to the tyranny of the market. The institutions were forced to play a totally different role, both in the realm of employment (the allocation system, control of geographic mobility, etc.), and in the protection of workers' rights and the welfare system. The market has been among the most powerful and appealing points of reference in the Chinese reform (often appealingly prefaced by the evocative word 'socialist'), but one of the most persistent taboos was its association with the word 'labour'. The marketisation of labour relations had already taken place in many practical fields when labour contracts were reintroduced into Chinese state industry, de facto recognizing that manpower could be sold just like any other 'production factor,' or, as a lengthy debate later concluded, as a 'commodity.' Despite the rampaging marketisation of labour relations, the state has not yet renounced its claim to a redistributive role and to a direct role in the organisation of labour allocation. This has resulted in a 'highly institutionalised' labour market, in which the role of institutions (either direct, as employer, or indirect, as service organiser) is extremely important and sometimes contradictory to the anarchy of market behaviour. The role of institutions (that is, of public bodies or enterprises) has been decoupled from the state's ability to maintain control over the employment system. The labour market (with the exception of certain sections, such as managerial and skilled personnel) is almost entirely independent from labour allocation plans. Nonetheless, local institutions and work-units, and the system of employment agencies, still play the major role in determining hiring practices, as shown by the prevalence of institutional practices for the hiring of personnel in the formal industrial sector. Clienteles and cronyism, once embedded in the upward mobility processes internal to the *danwei*, are now at work from the moment the unit is accessed, thereby anticipating and moving labour conflicts outside the work-unit and implying a higher rate of open competitiveness among workers.

1.2 Chinese Labour and the Making of a Market: An Overview and Some Basic Assumptions

Labour Policy and Institutions

China's labour market included over eight million private workers in 1952, almost three years after the Communist takeover, that is, over 35 percent of the total industrial work force. The traditional family-based labour market that dominated allocation patterns since ancient times – and had been challenged only in the nineteenth century by an increasing presence of foreign enterprises – had always been characterized by a high degree of informality, and had relied heavily on kinship and friendship.[12] After the founding of the PRC – and even more so after the nationalisation of Chinese industry in 1956 (that is during the so-called 'classic'[13] period of socialism) – the number of Chinese private workers was reduced progressively, until they virtually disappeared from the national statistics in the last years of the Cultural Revolution. As a consequence of the focus on state industry China assigned paramount importance to full-employment policies as a criterion for the allocation of the work force: work was considered a *general* right,[14] like food and housing, and policies fostered egalitarian access to it. A job, and an urban job in particular, represented a door to participation in the distribution of wealth throughout society. Food rations, free housing, and centrally planned work allocations were the basic parts of socialism: in this context work was not a production factor but rather a major component in the distribution system; work was not based on an individual choice guided by economic conditions, but the representation of social status.

During the initial steps of socialist construction and until the 1958 Great Leap Forward (GLF), the development of China's labour institutions was based mainly on the post-war 'high Stalinist' Soviet model, calling for the implementation of a wage-grade system, with income gaps for different duties among staff and workers. This system was widely implemented, but it was not always effective, resulting in the emergence of egalitarian practices; it was also one of the main reasons for the discontent during the intra-unit conflicts of the late 1950s,[15] until the implementation of the 'rational low-wage system' (a high-benefits low-wage scheme) which characterised China's salary policy until the end of the Cultural Revolution.[16]

The Soviet-style attempt to implement the principle of 'distribution according to labour' in the wage system is one – but not the only – feature inviting a comparison between the 1950s and the initial stage of labour reform in the 1980s. During the years prior to the GLF, temporary workers in fact were widely employed in industry and infrastructural construction, either for particular labour-intensive production needs or as seasonal workers in different locations and in response to manufacturing necessities.

Finally, the sharp increase in urban population during the 1950s, before the anti-urban policies (aimed in particular at defending urban privileges) came into effect, was analogous to a deregulated labour allocation situation, similar to that experienced in the 1980s. Urban administrative re-organisation and strict control of migration flows were the solutions adopted at the end of the GLF; deregulation and market development were part of the post-Cultural Revolution solutions.

The reform drive starting at the end of the 1970s changed China's planned economy into a state-controlled market system, the main scope of which was to boost the efficiency of the productive system and to prepare the economy for international competition. In the new political climate of economic reform, questions of labour organisation, recruitment and allocation became increasingly important, engendering many contradictions. On the one hand, labour was among the few economic factors China could rely on extensively; on the other, the entire social and economic equilibrium was based on bureaucratic, centralised, and 'unified' labour management.

In the initial years of reform, it very quickly became obvious that the attempt to maintain bureaucratic control over population and labour movements would conflict with the problem of the increased geographic distribution of work opportunities and thus create problems for the idea of state *supervision* over the market economy.

The production needs engendered by the opening up of the formerly closed and self sufficient Chinese economy – also in the field of labour – to international markets, meant the Communist leadership faced the challenge of undertaking a major re-writing of regulations, a radical modification of ideological assumptions, and a fundamental downgrading of the political involvement of the state in the field of economics, in order to attract the flow of foreign capital.

Mobility and opening to the outside world are useful here only as examples to help understand the paths along which the transformation effort of labour politics in China has been moving during the last twenty years: continuous revision of social and economic *policy* under pressure of practical contradictions is accompanied by theoretically 'justified' *deregulation* to respond to (internal and) international interests.

The official final aim of economic reform has never been the implementation of 'private free markets' (*ziyou siren shichang* – even though it might appear so currently) but rather of a 'socialist market economy under the conditions of socialist public ownership.'[17] Indeed, the larger part of the financial and productive potential of China is still under the control of the state, although the growth of the private sector is progressively overtaking the leading role of poorly-performing state industrial plants; however, the most dynamic sectors of the booming economy are all found in the private or 'collective' industries (most of the latter are hidden private enterprises in local state enterprises), while the state-owned enterprises are struggling to be profitable entities (44 percent experienced losses in 1994; in 1997 total losses in state sector exceeded total profits but these are now beginning to decline).[18] But, critical for the state and for its policy choices, these enterprises still provide 50 percent of state revenue.

The reform of labour institutions and the introduction of new administrative tools, such as the contract system, were aimed at differentiating allocation channels and at controlling the increasing labour mobility. The growing availability of labour outside the traditional recruitment channels progressively reduced the importance of the system of 'central-unified allocation' (*zhongyang tongyi fenpei*). This *dual market* took clear shape during the 1980s, when full employment and market opportunities clashed openly, negatively affecting the hiring and development plans of Chinese state enterprises. Prior to the reform, the number of workers employed in an enterprise was based on financial considerations by management. New allocations *according to the plan* accompanied by new funds were normally welcomed by enterprises that accepted the advantages of new financial means without direct costs for the unit.

Even in the first years of the reform – when enterprises still faced limited budget constraints – recruitment from the open (*out of plan*) market (which had grown during the economic reorganisation) was limited as the enterprises were plagued by redundant personnel and preferred to hire from inside, giving higher priority to the satisfaction of the internal needs of their own unit rather than to productive skills. 'Back-door' (*hou men*) hiring and a preference for the children of workers in the unit remained among the guiding principles of the State-owned enterprise (SOE) recruitment strategies.[19]

As noted by Granick,[20] the requirements for recruitment and, in particular, the priority given to certain skills or the profile of hired personnel differ according to the administrative level of the decision maker: quality and skills are preferred when local administrative criteria are involved, while allocation equalities are more highly valued at higher or central levels. The administrative nature of hiring procedures and the limited interest of enterprise management in market opportunities remained strongly influenced during the reform period by a preference for internal recruitment (*neizhao* or *dingti*[21] – substitution) of *women danwei de erzi* ('sons of our unit'), mainly for reasons related to the mayor-like role played by

12

the manager of large state units and their need to avoid internal struggle.

Granick also suggests that competition among people entitled to new jobs is a sign of the existence of a labour market in which individuals are willing to participate 'even if only at a single stage' of their working life.

A characteristic of employment in state enterprises which persisted after the reform is the contemporary *excess* of an unnecessary (principally unskilled) labour force and the *shortage* of necessary (skilled) workers; this is one of the features (together with the phenomenon of hoarding staff) which Janos Kornai associates with the chronic 'shortages' of socialist economies.[22] In such a situation (which changed considerably later in the 1980s and was dramatically reversed during the 1990s), the fundamental influence of interpersonal relationships and interest networks (what the Chinese usually call *guanxi*) in recruitment practices could not be ignored.

The effectiveness of informal networks – able to influence the evolution of work relationships and access by enterprises to skilled labourers or access by workers to the best enterprises – are, according to Christiansen,[23] a demonstration that the existence of one or more markets does not imply that labour mobility is governed by market forces.

Work-units and the Working Class

Reform of labour started as a way to alleviate the burden of state industry caused by the enormous costs of redundant personnel and by the low productivity of plants and individual labourers resulting from the egalitarian practices of the radical Maoist years. The closed labour system built around the comprehensive role of the *danwei* resulted in extremely low levels of labour mobility that continued well into the reform period. During the early 1980s, state enterprises continued to be a source of attraction to outsiders and newcomers to the work force (particularly the skilled among them), and prevented highly qualified labourers from leaving the unit (contributing decisively to this, was their politically privileged position in the unit). Only later did the rapid development of individual entrepreneurship make the 'dive into the sea' (*xia hai*) of the individual or non-state economy more attractive to workers, as labour mobility and flexibility become accepted features of the new approach to labour policy.

Aggravating the burden of labour immobility were the long-term consequences of the policies on administration of the population. For almost two decades, from the end of the 1950s throughout the 1960s and early 1970s, China's anti-urban policies had been successful in controlling and partially reducing the urban population. This achievement in controlling geographic mobility was to some extent due to the forced rustication process, but a major role was also played by such bureaucratic means as the 'family registration system' (*hukou dengji zhidu*) – hereafter *hukou* – the basic registration document of any Chinese, defining his or her status according to place of residence, with the main distinction being agricultural or nonagricultural, and under the strict control of the party's reach to the countryside. But, by the late 1970s, the population began moving into the cities and the earlier economic equilibrium changed rapidly, increasing the entropy of the system and its complexity.

Acknowledgement of the re-emergence of the concurrent actions of marketisation and urbanisation threw open an important question concerning the existence, formation, and role of a Chinese working class, as well as the process of *proletarianisation* of Chinese workers during the 1980s.

According to the 'classic' three-phase proletarianisation process proposed by Charles Tilly,[24] and applied to China by Walder the process takes place in industrial economies through 'the expropriation of rural producers, a reclassification of the rural population from peasants to wage labourers and the transfer of the rural population to urban areas.'[25]

Although much of the working class was a 1950s creation of the Chinese Communist Party (CCP), China's socialism formally opposed the process of 'making' a working class (a large class of wage labourers resulting from modernisation of the economy and industry), while facing, in practice, the necessity of increasing the number of workers involved in industrial production.

One of Walder's conclusions was that what differs in China's making of a proletarian working class is the absence of an accomplished urbanization process during the phase of classic socialism. Since the time of the Great Leap Forward, the industrial population in the cities had become an increasingly closed group, and the forced urban-to-rural migration policies of the 1960s were probably a result of the endogenous growth of the working population inside the cities, and not of further immigration.[26] In the actual process of making a Chinese working class the taming of the transformative power of markets and capitalism has been accomplished by a bureaucratic system that channels mobility into the narrow bounds of a status system based on residence and birth.[27]

Bureaucratic intervention during the 1960s and 1970s was apparently a way to 'channel' mobility and productive forces. But what happens if the bureaucratic control over local processes progressively decreases or changes its shape and objectives while market forces are allowed to exercise a higher (although 'socialist' and 'mechanical') influence?

Though labour flexibility was only gradually implemented, its theoretical acknowledgment and the implementation of practical policy steps are the major reasons why the issue of *full* proletarianisation was reintroduced in the evaluation of the years following the Cultural Revolution. I would call this process – which is only partly related to the traditional influence of industrial development – a *re*-proletarianisation, as it is the result of a second start (the first was interrupted by the deepening of the socialist planned economy in the late 1950s) of a process based also on (a) the massive floating of the rural population due to a relaxation of bureaucratic controls, a crisis in agricultural employment, geographic differentiation between development strategies (caused in part also by policy decisions and not simply by the modernization drive); (b) the progressive decentralization and informalisation of the economy, that is, the transformation of the aims and objectives of the work-unit and the emergence of an independent sector with less interest in production plans and more interest in profit-making activities; and (c) the re-emerging role of the family as a unit of production and household accumulation, whose readiness to work hard for money has become proverbial.

Sally Sargeson recently contributed an anthropological work on the transformation of the discourse on the proletariat in China, that correctly portrays how reforms – that at an increasing pace turned the socialist paternalist state into a quasi-capitalist, market-regulating, bureaucratic mechanism – 'have created the ideological, political, economic and institutional tools by which China's proletariat has been reworked' and, eventually, has passed from being the 'master' to being the exploitable sector of industrial society. 'The long term significance of these reforms' in Sargeson's words, 'is that China's proletariat has been reworked as a cheap, "manageable" work force that will produce profits for investors and enterprise owners.'[28]

Different and contrasting interpretations have been put forward regarding the ability of Chinese workers to stand up to various exploiters (be it the bureaucracy or the new despotic disorder of the labour market). The history of worker conflicts in the 1950s has been re-evaluated by Francois Gipouloux[29] and later by Elizabeth Perry,[30] who notes that the obsessive search for class consciousness in studies of the Chinese working class has led many to ignore how – although organized around such 'feudal' tools as 'regional gangs, guilds, and native place associations – workers joined other urbanites to protest as *citizens* or *consumers*, rather than as members of a working class,'[31] and that native place networks should therefore not be excluded from investigation as a form of organisation of an otherwise relatively unconscious working class' protest and participation in political life.

Along the same lines and more recently Jackie Sheehan has considered a longer period of China's worker history to conclude that intra-unit disputes and other conflicts 'tend quickly to develop into a confrontation between workers and the Party,'[32] and that their antagonistic nature is of utmost importance, despite the lack of an orthodox class construction.

An impressive and complex record of conflicts recently shed new light on the influence of worker unrest on the direction of political campaigns under CCP leadership (such as the sudden turn around of the Hundred Flowers campaign in 1957 or the 1989 crackdown on the student movement). Different forms of indirect action – intentional inefficiency, production slowdowns, non-compliance with assigned duties, second jobs – that have been referred to as 'unorganized but collective inaction'[33] also have to be considered among the determinants of labour policies. While the existence of significant – visible and invisible – conflicts does not make Chinese workers an organised class and a conscious antagonistic movement, the history of labour unrest and resistance[34] is relevant to this study as it helps validate the basic assumption that most of the policy steps taken by the reform leadership were a response to a generalized demand and were taken under the threat of discontent more than as an outcome of an all-encompassing drive towards social and economic planning. Policy decisions and regulatory measures were efficient in setting the hurdles for labour market development – more than in boosting its development – in particular by maintaining almost intact the administrative divides that after twenty years of reform still determine individual opportunities to participate in the market and tie the distribution of wealth to status.

The instability of labour relations and draconian exploitation encouraged the speeding up of mobility and, coupled with the preservation of administrative barriers, transformed the proletariat from an ideological elite into a multifaceted, complex blend of unprotected and often displaced wage workers.

Migration and Informalisation of the Urban Economy

In recent extensive research on the quest for citizenship among new urbanites who are increasingly migrating from the country-side to fill the ranks of an army of unemployed, Dorothy Solinger notes that 'both the extant state and the market were blocking the achievement of urban citizenship' and that this peculiar interaction basically contradicted the generally accepted assumption that development and marketisation produce an extension of citizen-ship to wider sections of the population.[35]

The *hukou*[36] had always been the main component of demo-graphic policies, but it proved a major economic disadvantage as soon as the centralized system faced the challenge of an increas-ingly deregulated society and it was a constraint on the mobility of the workforce in a free labour market. In the *hukou* system, the rural population is registered and administratively dependent on its rural territorial unit; the population registered as urban, on the other hand, enjoys the advantages of the larger urban labour market and is given free access to the public sector under the protec-tion of the state. After the process of deregulation began, demands for work were concentrated in places other than the countryside, or changed from one agricultural area or mining compound to another from season to season. Agricultural work opportunities decreased steadily after the contract system was implemented in the countryside (1980); unemployed farmers were therefore forced to leave their homes to seek temporary jobs in distant counties or cities, or to engage in different strategies of development, invari-ably beginning with migration. Very soon, the outdated *hukou* system could no longer control migration flows, and its abolition has since then been on the agenda of Chinese reformers.[37]

The contradiction between a stable residence and floating work opportunities caused, on the one hand, a sharp increase in the availability of cheap and unskilled labour, engendered by the inflow of the rural population into cities of all sizes (where a *bendi hukou* – local hukou – is still a major advantage in job seeking,[38] while it is also an administrative definition of the divisions within the labour market); on the other, the emergence of a parallel labour market which ignores the *hukou* registration as well as labour rights protection, and is based on informal practices. The continued direct influence of the *hukou* in the organisation and segmentation of the labour market is also a major reason for the higher competition among different players in the market (especially along the insider-outsider divide) and for the lack of a self-organised common interest among the re-born Chinese proletariat. 'The workers, when entering the factories are already differentiated as the bearers of distinctive, potentially antagonistic non-class identities and relations.'[39]

The critical and contradictory situations created by the crisis of household registration were initially tackled by emergency actions, such as the issue, during the 1980s, of *temporary urban certificates* to incoming rural workers to allow them to sell their labour in the urban labour 'market' without allowing them access to the associated welfare benefits.[40] Only later, did more stable forms of registration (ID cards and working permits) become available to non residents. For migrants, the corresponding increase in status granted by a permanent urban *hukou* and employment in a SOE invariably was mere wishful thinking; the probability of entering a state enterprise as a permanent worker decreased significantly as the reform moved towards a full marketisation of labour relations. Work in an SOE long remained the divide between people with and people without access to public services and facilities, and to goods available only by work-unit distribution. Recent major changes in housing allocations and welfare distributions pose gloomier prospects also for large numbers of urban dwellers. Their ability to get the greatest comparative advantages over migrants from the marketisation remains, however, unchanged, due to their traditional status and networks of connection.

As a result of the increased labour opportunities and restrictions on the redistributive role of the work-unit, labour relations during the reform period have undergone a process of informalisation.

Informalisation and second or 'grey' economies, as some authors have already pointed out,[41] greatly influenced the economy even during the radical years, when the number and nature of activities on the border of legality – not formally acknowledged but largely accepted by the authorities and therefore 'informal'- was significant. This process accelerated the re-emergence of large-scale individual private economies in rural areas after the beginning of reform and led to the transformation of the grey economies into a lively and flexible private sector. This trans-formation sometimes occurred with the complicity of historical, economic, and political factors, which granted some areas advan-tageous positions (as was the case in the coastal areas or the faster, and unexpected, growth of private economies in such areas as Wenzhou)[42] or simply more social motivation and cultural capital to make the change less disruptive and more profitable.

From the point of view of policymaking, informalisation should be considered a part of what Naughton calls the 'ex-post coher-ence'[43] of China's modernisation drive, as it was the result of tolerant behaviour on the part of the central and local state towards some sectors of the economy, under the consideration of peculiar situations, and not the result of coherent and conscious steps taken by the policymakers.

Indeed, after the reform process began, the second economy in the rural areas rapidly extended to the once monolithic and state-led cities, where the organisation of production and services had always been a monopoly of state-owned units; a market for services and labour rapidly emerged, profiting from the crisis of the urban state's redistributive functions.

I define informalisation as a progressive release of administra-tive power by the state that allows, under imperfect and largely deregulated market conditions, activities by non recognised market actors. While their status and rights are denied by social and polit-ical rules, their existence and activities are necessary to the fulfil-ment of certain requirements of capitalist development (the supply of basic services and of cheap labour, for example).

In addition to modernization theories of development, David Stark suggests 'an alternative interpretation of the relationship between modernity and informality, in which informalisation and proletarianisation grow in tandem rather than through mutual dis-placement.'[44] Progressive informalisation opened alternative paths to participation in production and the distribution of social wealth to the 'new proletarians' of the 1980s. This followed the develop-ment of 'second' urban economies in petty commerce and small workshops of the individual sector and marginal, illicit activities of an illegal economy (the entire range of unregistered enterprises, not only criminal activities).

It is my opinion that the process of debureaucratisation con-tributed to the emergence of informal economic players, and that the explosion of a *yinxing jingji* (shadow economy), which is not only an urban phenomenon, grew in response to widespread efforts to extend labour opportunities. The policy struggles against the second economy and economic informalisation targeted only smuggling and related tax evasions (even though migrant economies, for example, became major contributors to local public coffers[45]). But these struggles were challenged by unexpected factors, such as increasing organisation and quality of production (technology and commercial networks in particular) and by the number of people involved in informal activities (including many state workers who took on secondary activities). Some official data from the early 1990s put the share of total production 'coming from obscure roads' (*lailu bu ming*) at about 20 percent of total national output. Smuggling activities also changed the composition of the urban market with respect to commodities generally not associated with illegal activity – in the 1990s, alcohol has been surpassed in output value by, for example, leather shoes.[46] This seems to demonstrate that urban consumer markets are able to absorb a much larger quantity of consumer goods than those marketed by formal producers, and that the shadow economy is competing with the official productive structure not only in marginal and simple production but also in major consumer sectors. In particular, unregistered workshops rely on the increasing availability of a cheap and unprotected work force, and on expanding and concentrated urban markets, to produce and marketise popular, small goods with relatively low technological content. Productive and spatial organisation sometimes take the classic shape of the 'industrial districts' already observed in earlier stages of capitalist development and during the passage from craftsmanship to small industry in Western countries (the concentration of production, a family structure, a sharing of basic services, and self-organisation of distribution).[47]

The informalisation of the economy is yet another major component of proletarianisation, as it contributes to the deterioration of working conditions in urban centres and to unrestrained exploitation of privately contracted wage labour and maintains an 'informal population' in the cities – that is, a 'reserve army' of labourers 'waiting for employment' – at survival level.[48] The growth of the above in urban centres and the bureaucracy's inability to regain direct or indirect control are probably the reasons for the tacit agreement between the formal (bureaucratic and state-led) and informal (private and shadow) economies, as demonstrated by the well-known cases of the ethnic enclaves in the cities, where commercial activities grew as a result of the reduced ability of the state to play its distributive role.[49]

1.3 Labour Theory regarding the Market:
Some Preliminary Notes and a Breakdown into Periods

China is a socialist state and a reforming socialist economy. This duality reflects the double nature of the ideological 'environment' in which debate has been shaped.

The Chinese definition of socialism is deeply rooted in the socialist state as well as in Maoist tradition. The orthodoxy of state socialism and of the proletarian dictatorship has never been formally abandoned, although many major political decisions and ideological statements over the last twenty years have resulted from a much less strict definition of the term 'socialism.' Nevertheless, a situation I would call *double orthodoxy* was operating for the most part during the period of this study. On the one hand, socialism means a fully planned economy, public ownership of the means of production, and the political leadership of the CCP as the vanguard of the working class, whose political activity is the result of the leading role of 'Marxism-Leninism-Mao Zedong Thought.' On the other hand, pragmatic orthodoxy based on formal adherence to productivity and market-driven state-socialism advocated 'modernisation,' the development of a 'legal system,' and a 'socialist market economy' into the next century. These two frames of reference constituted the battlefield for the internal struggles in the party between 'reformists' and 'conservatives' who suggested two opposing and independent paths of development, but who often acted simultaneously in the formulation of policy options.

This was the founding paradox of the theoretical debates of the late 1970s and early 1980s. No wonder that, having to move in a glass house, the debate became mainly 'factionalist' (opinions were rarely individual), and 'specialistic' (on single fields of research) as the existence of a double orthodoxy (together with a harsh and dangerous environment for outspoken theorists in the initial years of reform) was generally enough to inhibit any attempts to advocate general or comprehensive theories. Both referential 'orthodoxies' had an influential role, as did their political sponsors and representatives, resulting in an even more complex framework.[50]

But the difficulty was not only connected with two (or more) conflicting lines inside the party; it often involved the forced coexistence of sometimes antithetical ideas on development that progressively weakened the ideological foundations of the debate.

The existence of a double orthodoxy had practical consequences in the background of the debate. Particularly in the initial
years of the reform period, the basic references were to Marx,
Engels, and Lenin, and rarely to Chinese economists, party leaders or even Chairman Mao. There were two main reasons for this
attitude: the first was the attempt to find justification for the new
economic policies as much as possible in the socialist tradition,
sanctioning them as the result of a traditional interpretation, from
which Mao was clearly considered to have diverged in his later
years, thus making him a difficult source of reference (this was the
process of *re-establishing* the old ideology); the second was that,
once the 'people's enemies' (namely the members of the 'Gang of
Four') had been eliminated, no one dared to criticise anyone, as
the political climate was still extremely sensitive. The use of
Marxist texts was not only the result of the statements about the
nature of 'reform' and of Deng's pragmatic economicism, repeatedly defined as the 'actual socialist system of thought,' that suited
Chinese tastes as an alternative to the leftist putschist attitudes of
the 'gang.' It was also the outcome of a general difficulty in
identifying 'enemies' and 'friends' in the wake of the collective
nightmare of the Cultural Revolution.

Later on, when it became clear that the initial uncertain steps of
the *gaige* (reform) had become a definitive ideological path of
development and codified slogans, the issue gradually became less
sensitive, but the need for a double justification of ideas remained,
and the terms of reference diverged even more sharply.

In an attempt to describe this twenty year-long debate, my primary classification is based on a breakdown of the post-Mao years
into three main periods (and their practical consequences).

Before introducing the specifics of each period, the limits and
common features of such a problematic division must be presented. A breakdown into periods never has general validity and,
in this case, as I state at the beginning of this study, the linearity of
time (as a component of the historical method of process analysis)
has an autonomous importance in the methodological approach.
Periods are therefore divided along the lines of: (a) frequency of discussion of some basic issues in the debate; (b) major development
in economic policy, policy cycles, and general policy language;
(c) major political campaigns accompanying policy implementation, and (d) turning points in labour policy implementation.

This means that the identification of periods is based on the existence of homogeneous features in these four fields of analysis

(debate, policy, campaigns, and implementation). But it also means that instead of the major *discontinuities* in the historical cycle generally used for a breakdown into periods, I will use *major developments* along the lines of continuity as time markers.

Thus, the period from 1977 through 1995 will be divided into three main parts: (1) the period of *re-establishment* (1977–1983), during which an orthodoxy based on pre-Cultural Revolution socialist practices was implemented and harsh criticism was directed at policies driven by class struggle. The main topic of debate during this period was the theoretical evaluation and technical implementation of the Marxist principle of 'distribution according to labour;' (2) the period of *contractualisation* (1984–1991), characterised by the beginning of a structural reform of state enterprises, by the emergence of generalised contracting in the Chinese economy, and by theoretical disputes regarding whether or not labour is a commodity; and (3) the period of *marketisation* (1992–1995, and thereafter) of the Chinese economy and greater deregulation of social and economic mechanisms, paralleled by a debate – largely economic in nature – on the implementation of labour market (*laodongli shichang*) policies, and on a more pragmatic though populist acceptance of the issue of unemployment.

In order to be the first critic of my own divisions, it must be clearly understood that while this periodisation reflects a three-stage economic development of Chinese reform (planned economy – planned commodity economy – socialist market economy), no such clear-cut division can be accepted for the debate. Actually, the three characteristic topics (the law of 'distribution according to labour', the commoditisation of labour, and the labour market) are not exclusive to the debate in each phase, that is, topics often overlap. The time segments chosen here conform to the periods when each issue was supported by contending positions, while the ends of the periods roughly correspond to the *resolution* of the disputes and general acknowledgement, in turn, of the three successive principles. Not irrelevant to this pre-assumption is, of course, that each period is linked to relevant political events and to the approval of major political documents!

As for the definition of the periods, at the risk of oversimplification, I have decided to use the categories generally associated with the idea of 'market socialism' (socialist state, contract system, market mechanisms)[51] to mark the evolution towards a specific model of Chinese development which after its twentieth anniversary and after the death of its major advocate, Deng Xiaoping, appears in historical perspective as a single, though complex and contradictory, path. Market socialism is the attempt to let 'fire and water' interact to build an economic system able to apply the 'rationality' of the market to the 'superiority' of the planned economy and public ownership.

The 'Restoration' Stage (1977–1983)

The first period starts with the end of the Cultural Revolution and ends with the Third Plenum of the Twelfth CCP Congress in October 1984 that affirmed the transformation of the Chinese economy into a 'planned *commodity* economy.'

This is the period when the foundations of reform were laid, as the economic and social system of socialist China underwent dramatic changes.

Even in the labour debates (as in other theoretical issues) the founding event was the defeat and political condemnation of the 'Gang of Four,' culminating in the 1980 trial.[52] This political act was the basis for any criticism of 'previous' views, the factor creating the ideological distinction between 'yesterday' and 'today,' and the symbolic element identifying a collectively condemned *enemy*. During this period, the debate over labour was very general. The Marxist category of 'distribution according to labour' (*an lao fenpei* – hereafter DATL) had been widely and extensively replaced during the years of Maoist egalitarianism, at both a theoretical and practical level, by the practice of 'to each according to his needs' or, as Deng himself later depicted, 'distribution according to politics' (*anzheng fenpei*).[53] The reassessment of a Marxist interpretation and the condemnation of previous distribution practices accompanied elements of the initial steps to reform labour to pre-Cultural Revolution organisation. DATL was a central topic in the overall discussion of the reform process. Particularly in the initial years of economic recovery (namely 1977–78) the issue was given increasing attention, to the point that the newly mobilized intelligentsia convened four major conferences on this topic between April 1977 and October 1978, all assessing the fundamental role of this economic law in the 'socialist' (i.e. precommunist) stage of the Chinese revolution.

This was a period when theoretical debate was mainly shaped by the need to go beyond earlier ideological constructions, negating issue by issue the negative interpretation of the objective economic law of DATL. Many of the ideas raised in these months of lively (though obsessively repetitive) academic discussions were to become very important for the reassessment of economic and political reform. For example, the reintroduction of the concept of bourgeois rights (*das bürgerliche Recht*)[54] which had been associated by Cultural Revolution theoreticians with DATL according to a rather peculiar interpretation of Marxist texts, allowed an opportunity to discuss wider and more complex *Recht*-related issues of China's economic and legal reform.

The reinstatement of DATL as the guiding principle of the economic distribution of social wealth was accompanied by the emergence of several other issues: general egalitarian distribution was compared with labour-based egalitarianism; the hierarchical implications of DATL advocated during the previous decade were openly criticised and instead the non-hierarchical nature of economic relationships under DATL was affirmed; the capitalist or bourgeois nature of economic relationships and of the political mentality or attitude under the influence of 'bourgeois' DATL was denied; the question of property rights was cautiously raised, as DATL law allowed for the private possession of consumer goods.

There was no real contention about the superiority of the old Marxist principle of distribution in itself, as most of the 'enemies' were serving prison terms or were not taking part in the discussion. During these years, the debate on labour became a powerful tool for legitimation of the new policy; despite a general consensus on the central issue (the adoption of DATL as the guiding principle and the consequent functional link between labour performance and remuneration), at the level of policy decisions, the contradictions between different lines of thought were much more evident.

The topic of DATL dominated the discussion during the entire period and had both ideological and practical implications. One side of the debate concentrated on its nature, its superiority as a guiding redistributive principle under socialism, and its origin and meaning; the other discussed the applicability and computability of DATL, with particular reference to understanding and calculating the basic term 'labour.' The major theoretical point was in fact the measurement of labour (*lao*), that is, *whether* labour has monetary value, the meaning of wages, how to calculate wages and what 'quantity and quality' mean as far as wage levels are concerned.

Some source of theoretical dispute was represented, for example, by the tools needed to make wages and distribution *formally* non-egalitarian (the issue of production bonuses, the reform of the rational low-wage system and piece-rates) and by the link between the performance of the individual and that of the enterprise in the calculation of wages.

A major turning point in this period was the Third Plenum of the Eleventh Congress of the CCP at the end of 1978. Until then, the debate over DATL had been mainly academic, aimed at a re-evaluation of the concept, while denying the capitalist nature of both its basic principle and its mechanisms. After the plenum, that is, after the official public declaration of the exclusive socialist nature of DATL, the term was generally recognised as a guiding principle and the main foci became *how* it was to be implemented and *what* its real meaning was 'under the new conditions of a complex economic system,'[55]

This shift had consequences not only for the substance of the issues already on the table, but also for the implementation of the initial steps of the labour reform policy. The main concern of policymakers at that point was distribution and wages: since the end of the 1950s, Chinese workers had been working under a so-called 'rational system of low wages and high employment,' an egalitarian distribution mechanism based on a significant quota of subsidies, for which the main justification was the low level of development of Chinese productive forces and the need to solve the structural unemployment problem. Subsequently, during the Cultural Revolution, wages had been progressively linked to noneconomic factors, such as the so-called *zhengzhi biaoxian*, or 'political performance.' With the re-adoption of DATL as the guiding principle China could re-evaluate such industrial labour wage mechanisms as bonuses and piece-rates, that had previously been rejected as 'capitalist petty bourgeois.'

The re-evaluation of bonus and piece-rate wages was structurally connected both with the reform of the relationship between the central authority and enterprises, and with the restructuring of unit-level organisation in the production system.

As early as the end of 1978, some enterprises had already started experimenting with a 'profit retention system.' The first of many successive steps aimed at granting local enterprises financial autonomy, this measure allowed enterprises to retain a small percentage of their resources (initially 5 percent of total payroll) as welfare and bonus funds.

To complete the *recovery* of pre-Cultural Revolution practices, in 1978 the All-China Federation of Trade Unions (ACFTU), the official workers' organisation which had been dismantled during the Cultural Revolution, was finally re-established to become a tool of the new policy.

Later, in 1981, the reform of industrial enterprises was deepened with regulations on the so-called Economic Responsibility System (*jingji zeren zhi*). The increased autonomy accorded to enterprise management implied an interpretation of DATL in which the term labour, as well as the question of productivity and consequently of wages, were closely linked to enterprise performance, and not only to individual or group performance.

This initial period of labour reform featured the re-establishment of a labour system and of a labour theory that were quite similar to those of the 1950s, the initial years of the socialist economic construction. The theoretical assumptions, as well as the organisation and distribution, confronted many structural problems comparable to those of the late 1950s; many common features of the two systems allow us to refer to this period as a *restoration*.[56] These years also featured the emergence of the terms and practice of economic modernisation. This was stated at the 1978 Plenum, when the focus on class struggle was replaced by a focus on modernisation of the economy. The initial steps in the discussion of the nature and the practice of socialist labour were propaedeutic for major and faster development of the labour reform after the 1978 Plenum sanctioned the nature of the 'planned commodity economy' in the Chinese system.

The 'Contractualisation' Period (1984–91)

From the point of view of labour reform, the most important element during this second period was the formulation and implementation of a 'contract labour system' (*hetong laodong zhidu*) for all state workers and the consequent transformation of labour relations inside enterprises. It is important to underline here that the new employment mechanism after 1986 required state-owned enterprises to hire workers on a contract basis and to limit the length of the period of the contract. Some major consequences were soon apparent: (a) a temporary (though long-term) differentiation among the workforce, between newly hired contract or temporary workers and those previously hired on a life-tenure basis. This resulted in labourers doing the same work while enjoying different status in the same unit; (b) despite resistance and informal networks greatly influencing the recruitment process, competition was stimulated among the growing number of unemployed workers outside the factories (a premise for the formation of a labour market); (c) contracts eventually forced an acknowledgement that enterprises and workers are bound by an employer-employee relationship, therefore casting doubts on the position of workers as 'masters' of the enterprise.

The policy shift resulted, during the initial years after the reform, in firm resistance from the established 'elites' of fixed workers, who felt threatened by the prospect of having to share the privileges of urban residence with a growing mass of newly arrived farmers.

The debate accompanying the initiation, formation and implementation of this policy can be summed up by the question: 'Is labour a commodity?'

If during the Maoist period, under the effect of Leninist state ideology labour had been considered a 'general right', during the post-1978 reform, labour was generally thought of as a 'commodity' (*shangpin*). The Leninist concept is based on the assumption that industrial workers have multiple roles, that is, they are at one and the same time buyers and sellers of their workforce, owners of the means of production and masters of the enterprise in which they are working. In the description of the production process, this classic mechanism resulted in less interest in economic parameters such as labour productivity per worker, and in the ideological assumption that progress and development are mainly the result of subjective attitudes such as enthusiasm, engagement, mutual help – in a word, the *mass* line. Nothing was considered impossible; economic laws governing labour allocation were generally ignored and extraordinary cases, providing evidence of the superior moral values of socialist labour, became the models. This was one of the obvious reasons for the defeat of the egalitarian model of the Maoist period, when labour intensity was considered a *panacea* that could ignite the increasing development of Chinese society, regardless of quality in manufacturing, gaps in technology, and lack of raw materials. People have always been China's major resource and the idea of sharing formal ownership while granting a job, as well as housing and food, were considered a way to tackle underdevelopment, aimed at a positive exploitation of 'available factors.'

The years after 1949 were characterised by two different patterns of industrial development and production management. The First Five-Year Plan can be considered the most comprehensive attempt to learn from the Stalinist model of industrial management and to modernise underdeveloped Chinese industry.[57] This first period saw party control over management, militarisation of production, and mass methods to raise productivity. The scientific attitude towards capital accumulation and labour allocation – the Soviet road[58] – distinguished the policies of this period from those of the later 'Great Leap Forward' when mobilisation through mass campaigns and an attempt to create the double oxymoron of the 'urban-rural' 'worker-peasant' socialist labourer gained privileged status in the organisational theory of people's rural and urban communes.

The change in the general line of the Chinese leadership after the Cultural Revolution, prompted a re-evaluation of the interpretation of the 'labour force' (*laodong li*) in terms of *production factors* (*shengchan ziyuan*), and an evaluation of its rational allocation, not only or no longer based on the common interest, but also with an eye to productivity indicators.

Labour allocation became the target of a new 'scientific' approach based on recognition on the ideological front of:

(a) unemployment as a 'necessary' prerequisite under the new economic conditions;
(b) the worker as a party to the contract (no longer a mere buyer/seller of the workforce), with obvious implications for his/her position as master of the enterprise;
(c) the state as 'supervisor' of a multiple-actor allocation system, rather than general and sole employing agency: the 'clay' rice bowl was seen as increasingly fragile;
(d) work as increasingly associated (at least 'technically') with a commodity, as value and use-value began to differ progressively, and ownership of the means of production extended from only national and collective (both state and collective) to international and private;
(e) labour as a tool for accomplishment by the individual rather than the common interest of socialist society, as moral values traditionally associated with socialist work changed dramatically after the reforms and the party-state was unable to determine work behaviour.[59]

Debate intensified in the years of most intensive contract-oriented reform – starting with the 1986 regulations – when a major focus of intellectual activities on these questions was stimulated by the existence of a practical, daily-life reference (the implementation of the contract labour regulations) and by the sharp contradictions they introduced in the newly re-defined Marxist ortho-doxy, as well as by the consolidated practice of enterprise allocation of labour.

The debate on contracts originated from analysis of 'labour mobility' (*laodong li liudong*). Labour mobility rates have always been very low in China, not only in absolute terms but even com-pared, for example, to those in the USSR and other East European socialist countries.[60] The state allocation plan and the workers' high rate of dependence on enterprises were among the reasons for the limited interest of workers (in particular those working in the urban industrial state sector) in changing their jobs or moving from one unit to another. The need for higher production flexibility in accor-dance with the changing necessities of society and economic cycles during the reform period resulted in a theoretical hostility to work-force immobility, which was seen as a limitation on the possibility of achieving rationality in factor allocation in the Chinese econ-omy.[61] In fact, irrational overemployment policies were often accepted by enterprise managers who saw the assignment of new workers as a steady source of income from the state and, despite the counter-economic contribution of surplus worker, they were not willing to release workers as long as they received financial help in exchange;[62] while the workers' micro-economic behaviour tended to keep the level of satisfaction of their needs as high as possible without their leaving the unit.[63] The method of contracting was generally viewed as a rational tool to solve the issue of both low mobility and of the internal 'softness' of labour factor constraints.

The debate on labour reform in this period was therefore focused on two principal theoretical issues with clear policy impli-cations:

(a) the intrinsic nature of individual labour, that is, the question of a human being's possession of his/her working capability, and the economic relationship between the person and labour – elements that are hardly distinguishable and that can, neither jointly nor separately, become the object of trade;
(b) the transformation of the nature of socialist enterprises, in which market relationships were allegedly transforming workers from masters of the enterprise into suppliers of labour.

This framework also influenced the question of whether labour is or is not a commodity under 'socialist market' conditions, and the debate followed the rapid modifications in the official answer from 'no' to 'yes,'[64] despite the fact that both thesis and antithesis were still mainly based on Marxist-Leninist textbooks.

I set the Fourteenth Party Congress as the endpoint of this period, when market socialism was eventually adopted without restrictions and the structure of the economy again entered a new stage. The final decision to adopt labour market policies required a clear statement that labour *is* a commodity;[65] thereafter the discussion turned more concretely to *what* a *socialist* labour market had to be like.[66]

The Stage of Marketisation (1992–1995)

The years since 1992 are characterized by deepening economic reform and by a further bifurcation between the policy line and the dramatic movements of the labour markets.

Since the Fourteenth Party Congress (1992), China has acknowledged that the developmental model of its economy is 'market socialism.' This model grants equal status to the 'socialist state' and 'market mechanisms', a status that has allowed a dramatic increase in market-driven activities, as well as the further internationalisation of the economy, with far-reaching consequences for the labour market.

This period has been characterised by – if possible – even faster economic development of the Chinese economy, a growing role of the market, and a decrease in the role of the state. As a consequence of a more pragmatic attitude, the debate on labour has also abandoned most of its previous ideological assumptions, but has not been separated from its organic ties with the policymaking process. Once the nature of individual labour as a commodity became an accepted concept, discussion rapidly turned to the need for a 'market of production factors.'

The use of the term 'labour market' (*laodong shichang*), or 'labour force market' (*laodong li shichang*) was still contentious prior to the Fourteenth Congress. Actually, the dispute was less about the word 'market' than about the word *laodong* (labour) and the economic relationships it involved, such as the relationship between workers and their labour capacities. In fact it was only in 1992 that the alternative term *laowu shichang* (labour functions market) was replaced by the term labour market, eliminating the last theoretical resistance to the marketisation of labour.[67]

After 1980 China's labour discourse generally accepted that the labour force is allocated 'under the guidance of a state unified plan, through the combination of activities of labour departments, voluntary employment organisations, and self-employment.'[68] It was called a 'three in one' (*sanjiehe*) allocation system, featuring the existence of a general employment plan, as well as *bureaucratic* intervention of state agencies such as labour bureaus (*laodong ju*).

In the early 1990s, this picture of an efficient mixed allocation scheme was maintained, with one major evolution, the combination between 'market' and, not plan but, 'administrative adjustment,' (*xingzheng tiaojie*). Market actions are based on free labour mobility and autonomous decisions regarding employment, while the 'administrative adjustment' consists of the bureaucratic interventions of state bureaus influencing decisions by workers and enterprises about hiring and firing, work conditions, and labour relations.[69] This situation is a consequence of the general features of the contemporary path of the Chinese economy, precipitated by the definition of a 'double-track system' (*shuanggui zhidu*) to represent the present transitional stage, somewhere between a fully planned socialist system and a market economy. The identification and recognition of a *transitional* stage has been a further step to allow theoretical disputes to focus on the economic and social problems related to the issue of the labour market, without any longer having to be justified in the narrow frame of purely socialist ideology. After the Fourteenth Congress, market socialism became a 'major development in Marxist theory,' a definition that, on one side, reiterates the Marxist origins of China's socialism and, on the other, establishes a (probably definitive) distinction from the Marxist-Leninist understanding of labour and production relations and allows for 'further development' along an autonomous path.

In order for the role of market mechanisms to grow, a clear statement was required concerning who the actors in labour relations are: these were identified as 'free workers' (*ziyou gongren*) and enterprises; the latter were named 'units employing people' (*yong ren danwei*) in the 1994 Labour Law.

The debate focused on the *making* of free workers. Major difficulties in this respect were the high dependency of workers on enterprise benefits, such as housing facilities and services and the lack of a national social welfare system (*quanguo shehui baozhang jigou*). In fact, while dependence can be considered an advantage for individual workers, the difficulties in finding individual access to services outside the bureaucratic allocation by employing units is instead a disadvantage for the employer. Housing, medical care, and a protection system for the elderly and the retired are areas in which non-factory based welfare is underdeveloped.[70]

At this point, the term 'free worker,' which some Chinese authors use in a Marxist sense,[71] lost its significance as a person 'liberated from wage labour' and took on a meaning that can be summarised as a person free to act in the market and to make economic decisions without political and bureaucratic constraints.

The reform policies originating from such a turning point in the guiding economic assumptions involved are, on one side, the institution of new labour markets and, on the other, the implementation of fundamental legal tools to govern the market and rewrite a largely inadequate and old labour legislation.

On the institutional front, great attention was paid to the development of a wide net of urban service organisations of different kinds, with slightly different functions: urban 'labour markets' (*laodong li shichang*), administrative tools aimed at easing the demand and supply of labour, both skilled and unskilled; 'talent exchange centres' (*rencai zhongxin*), in charge of the 'rational mobility' (*heli liudong*) of skilled personnel as well as of training activities (talent exchange centres formally existed since 1983 but have grown in number and quality only in the 1990s, constituting an apparently more efficient system of recruitment for skilled labour); 'introduction bureaus,' (*laodong jieshao suo*) generally managed by local trade unions or by other mass organisations; 'labour service companies' (*laodong fuwu gongsi*) the original purpose of which was to help solve urban and rural unemployment, but have since developed on some occasions into autonomous organisers of productive activities and self-reliant 'units employing people.'

On the other major reform path, that of the creation of a legal system, a new labour law was approved in 1994 and implemented in 1995. This new law not only adopted legal mechanisms to manage labour markets and labour disputes but also provided an opportunity to introduce 'legal labour relations' (*laodong falü guanxi*) and 'labour relations' (*laodong guanxi*). More than for other reasons, this distinction was important because it was a formal statement of the existence both of persons acting rationally in a market according to 'rights and duties' regulated by law, and also of workers acting in the production process according to economic 'advantages and disadvantages' formally defined in the agreement (contract) with the enterprise and protected by the law.[72]

Furthermore, the 1994 Labour Law contains a formal definition of 'collective contract and bargaining,' assigning to trade unions the unusual role of collective contractor in the name of the workers.[73] This was the first, albeit only formal, recognition of the role that the ACFTU had been seeking since its own 1988 congress.

Theoretical, institutional, and legal reforms constitute only the 'formal side' of a dramatic transformation of practices and of the social role of labour during the entire reform period. This change has been much faster and has had much deeper consequences for living standards in recent years than expected, and the emergence of a formal side can be seen as an acknowledgement of the new features of the reality of urban labour. During the years of contractualisation and marketisation, in fact, the labour economy moved towards the goals of progressive deregulation of administrative controls, while the corresponding downgrading of the role of the bureaucracy boosted the development of informal forces, whose influence has been an important factor in reshaping economic, political, and cultural labour behaviour.

China's development is still progressing and any attempt to provide a comprehensive explanation of the entire process always generates problematic questions and contradictions. Nevertheless, the labour reform offers a complete set of parameters which can be used as a lens for viewing, and thus as an aid to understanding, the entire transformation of the 1980s and 1990s.

This work deals with only a few of these contradictions and uses only some of the lenses at the disposal of China specialists during these years. By collecting and presenting documentation as well as empirical data, I have tried to bring a long-neglected theoretical debate on labour back into the general picture of the contradictory roots of labour policy, of its development and of its achievements, where a sometimes Byzantine approach to theoretical analysis was accompanied by a pragmatic and incremental approach to policymaking. China, with its rapidly changing society and economy driving the fearful hand of the policymaker, is in the background. To complete this picture there is a need to further investigate the way institutions (those involved in industrial labour relations, such as work-units, trade unions, and families; and those involved in the market, such as local governments, and the agents of labour distribution and mobility) deal with policy. By dealing with labour reform this book thus firstly devotes its attention to the way socialism in China successfully eliminated its own basic features without abandoning the ideological framework that had created and legitimated its power; secondly to how deregulation made this demise possible in a constant loop of experiment, justification and crisis; and lastly to how this process is relevant for the evaluation of the recipe of the reform strategy, its apparent success, and its contradictory paths. For this reason, I will pay more attention to how the processes take shape and can be described during the entire period, rather than focusing on the structure of Chinese society and its components; I will use the amplifying effect of time to magnify the growing gaps between theory formulation and policy outcomes. To do this I am – partly illicitly – borrowing the eye of the historian in a field of analysis that belongs more to the sociologist and the economist.

1.4 Précis of the Research

I devote two chapters to each of the phases introduced above. The even chapters within each period (that is, Chapters 2, 4, and 6) are intended to address the political and ideological relevance of the steps of the labour reform, to report on the major ideological evolutions and to focus on the debates about the central issues. Chapter 2 deals with the re-emergence of a theoretical line based on the principle of 'distribution according to labour' that had been abandoned after the Great Leap Forward. Chapter 4 is largely a discussion about the nature of labour relations, and the theoretical question of whether or not labour can be considered a commodity. Chapter 6 reveals the surfacing of a clearly more economy-driven approach to the issue of labour, and the recognition of its nature of production factor, under the condition of the socialist commodity economy.

The odd chapters (3, 5, and 7) contain a parallel attempt to investigate how the evolutions in ideology and the gradual abandonment of the Leninist interpretation of labour became conscious policies of the state, how these policies often pushed much further than their theoretical premises and faced social and economic developments that created difficulties and engendered paradoxes. Chapter 3 investigates the economic rationale behind the initial steps of the labour reform, mainly related to wage and salary composition and distribution, after a decade of immobility and egalitarianism. In Chapter 5 the contractualisation of labour relations is considered, including the contradictions due to the co-emergence of an incomplete reform of the allocation mechanism and an increasing demand for flexibility from the 'buyers' of labour. The Epilogue (Chapter 7) presents final considerations on the most recent developments in the labour markets and analyses the role of labour in a phase of the transition in which the market is in full swing but bureaucratic intervention is still attempting to reduce the domino effect of a fully deregulated market. Drawing from different sets of data on labour markets this chapter attempts to present an understanding of the roles of the market and the state in the emerging labour allocation patterns, and to draw some conclusions on the divergence between socialist discourse and market deregulation in the 1990s.

2

DISTRIBUTION ACCORDING TO WHAT?

From Politics to Labour

2.1 Ownership and Distribution: The Limits of the Chinese Debate

The shape and mechanisms of the capitalist labour process as described by Marx long remained unchallenged in the Marxist system of thought, and existing socialist systems assumed this particular analysis of labour as a point of reference for all that is most evil in a production process based on exploitation. That evil side of the old societies was, however, according to a Marxist interpretation, also the highest expression of the capitalist phase of an inexorable evolution towards socialism, the role of which was to develop the forces of production.

Socialist labour theory was characterised by two major points. At the production level, acknowledgement of the 'technical' superiority of capitalist labour organisation, together with an emphasis on technological improvement of production methods, made the socialist labour process implemented on the shop floor very similar to the capitalist labour process, at least in the sphere of industrial production. Indeed, Lenin's admiration for Taylorist production techniques was frequently referred to in the labour process debate, as well as his condemnations of the alienating effects of such wage systems as full piece-rate, without focusing on the substantial, apparent contradiction.

At the higher level of the labour economy, the 'superiority' of the socialist system was mainly justified within the framework of the two issues of *ownership* and *distribution*; the nature and contradictions of *production relations* were mainly ignored, as it was assumed that they were no longer problematic in societies that had eliminated conflicts between labour and capital.

These general features of the attitude of later Marxism endured for a long time after Marx. Actually, Marx's analysis of the labour process under capitalism in the first volume of *Capital* did not evolve substantially during the next hundred years and not at all in the socialist countries after 1917. In the Soviet Union the approach was inclined towards a positive evaluation of capitalist achievements in the organisation of production, while it contributed to the emergence of a mystique about Marx's description of capital-labour relations.

Outside the Soviet Union, the socialist theory of labour organisation instead became an idealised model. As argued by sociologist Michael Burawoy, who was among the major voices in the renewed debate on capitalist and socialist labour relations in the 1970s, the general Marxist view of the socialist labour process developed along an irrational path.

> Whatever was taken to be the defining nature of the capitalist labour process was mechanically inverted to yield a productivist vision of socialism. Work became the arena of emancipation to the exclusion of all else. Thus if the capitalist labour process was defined by the separation of conception and execution, then the socialist labour process had to be the opposite – the reunification of conception and execution; if the capitalist labour process was defined by de-skilling, then socialism had to herald the restoration of the craftsman – a romantic resurrection of the past; if the capitalist labour process was defined by hierarchy, then the socialist labour process was defined by the abolition of hierarchy; control by capital gave way to control by workers. And if capitalist technology made it impossible to realize worker control, the abolition of hierarchy, or the reunification of conception and execution, then a new technology would be required to inaugurate socialism. In each instance, the realities of capitalism were juxtaposed with some utopian construction of socialism obtained through the miraculous abolition of alienation, atomization, subordination, or whatever.[1]

It was only in the 1970s, after some comparisons between labour relations under capitalism and under socialism were publicly advocated, that the international debate about the Marxist interpretation of capitalist labour relations was reinvigorated and developed. That such contradictions as alienation and subordination also existed in socialist countries was made evident by the famous work of Miklos Haraszti[2] who reported his experience in a Hungarian tractor factory[3] where labour relations were dominated by the 'despotism' of a piece-rate wage system. Although some regard the particular nature of work relations in that factory to be 'unusually despotic,'[4] this was probably the first time that socialist labour relations were looked at realistically.

The widespread debate on the labour process under monopoly capitalism and state socialism that developed after Haraszti's work as well as after the 1974 groundbreaking work by Harry Braverman[5] involved an evaluation of such general features as de-skilling and the separation of conception and execution in capitalist production, and rapidly expanded to include socialist labour systems. The latter debate was based particularly on the works of Hungarian sociologists and economists[6] who initiated a discussion on socialist economies and labour society that was to extend its influence also into China, but only in a much later phase. In fact, although this debate was in full swing during the years of the Chinese economic recovery from the Cultural Revolution (1966–1976), it had no real influence on China until the second half of the 1980s, and was probably largely unknown to policymakers, at least in its initial years.[7]

The main reason for this can easily be identified as the cultural isolation of China not only from the West, but also from other socialist countries after the door had been closed to the outside world during the radical years between 1966 and 1976. But other factors also contributed to defining the framework for the Chinese labour debate in the initial years after the Cultural Revolution.

To understand these factors, and to safely navigate through the long pages of Chinese characters written on this argument during these years, a preliminary evaluation must be made on the basis of what is and what is not found in this period of the debate, that is in the years after 1977.

The first distinction is one that has already been mentioned: the debate over labour concentrated on such issues as ownership and distribution; we should not expect to find a direct discussion of 'labour relations,' of 'production relations,' or of 'labour conditions.'

Furthermore, even the policy measures that were intended to affect the labour process directly, such as the re-introduction of piece-rate wages, the re-organisation of individual and group bonuses, and the assignment of material incentives, were generally seen as tools of socialist *distribution*, and their controversial, non-egalitarian, and partially despotic nature were generally justified by a belief in the intrinsic superiority of socialist ownership of the means and modes of production.

Nor was there any theoretical reference in the debate other than to Marx and to the Leninist interpretation of his works, or any other scientific tool of analysis other than that of Marxism-Leninism. Such 'bourgeois' sciences as labour sociology had not yet been developed and it took several years before the scientific community was able to fully recover from the devastation to academic and research institutions caused by the Cultural Revolution.

This was a clear disadvantage in systemic and political analysis as well, as Marx's framework for evaluation of a *socialist* system is rather weak and limited to some asystematic notes on future socialism which penetrated China through Lenin's interpretative work. Consequently, the socialist nature of the Chinese system had to be demonstrated at the theoretical level by its anti-capitalist nature, in a dialectic way that recalls Burawoy's 'mechanic inversion' of capitalism quoted earlier. A significant example of the pervasiveness of this influence can be found in a work by Su Shaozhi and Feng Lanrui, among the most astute and most critical intellectuals of the reform period, who in 1977 expressed their view on the 'Gang of Four's accusation of the 'capitalist nature of distribution according to labour' (DATL). Their defence of the principle was mainly based on Marx's description of the capitalist production and distribution processes, concluding with the statement that capitalist and socialist production are 'basically *different in nature; the first is based on exploitation, the second is *not* based on exploitation*'![18]

This 'quick exit' from the problem characterized the entire debate during 1977. Thereafter, greater attention was focused on the *mechanisms* of the distribution system, while production problems and labour analysis in a larger economic context were not considered until implementation of the contract system in 1983–86.

What are the reasons for such a narrow dimension to the labour debate?

China's isolation has already been mentioned, but another consequence of the previous ten years of turmoil was a sort of homogenisation of arguments raised by commentators; whatever the argument, it could be reduced to criticism of the 'Gang of Four' and the re-establishment of the socialist truth about egalitarianism and non-egalitarianism through reference to Marx's 'Critique of the Gotha Program' and Lenin's 'State and Revolution'. The latter is the classic Bolshevik interpretation of the former, and both were maniacally quoted. The three pages containing Marx's statement about social labour as the only criterion for the allocation of wealth in a socialist state were cited an infinite number of times, together with criticism of Lassalle's 'integral labour profit' principle.[9] This was a self-imposed limit on the entire debate during a period when political instability and uncertainty about the future party leadership suggested caution in developing new and far-reaching theoretical initiatives.

The attitude towards theory and the consequent political practice during 1977 and the initial months of 1978, before the Third Plenum of the Eleventh Party Congress defined the objective of modernisation as the guiding principle in the economy and society and gave Deng Xiaoping sufficient legitimacy to lead the CCP, was mainly destructive: it was aimed at destroying the apparatus, political networks, and ideological influence around such leaders as Zhang Chunqiao, Wang Hongwen, and Yao Wenyuan, the members (along with Jiang Qing, Mao's widow) of the clique embodying all the negative products of radical leftism, namely, the 'Gang of Four.'[10]

At times, some of the participants in the debate seemed to forget their 'scientific' demeanour and the 'natural superiority' of the principle of distribution according to labour and to embrace the weapons of anti-radicalism in order to label the gang's members and supporters with such apparently common designations at that time as 'traitor' or 'Nationalist spy.' Although this reflected a consolidated style of debate inside the CCP, sometimes such behaviour went beyond the scope of political struggle, and personal accusations became scientific demonstrations of the illegitimacy of theoretical points. The violence of such attacks is but one of the expressions of the political and cultural climate of that period, when personal resentment over the tragedy of Cultural Revolution policies was paralleled by manoeuvring in the bureaucracy and political takeovers.

In this context Mao's 1956 discourse 'On the Ten Great Relationships' was republished, which became an important formal point of reference for the debate, at least for some months between 1977 and the Third Plenum of December 1978, under the auspices of Mao's chosen successor, Hua Guofeng, who was willing to prove the theoretical independence of Mao's (and consequently his own) political line from the leftist radicalism of the gang. The political struggle and the violent diatribes of dialectic criticism against the gang were also aimed at maintaining the only autonomous theoretical basis still existing after the disaster of the Cultural Revolution, namely, Mao's 'socialism with Chinese characteristics,' a legacy of the early revolutionary stage of China's socialist experience.

As at other moments of radical change in revolutionary societies, a re-elaboration of orthodoxy led to a null-point in theory, that is, a moment in which even the most obvious among the basic concepts needed to be restated and accepted, not so much for their founding importance as to destroy the legitimacy of the previous (*ancien*) regime.

Further reducing the range of issues in the debate was China's traditional limited knowledge of Marxist texts and Marxist tradition. In the 1950s, China had learned how to build a socialist state from Soviet manuals (and from the unidirectional visits of Soviet technicians to China) rather than from Soviet 'experience,'[11] while knowledge of Marxism and Marxist texts was always limited by the comprehensive role of the so-called Maoist adaptation of Marxism-Leninism.

> Is distribution according to labour a socialist or a capitalist principle? This seems a laughable question: we already experienced twenty-eight years of socialist revolution and someone who supports the Gang of Four still doesn't know what principle this is! But, in fact, so it is![12]

Li Honglin put the question for a different objective, but in fact the lack of knowledge of Marxist theory and evolution sometimes turned the debates into scholarly exercises that lacked the tools with which to analyse a complex reality and thus could not further an understanding of the social and economic evolution until the industrial labour and production systems were faced with the need for a radical reform based on economic factors.

The focus on issues mainly related to distribution and ownership was also a sign of a poor understanding and lack of investigation into the dynamics of all the components of the labour process (organisation, technology factors, role and nature of the bureaucracy, influence of external factors, etc).

Since the 1980s, the internationalisation of the Chinese economy has shown that technology and organisation in China were plagued by many of the same problems found in the monopoly capitalist system. Mao's statement that 'the difference between now and before is in the *ownership* of the means of productions' rapidly became insufficient to justify the superiority of the socialist labour process *vis à vis* the competitive western enterprises with their culture of efficiency and hard-budget constraints. But during the initial years of the debate ownership remained a central topic, and *the* main difference between the socialist and capitalist conceptions of labour.

2.2 'Distribution According to Labour' (DATL): Rehabilitation of a Socialist Principle

While emphasis was focused on economic modernisation after the end of the Cultural Revolution, the origins of the new drive were political, so that the economic reassessment of DATL as the guiding distributive principle was still mainly considered a result of political decisions rather than of simple economic or social considerations. The economy-first approach did not correspond – during the first phase – to a larger independence of the economy from politics, but, on the contrary, it contributed to the devolution of further political attention to economic issues.

Ironically, the explosion of DATL, both in terms of ideological relevance and of the 'quantity' of words expended, was to provoke a downgrading of the redistributive functions in socialist economic construction. In fact, it was important that fundamental and radical opposition to such issues as income and wage differentials, the rationalisation of production, and the decentralisation of industrial decisions be eliminated. This could be done only by placing the redistributive principle in the appropriate place within the general ideological framework, whereby distribution was featured as a *part* of the economic production process rather than as *the* characteristic feature of socialism. This theoretical effort resulted in a dialectic reduction in the importance of the redistributive principle and in a reassessment of the positive role of 'unequal' distribution (as opposed to purely egalitarian distribution) to stimulate the 'liberation of productive forces' (*shengchan li de jiefang*).

DATL was re-evaluated at a time when the role played by Chinese academics in the policy process was growing significantly. In 1977 alone (the year the Chinese Academy of Social Sciences – CASS – was founded), three major conferences were held in Beijing to 'Discuss the Socialist Principle of Distribution According to Labour' (*lun anlao fenpei shehui zhuyi yuanze*). The conferences took place in April, June, and October-November, and were organised mainly by former leading cadres and members of the State Council Political Research Office (*Guowuyuan zhengzhi yanjiu suo*), a think-tank inspired by Deng Xiaoping in 1975. A critical role in the 1977 conferences, as well as in the fourth and fifth conferences (in 1978 and 1983, respectively) was played by Yu Guangyuan, a senior cadre in the office and later a vice president of CASS, who wrote the opening and closing addresses of each conference.[13] The conferences and the debate as a whole led to a mobilisation of policymakers and academics, as demonstrated by participation both in the events themselves and in the public follow-up, of such leading intellectuals as the economists Su Shaozhi[14] (later director of the Institute of Marxism-Leninism and Mao Zedong Thought at CASS), Wu Jinglian (one of Su's most prominent students), Feng Lanrui (later a deputy at Su's institute), Zhao Lükuan, and others. Among the party leaders, Yu Guangyuan represented other major figures involved in the Political Research Office, such as Hu Qiaomu and Deng Liqun, who became leading ideologists of the post Cultural Revolution CCP (although their views were soon to diverge greatly).[15] 'Academics were mobilised by an academic member of the policy elite,'[16] such as Yu Guangyuan, while theoretical disputes were not only a simple step in policy formation but also contributed to rehabilitating and supporting Deng's position within the party.

The conferences and their results were accompanied by a large number of influential essays and articles in the major scientific journals, as well as in the official party newspapers. An authoritative article signed by an anonymous 'People's Daily special commentator' (*Renmin ribao teyue pinglun yuan*) on 5 May 1978[17] summarizes the results of the debate during the 1977 conferences. Not surprisingly, the article opened with a positive affirmation of the socialist nature of DATL as a socialist principle, and with a paradigmatic quotation from the three leading referential texts:

Under socialism each individual producer obtains from society – after due detractions – exactly as much as he contributed. [Marx[18]]

... Human society can only develop from capitalism to socialism, that is to evolve towards public property of the means of production and towards distribution according to labour. [Lenin[19]]

... Under socialism, material distribution must also be based on the principle 'from each according to his capability, to each according to his work', there cannot be an absolute egalitarianism [Mao[20]].[21]

The three references are familiar to any follower of the debate in those months, and – despite their conciseness – actually constitute a notable part of what has been written about this principle in what we will refer to as the 'classic' Marxist-Leninist literature.

Due to the dimension of the debate itself, which involved a large number of actors and resulted in the publication of thousands of pages in the Chinese press (as well as many books), it is sometimes impossible to distinguish original statements from slavish reproductions of generally recognised and propagandistic ideas.

Before evaluating its contents, some kind of schematisation must be undertaken – even if a bit forcibly – of the issues, structure, and aims as well as of the general path followed by the debate in correspondence to policy shifts and the various phases of the intensifying political struggle:

(a) As already noted, the debate was mainly negative and aimed at the prosecution and condemnation of the leftist positions as expressed by the members of the gang. Two major interests played concurrent roles: those of the new leadership emerging after the end of the Cultural Revolution, with the standing of a feeble Hua Guofeng progressively challenged and finally replaced by Deng Xiaoping's behind-the-scenes political manoeuvres; and those of a re-emerging cultural elite, slowly recovering from disgrace during the Cultural Revolution and willing to lend the new leadership their effective support through massive participation in the re-legitimation effort.

(b) During the 1977 conferences this concurrence generated an almost monolithic line around solid, politically justified positions. DATL had to be reinstated, mainly because it had been one of the major targets of the egalitarian drive publicly identified with the gang.

As noted by Sheehan, the old system was itself linked to the 'era of Cultural Revolution leftism, so that it became difficult to defend egalitarianism or social security without appearing to be defending late Maoism....'[22] This often was more relevant than the rational economic reasons behind it: the rigidity of the centrally-planned wage system, as well as the deterioration of living standards among workers as a consequence of the economic crisis, had to be alleviated, and while a major wage reform was immediately approved on the policy front,[23] the open visibility of this debate on the propaganda front became the principal vehicle to 'prepare' public opinion for the major changes in the labour system to be decided in and after 1978.

For these reasons (converging interests and propagandistic purposes) the debate in 1977 was deprived of real disputation, and was generally based on nearly static and unsupported opinions attributed to the gang. Attention was focused on such apparently hollow issues as the alleged nature of 'bourgeois rights' (*zichan jieji quanli*) in DATL, the role of public ownership in defining whether or not industrial labour falls under the label of exploitation, and the role of DATL in creating income differentials and producing a 'division into two classes' (*liangji fenhua*).

(c) A larger controversy emerged when the discussion (after the fourth conference in 1978) turned to the policy steps to be taken, and included such labour-process related issues as the reinstatement of piece-rate wages, production bonuses, and so-called material incentives (*wuzhi cizhi*). At that point, the discussion became a more direct component of the policy process, specifically of the preparatory work for the coming Third Plenum, coinciding with experimentation inside production units, for the reform of both labour and management systems. The debate at the 1978 conference served a purpose that paralleled that on the pragmatic nature of socialism, which resulted in the resurrection of the famous slogan 'practice is the sole criterion of truth.' Many references were made to the criterion discussion during this conference,[24] which in terms of its size, involvement, and political participation had a decisive influence on the elaboration of the economic policy of modernisation and reform that was discussed and approved only a few weeks later at the plenum.

(d) The entire period of Chinese reform until 1984 was characterized by the absence of legislative measures or 'definitive' regulations. Most of the policy measures were *experimental* steps and there was a relative fluctuation and differentiation in the application of generally recognised principles. The debate was therefore increasingly influenced by the need to express both proposals and evaluations of the policy process, as well as by the existence of referential experiments already underway. The line was set by the party's central bodies but major shifts and adjustments took place at the local level, both in the field of wages and distribution and in that of management and enterprise autonomy.

This shift from *justification* to *evaluation* appeared clearly at the fifth conference held in Beijing from 18–23 July 1983. At that time, the political struggle had apparently subsided and the five years of experimentation were leading the economic strategy of Chinese socialism on a more stable reform path. DATL remained *the* principle and the classic literature remained *the* reference, but the discussion took account of the method of evaluation of the economic results of policies. Similarly, the technique of *diaocha* (investigation) became fashionable and was used extensively, but it remained a nominal practice for some time, with a mainly 'organic' point of view. Eventually, the focus moved to 'what has been done' and 'what remains to be done.' The policy measures taken heretofore appeared to be 'initial steps' on an already defined path, that would be followed further with the decisions of the 1984 plenum and the opening of a new phase.

2.3 The 1977 Conferences: The Rehabilitation of Dismantled Ideologies

As already mentioned, one of the purely theoretical disputes at the origin of the debate on the nature of DATL was raised by the interpretation of Marx's words in his 'Critique of the Gotha Programme:'

Here [in socialist society] obviously the same principle prevails as that which regulates the exchange of commodities, as far as this is exchange of equal values.

Content and form are changed, because, under the altered circumstances no one can give anything except his labour, and because, on the other hand, nothing can pass to the ownership of individuals except individual means of consumption. But as far as the distribution of the latter among the individual producers is concerned, the same principle prevails as in the exchange of commodity equivalents: so much labour in one form is exchanged for an equal amount of labour in another form. Hence the *equal right* here is still in principle *bourgeois righ*t, although principle and practice are no longer at logger-heads, while the exchange of equivalents in commodity exchange only exists *on the average* and not in the individual case.

In spite of this advance, this *equal right* is still stigmatised by a bourgeois limitation. The right of the producers is proportional to the labour they supply; the equality consists in the fact that measurement is made with an equal standard, labour.[25]

This brief statement and the concept of bourgeois right laid the foundations for the attacks on the principle by the gang. The stress on egalitarianism by Zhang Chunqiao and Wang Hongwen in 1975 was consistent with their historical evaluation about *what point* socialist evolution had reached at that time. The socialist nature of the 'initial phase of socialism' was debated and denied by Zhang and Wang on the basis of the bourgeois right (*das bürger-liche Recht*) described in Marx's booklet; this position was the main political target during the 1977 conferences and later.[26]

One of the academics who actively took part in the discussion pointed out in a later book that the discussion was partially affected by a problem of terminology arising from difficulties in the translation and understanding of the term.[27] In the Chinese edition of 'Gotha,' first published in 1950 as translated by He Sijing and Xu Bing, the German words *das bürgerliche Recht* were translated as *zichan zhe quanli* (literally, right of the bourgeoisie), while in the following revised version it was changed to *zichan jieji faquan* (legal rights of the bourgeois class). A special meeting of the Bureau of Translation of the Works of Marx, Engels Lenin, and Stalin' was held in 1956 to discuss this specific issue but no solution was reached and the word legal (*fa*) was not replaced until the 1977 debate and a comparison with the English translations.

According to Feng's interpretation, this misunderstanding might have resulted from the several meanings of the word *Recht*:

> The German word *Recht* has many meanings, such as law (*fa*), right (*quanli*), correct (*dui*), justice (*gongdao*). ... Marx, when raising the point of *das bürgerliche Recht* in his *Critique of the Gotha Programme*, was comparing the exchange on the basis of equal quantities of labour and the principle of equal price commodity exchange; that means he was dealing with *quanli* (rights) relationships and not with legal (*fa*) relationships.[29]

This was probably not the first time that mistakes in translation have lead to wrong policy formulations, but Feng is probably trying to blame Cultural Revolution theorists not only for their limited knowledge of Marxist literature, but also for their narrow attention to nothing but words, instead of 'seeking truth from facts.'

Apparently basing their ideas on this 'wrong' translation, the members of the Gang of Four started to build an 'all-embracing theory of bourgeois legal rights'[30]: their criticism of DATL developed along three major lines: (a) the nature of the principle as an 'old thing' (*jiu shiwu*), that is, a product of the old, bourgeois society and not of the socialist revolution; (b) the risk of a growth in income differentials, that is, of the separation of the two social strata and, consequently, (c) the inevitable emergence of a new bourgeois class.

The attention of later critics concentrated on these three main points. The debate constituted a major conflict between two main interpretations of socialism, not merely a technical dispute between different policy options. Actually these options were determined by the struggle that took place within the party, while justification for the new attitude was less simple than today's account of that period might lead us to expect.

The 1978 article in the *People's Daily* was very careful to search for Mao's own ideas on the issue, and the result was that all the quotes come from the pre-Cultural Revolution years, sometimes ironically re-evaluating the Great Leap Forward radicalism.[31] This enthusiasm for Mao's understanding of the very features of socialism was not coincidental as it corresponded to Hua Guofeng's attempt to redefine his weak political position in the shadow of the Great Helmsman. It was later gradually abandoned as Deng solidified his position and a new ideological environment was created whereby Mao became more of a symbol than a cultural or political reference.

In fact, after the 1977 conferences there were still controversial attitudes towards DATL, not only in regard to the way to implement it, but even in the nature of the principle itself.

Summing up the positions at the 1977 conferences, Wen Min wrote in 1978:

> ... DATL has a positive effect but also some negative effects. DATL is the direct result of public ownership of the means of production. It abolishes exploitation and any distribution system of the previous societies based on private ownership. The implementation of DATL makes positive contributions to the elimination of capitalism and to the development of socialist production. Nevertheless, DATL has not yet cast off the narrow mentality of bourgeois rights and has some negative effects. Some comrades believe the negative effects are secondary to the positive effects. Some comrades also think that income differences are a step backward from the Communist principle of 'to each according to his needs,' but still an advance if compared to the wide gap between the rich and poor under capitalism.[32]

Later, 'unstable' positions such as this were doomed to be criticized as theoretical errors.

There were cases of essays in which the first part claimed that DATL had no negative effects, while various defects were pointed out in the second part; others in which piece-rate wages were initially supported and then defined as no more than an accessory form of salary; and yet others in which, after claims that distribution must not rely on politics, the idea of distribution according to political attitude was supported. Timid and mitigated analysis often resulted in self-contradictory theoretical positions, indulging in vagueness and ambiguity.[33]

Criticism of the radical positions was not yet accompanied by a redefinition of the guiding policies for labour and distribution; nor was there a clear reassessment of the scope and aims of Chinese socialism. These became clear only in the months immediately preceding the Third Plenum of the Eleventh Party Congress in late 1978. This was still a transitional stage in which signs of continuity were probably more important than historical breaks.

2.4 The 1978 Fourth Conference on DATL: Writing the Line for the Plenum

As seen earlier, there was a significant difference between the three initial sessions of the DATL conferences and the fourth, held from 25 October to 3 November 1978. This difference originated not only in the subject, organisation, and issues that the conference dealt with, but also in the different political environment and strategic tasks determined by the imminent path-breaking Third Plenum of the Eleventh Party Congress.

It is probably fair to go so far in evaluating the organic role of this eight-day conference as to consider it a part of the 'working meeting' which prepared for the plenum that started only seven days later, and was to last for about one month.

The leadership and equilibrium as well as the policy line were going to be dramatically changed within a few weeks and a definitive re-evaluation of Deng Xiaoping was to once again make him, the most powerful among the new reformists. At the opening session of the plenum Deng released a powerful and appealing speech, focusing on pragmatism in politics ('seeking truth from facts', was the new slogan), flexibility and economic decentralization.[34]

The DATL conference, with its increasingly pragmatic attitude, also resulted in a sort of preparatory policy statement for the plenum. This is evidently why a reappraisal of such tools as material incentives, piece-rate wages, and bonuses accompanied the theoretical redefinition of DATL as a guiding socialist distribution principle.

The discussion, as well as the experimental implementation of material benefits, had already begun in 1977, but an acceleration of both the experiments and theoretical developments became evident during the following year.

A major thrust came, on the one hand, from Hu Qiaomu's speech on economic guidelines, published in October, advocating the concurrent re-implementation of DATL as a distribution principle[35] and the expansion of the autonomy of enterprises 'so that enterprise leadership as well as staff and workers would take a more active interest in economic results,'[36] and, on the other, from Deng Xiaoping's earlier condemnation of the practice of 'to each according to politics,' that is the policy of granting wage differentials only for political correctness or 'performance' (*zhengzhi biaoxian*). It is significant that the official guidelines for the 1977 wage adjustment still explicitly referred to *zhengzhi biaoxian*, while the term disappeared from all labour documents following the Third Plenum.[37]

Consequently, the origins of the 1978 debate were deeply rooted in previous political statements of a theoretical (political) as well as economic nature. The topics that had not yet 'achieved a thorough comprehension' were at this point not only 'the general law of DATL,' but more specifically its 'relations to material incentives,' 'the most suitable form of salary,' as well as the extension of the principle to the agricultural sector.[38]

Although still focusing on distribution, this conference devoted much more attention to the *mechanism* rather than to the *principle*. Thus, it clearly appeared, that the implementation of DATL was intended to increase labour efficiency; a way to deal with the labour concept, to determine its role and meaning within the DATL formula such that it was overtly considered as a measurement unit for the calculation of individual and collective contributions to production.

This helped to focus part of the discussion on wage rates and their positive or negative influence on such parameters as productivity, performance, worker motivation, participation, and on recently addressed issues such as workers' individual economic interests. Furthermore, Hu Qiaomu's speech was largely used as an official endorsement of the initial steps of economic decentralisation of the distribution process through enterprise autonomy.

Individual interests (*geren liyi*) as well as material incentives (*wuzhi ciji*) were at the centre of the 1978 re-evaluation, while many commentators, believing the theoretical issues were already settled, turned to slightly more technical problems in the implementation of piece-rates and bonuses.

As for piece-rates, initial experiments induced optimism among observers about the possibility of raising worker motivation, and pushed the focus to the fields of possible application (hard manual labour only or mechanized and intellectual, labour?), to ways of implementation (limited to extra-quota production or unlimited?), and to the basis of calculation (individual or collective performance?). The result was an assessment of the 'protection of workers' individual interests' as the main task of socialism, on the one hand, in reaction to the ten years of radical negation of individual benefits, and, on the other, of a different approach to the role of individual and collective economic entities:

Socialist 'material benefits' have the workers' own labour as a basis, under the conditions of public property of the means of production and collective labour. ... Regardless of whether they are individual or collective workers, their material benefits are decided by the quantity, quality, and efficiency of their labour. In other words, public ownership of the means of production is decisive for the socialist nature of material interests and all objectives of socialist production aim at protecting and increasing the workers' material interests; the principle of distribution according to labour, consequently, is the correct measure for calculating the part of global production to be distributed to single or collective workers. The more and the better their work, the higher their material benefits; the lower and the worse their work, the lower their material benefits.[39]

This position, adding the quality factor to the principle of *duolao duode, shaolao shaode* ('who works more gets more, who works less gets less'), accompanied the first steps of an 'economy-first' wage policy, in which 'economic interest is an objective economic category' and 'all individual interests have an economic nature.'[40]

A description of the economic characteristics of 'non-developed socialist society' (*fei fada shehui zhuyi shehui*) can help provide an understanding of the basic features of this new economic, developmental attitude towards socialist labour:

Non-developed socialist societies have the following major characteristics:
1. There is still a large quantity of manual labour, in particular in the agricultural sector ....
2. Due to the low level of the productive forces, workers have low cultural and technical skills, while their differences in natural labour ability are also very great; the outcome of individual labour is, by consequence, also very different ....
3. The means of production are still under two different ownership systems ....
4. The socialist commodity economy and the effects of the price law still exist.
5. The capitalist economy, classes and class struggle, as well as exploitation of man over man, still exist.[41]

This evaluation, which considers socialism to be one of the historical phases of economic development, was to be a part of the 'modernisation' approach, the winning trend at the Third Plenum. Development and growth of the economy was the correct road to advance to the stage of a 'developed socialist society' (*fada shehui zhuyi shehui*). The idea that generally came to be accepted during these months focused on increasing the flexibility of administrative measures and extending the independence enjoyed by each unit, which needed to be free

> to choose the most suitable form of salary for its workers in accordance with its specificity in the fields of product characteristics, production duties, technological conditions, [and] administrative levels,[42]

The matter of the independence of production units and of income distribution had practical implications for DATL:

> After a short period of discussion, some problems [concerning DATL] were made clear (e.g., DATL is not the economic foundation of capitalism; socialist society has to implement material incentives together with spiritual incentives and time rates together with piece-rate wage systems etc.). But on some other points there was not yet a complete opening ..., 1) how to create a link between individual income and the economic management of the enterprise, and 2) how to implement material incentives for cadres ....[43]

> The socialist economy is organised in the entire society through planning; this is the root of its superiority over capitalism. But we cannot use this point to deny the role and position of enterprises. Enterprises are the constituent units of a socialist economy, as well as the economic foundation of the society as a whole.[44]

This is only one of the earliest statements that cleared the path for the theoretical demise of the long-lasting central policy of 'rational low wages' and for the introduction of a new enterprise policy in the following months and years.

To sum up, from the point of view of an outside observer, the labour debate, before and after it passed the 'historical turning point' at the Third Plenum, was characterised more by what it did not deal with than by what it did deal with. While the importance of labour as an economic factor was becoming increasingly clear in the minds of commentators and in the official line, distribution issues were still of overwhelming importance, and economic contradictions at the level of labour relations continued to be ignored. The reasons for this direction in the debate are partly to be found in the dogmatic nature of the ideological references as well as in the assumption of the fundamental superiority of socialist property and production. But still it is surprising not to find any reference (either positive or negative) to the debate on the socialist labour process that was developing in the same months in Eastern Europe and among Western Marxists.

That is why the definition of labour most suitable for summarizing the present stage of the debate remains one of pure Leninist origins:

> ... Under DATL, labour is the quantity and quality of labour translated into its mobile shape, that is the time worked.[45]

The specific importance of the 1978 conference lies in its policy-oriented approach. The scientific community was collectively organised to help write the new party line, to set the concrete objectives of the reform. While the written results of this collective effort were still full of ideological references and political aims, the attempt to submit 'objective' (*keguan*) economic analysis seems to be the major innovation in the methodological field. The conference was presented as one in which the institutional and the production world, as well as other elements from economic circles (*jingji jie*), were called to contribute their experiences. It was what we would call a lobbying activity, with a specific political reference to those people due to shortly take over the leadership of the CCP. It was one of the first initiatives that involved the newly founded CASS. There were also some organisational difficulties and 'unofficial' features; blooming ideas and contending intellectuals were mobilised in the common effort of the political takeover, with some evident contradictions to Hua Guofeng's line of continuity, and against it.

As Yu Guangyuan himself later recalled:

> You all still remember that our situation at the time of that conference was still very hard: we had no funds; the

> meeting hall, materials, and personnel were up to the ini-
> tiative of the participants and relied on the help of the
> individual work-units. Comrades from outside of Beijing
> all paid for their own board and lodging. At that time, the
> CCP leaders were maintaining the 'two whatever'[46]
> approach, and there was no other way [to discuss].[47]

Yu's comments clearly indicate that the problem was more than one of logistics. These were years of intense political struggle that resulted in the final success of Deng Xiaoping and his reformist supporters. Labour was one of the issues at the top of the reformist agenda, because of the need to face the general discontent among workers due to the long-standing stagnation of salaries, and of its great political importance as an anti-leftist approach. Furthermore, this, together with the almost contemporary debate on 'practice as the sole criterion of truth,' was probably one of the first public appearances of the alliance between party reformists and intellec-tuals that characterised the initial years of economic reform. Not surprisingly, therefore, the associated difficulties in organising such a conference were much greater in 1977 and 1978 than they were to be in 1983 when this alliance was well established.

2.5 Towards an Enlargement of the Labour Debate

In the following years, labour reform kept advancing along the lines of economic reorganisation and decentralisation and was mainly associated with wage reform and wage adjustment. By January 1979, as a direct consequence of the new line set down by the Third Plenum, a 'Forum on Labour and Wages' discussed how to eliminate the 'low wage, high employment policy.'

Some important steps in a redefinition of labour policies took place in the five years between the fourth and the fifth DATL conferences. In October 1978 the All-China Federation of Trade Unions (ACFTU) was re-established. The re-establishment of the ACFTU was part of the recovery of mass organisations after the turbulent years of the Cultural Revolution, and corresponded with the emergence of a more conflictual labour economy. After a decade of dismantlement, and lacking revolutionary status (unlike the Russian Unions after the 1917 Revolution), the posi-tion of the unions was extremely weak. The leadership of the ACFTU did not advocate any independent role for the unions until very late in the 1980s, and instead aligned itself with the

Leninist role of a 'transmission belt' between the party and the working masses.[48]

The wage system evolved towards progressive diversification, the main reason for this being the increasing independence of enterprise management and the different strategies in the central allocation of resources to the localities and to enterprises. The main steps in this evolution were the so-called 'profit retention' policy (1979–81), which allowed enterprises to decide independently on the allocation of a portion of their profits, and the new 'factory director responsibility system' (1981), which gave managers responsibility over their enterprise's performance. Both systems allowed for more independent behaviour in the field of labour allocation (although the allocation of general resources, including labour, was still mainly a central prerogative).

The new policies also provided an occasion for many local leaders to climb the ladder of central power. The success of the reformers at the Third Plenum was soon followed by the replacement of the leftists in the party with new leaders, culminating in the removal of Hua Guofeng from his post as prime minister and his replacement by Zhao Ziyang in 1980. While leftist attitudes and central planning still played an important role, there was limited contention over the general needs expressed by the reformist line. The renewed debate in the labour field was characterised by attention to emerging economic contradictions and political and economic evaluations on the ongoing experimental stage.

As already argued, the Chinese debate over labour was not independent of policy options or the political struggle. Even the choice of issues to be raised during these years, in the framework established by the reappraisal of DATL, did not deviate from this rule.

As an example of this functional link, the insistence on a distinction between productive and nonproductive labour between 1979 and 1980 reflected a need to deepen the understanding of the general rule as applied not only to 'labour processes' (*laodong chengdu*) and 'labour relations' (*laodong guanxi*), but also to some practical difficulties in the growing industrial structure in China. In fact, the extension of the definition of 'productive labour' – from 'direct production activities' (*zhijie shengchan*) to 'social activities that satisfy any material or cultural need of the society' – responded to specific economic and social requirements: the need for technology and consequently for skilled and motivated technicians to boost the development of modern industry, and the need to eliminate the ideological superiority of manual labour over management and white-collar workers.

A third factor in the re-evaluation of intellectual labour was the recognition of the economic rights of the intellectual elite who had supported the initial steps of the economic reform. At the 1983 conference, where, as mentioned, great attention was devoted to evaluation of the results of labour policy since 1977, several authors criticized the paradox of the existence of sharp income gaps between non-skilled manual labour and intellectual labour, arguing that 'intellectual labour is not a simple type of labour force. It is skilled, developed, and educated labour,'[49] and as such it has to be considered and remunerated.

Some important new issues characterised the labour debate during these years. Some of these were merely theoretical reassessments, others were a more direct response to social and economic phenomena. An interesting statement on the state of the art in the labour debate was issued at the founding meeting of the Chinese Labour Research Association (*Zhongguo laodong xuehui*), held in Beijing from 14 to 19 January 1982.

A much more complicated dimension of the labour issue emerged from that discussion. The labour issue was extended beyond the field of distribution; for the first time the principles of central 'unified allocation' (*tongbao tongpei*) of the labour force and employment (*jiuye*) were problematic.

> What is the meaning of 'waiting for employment' [*daiye*] and 'unemployment' [*shiye*]? Some believe they have the same meaning, because they both indicate people whose working ability cannot be integrated with the means of production, whose labour force cannot become a means of life. But the distinction between the two is in the social conditions that create them, in the methods for solving them .... Unemployment originates from a capitalist crisis, as a result of capital accumulation. It is an irresolvable problem under that system and its increase or decrease depends on the cycles of the economic crisis.
>
> The phenomenon of people 'waiting for employment' in our country, in contrast, is a consequence of the rapid growth of the labour force and of economic development. The increase or decrease in the number of people waiting for employment depends on control over reproduction of the labour force and the development of the national

economy. The cycle is [at present] relatively long, but the problem can be solved under a socialist system.[50]

There was still no admission of the emergence of such phenomena as unemployment or the hoarding of the workforce in the industrial sector, but 'full employment' (*chongfen jiuye*), the unchallenged policy option since 1958, was being contested. The dispute was mainly over the influence of full employment on the productivity rate of industrial labour. On the one hand, some believed that the contradiction was not between the two needs, but 'between the practices used to solve employment problems on one side and the growth of productivity on the other.' Such practices included 'substitution' (*dingti*), that is, the custom of leaving the father's workplace to another member of the family, and the 'iron rice bowl' (*tie fanwan*) (that is, almost unconditional life tenure). The possibility of increasing productivity was linked to the elimination of such practices. This interpretation focused on the work-unit's internal organisation and bargaining with the state. On the other hand, a view that put more emphasis on 'external' factors, that is, on the economic role of *demand* and *supply* of labour, was slowly emerging.

> One aspect is that the increase in labour productivity might reduce the demand for labour and, consequently, the total number of employed people; another aspect is that, if fixed assets are given, the creation of new workplaces might reduce the coefficient of equipment exploitation per worker, also affecting the productivity of labour.
>
> There are two points that must be carefully evaluated: (1) if, in a situation of labour supply balanced with demand, and without regard to the state of financial and material resources, social unemployment (*daiye*) is turned into excess labour inside the enterprise, the result will be overstaffing, and the consequent reduction of productivity rates; (2) low-capital labour-intensive activities must be developed to create even more workplaces.[51]

As we shall see, some ten more years of theoretical and economic development were needed before this initial admission became a definitive recognition of the mechanisms of the socialist labour market. Although the issue was still very much disputed, the fields involved in the labour debate were growing to include the recruitment system and the implementation of a labour law, while in the theoretical field some initial steps were taken regarding the 'nature of labour relations under socialism.'

The main question at this time concerned the existence of an 'ownership relation' between the worker and his own labour force, and three positions were debated during these years:[52] one supported the idea that the labour force belongs to the field of public ownership (*gongyouzhi*) as it is a 'condition of production;' the second argued that it is 'part public and part individual;' and the third claimed that the labour force is an individual ownership.[53]

The first position insisted on a 'strict interdependence' (*miqie huxiang guanxi*) between the ownership level of the means of production and that of the labour force. This implied that 'only society is responsible for the production and reproduction of the labour force, and the right to allocate and use labour belongs exclusively to the society (state) [sic] and to the enterprise.' This position was the necessary starting point for the 'central planners' to justify the policy of the 'joint allocation' of the labour force, and the intervention of the state in the worker-enterprise relationship at the 'market' level.

The midway attitude was a sort of mediation in which, 'as the responsibility for production and reproduction of labour force is partly with the state and partly with the families,' the ownership of labour is also divided between individuals and the state.[54]

A major criticism of both these positions was based on the idea of a 'determinism of distribution' (*fenpei jueding lun*).

> The nature of ownership, no matter whether we deal with labour or ownership of the means of production, is decided by the nature and level of the production forces. The question of who is responsible for the reproduction costs is a distributive issue, and it is decided jointly by the ownership of labour and by that of the means of production. Explaining the forms of ownership through analysis of who is responsible for reproduction costs is like putting the cart before the horse, it is a 'dictatorship of distribution.'[55]

The third and well supported position, which emerged from this criticism, represented not only a theoretical step toward the future debate on the commodity nature of labour, but also an enlargement of the theoretical outlook, which was probably a result of the greater involvement of the academic world in the policy process and in analysis of the advancement of labour reform.

The fifth conference on DATL, in July 1983, took place in the middle of the Sixth Five-Year Plan and followed the work report released by Zhao Ziyang at the end of 1982 upholding the breakup of the 'iron rice bowl' and the 'big pot'[56] in Chinese industry. The conference faced a very different situation: the economic system had already undergone a deep transformation (not least of which was the building of a nonstate sector), and the experimental stage of labour reform was creating a wide range of examples, both positive and negative. A multifaceted reality, as well as a much more consolidated role for academic and research institutions, resulted in the emergence of contending ideas, although the main driving concept remained that of DATL, with increasing attention, on one side to the mechanisms of its implementation and on the other to the theoretical issues emerging from the progressive decentralisation and autonomy of the productive processes. A great deal of attention was still placed on distribution (and on the wage system), but the conference was far more specifically focused on an *evaluation* of concrete cases rather than on the earlier *justificatory* approach.

The conference expressed, in particular, supportive opinions for the so-called 'floating wages' that had been strongly endorsed by Party Secretary Hu Yaobang.[57] This was a broad term referring to systems that linked wages to both individual and enterprise performance. While the concept of floating wages was relatively short-lived, the principle was nonetheless a summary of the achievements in the debate of this initial phase of reform:

> [Wages] must first of all be 'floating,' that is not fixed. Second, while they must be floating they can be partially or totally floating, but, third, they have to respect the principle of DATL and their quantity must be determined not only by individual performance but also by the good or bad results of the enterprise.[58]

Unlike at previous conferences, discussion of DATL was no longer sufficient to encompass all that was going on in the field of labour. As early as February 1983, for example, new provisional regulations for the hiring of contract workers were issued.[59] This was still a small step but the direction would be followed in future years, that is, the contractualisation of the demand and supply of labour and the progressive abandonment of central allocations of labour.

The entire debate until this point mirrored both the evolution of the political struggles and the formulation of experimental policies. These were moulded on the experiences of the 1950s and early 1960s, the only tangible source of inspiration for policymakers and economic actors of this period, as opposed to the egalitarian policy of the Cultural Revolution. But this common experience did not prevent the emergence of contradictory paths and of different forms of adaptation to the changing economic and administrative environment.

3

BACK TO THE FUTURE

The Initial Paths of Labour Reform
(1977–1983)

3.1 Productivity Boost and Social Discontent:
The Contradictory Roots of Labour Reform

The Chinese leadership on the eve of the decisive 1978 CCP plenum was facing serious difficulties in coping with the conflicting needs of restarting the engine of the Chinese industrial economy through rationalization while, at the same time, limiting the effects of rampaging social discontent among those groups that had been the preferred target of the egalitarian policies during the Cultural Revolution. No comprehensive assessment of the decisions taken during 1977 and 1978 could avoid considering the risks implied in a restrictive redistributive policy in the cities. In 1977, when the first wage adjustment for workers in SOEs took place, the changes introduced in the criteria for distribution were insignificant with respect to both the social needs and the already proposed aims of the reform. No adjustment had taken place since 1971, and monetary wages had been reduced to an even smaller proportion of workers' income, while dependency on the *danwei* system of employment and welfare had peaked. Average monetary wages steadily decreased every year until 1977, during the last five years in particular. Despite the increase decided upon in 1971, the average annual monetary wage of SOE workers was 602 yuan – (478 yuan in collective units – COEs) in 1977, whilst it had been 661 yuan in 1964.[1] Although always low and relatively unimportant with respect to non-monetary benefits in the redistributive system of Chinese socialism, monetary wages remained the only parameter of workers' economic conditions that the government could rapidly act on in order to calm societal pressures.

During the 1960s and 1970s, industrial enterprises were the most important contributors to state coffers, as their productivity (as a result of favourable central policies and the absence of competition) soared. Despite their proverbial economic inefficiency, per-worker profits and taxes remained above 2,500 yuan per year between 1965 and 1978, almost four times the average worker wage.[2] Part of this surplus was reinvested (both formally and informally) by the enterprises for welfare and services, but it never entered the workers' pockets in the form of cash. Workers in large, heavy industrial SOEs enjoyed far better services than those in small and medium light industrial enterprises (larger housing, better health care, education and recreation facilities).[3]

An unbalanced distribution of resources (2 percent of the enterprises accounted for two thirds of profits and taxes), control of monetary income by the central government, and the precarious and varying ability of enterprises to assign non-monetary wage items further necessitated centrally-initiated adjustments, even though the general indicators of China's state economy (industrial and agricultural production) were not encouraging.

The 1977 wage raise can be considered to be the first step in labour reform, at least in as much as the State Council circular which defined it contained – for the first time after the Cultural Revolution – a positive reference to the principle of 'distribution according to labour.'[4] Nonetheless, the adjustment also targeted the 'livelihood of the people' (according to the Maoist slogan quoted at the beginning of the circular), and only formally stimulated the application of more 'rational' distributive principles. Significantly, the differences between each rung of the nationwide Soviet-style wage ladder were very limited, to the point that the adjustment remained 'limited to a range of 5 to 7 yuan.'[5] Slightly more significant adjustments were assigned to those workers who had 'participated in production' (*canjia shengchan*) since before 1966, as their purchasing power had suffered from the egalitarian policies for a longer period.

Although the revitalisation of DATL inspired this circular only with regard to the introduction of new criteria for the assignment of wage increases, some of the criteria still referred to political 'merit' and 'performance' rather than productivity.

The contradiction between the social and political objective of 'improving the livelihood of the people' and the economic imperative of increasing productivity and rationalising production was openly apparent in the circular. The adjustment (*tiaozheng*) was to be granted only to those workers who 'performed well or relatively well,' while it was to be 'postponed' (*huantiao*) for the others. In any case, the circular prudently stated that the 'proportion of workers who will see the increase postponed should not be higher than 10 percent of the total'![6]

The implementation of this policy, that due to these premises was to express the contrast between evaluation of individual performance and the context of 'common interest,' generated numerous intra-unit conflicts; in fact, from the point of view of the individuals and of the enterprises, it was hardly imaginable that a large part of the workers could be excluded from the wage increase.

Furthermore, the initiative to raise salaries was taken only after violent protests over the decrease in purchasing power had occurred in cities during 1975 and 1976, as workers organised spontaneous demonstrations and hoisted big-character posters (*dazibao*) even in such major cities as Shanghai and Hangzhou in mid-1977.[7] The situation in the cities and in many important industrial units was serious and the risks of larger-scale repercussions on stability urged intervention on the very sensitive question of wages. Issues relevant to the position of workers within socialist society, as well as their material discontent also had been regularly raised in the unofficial publications of the Democracy Wall movement (1978–1980).[8]

Although the campaign for a raise in monetary salaries was launched under the auspices of the new principle of DATL, its limited results reinforced the stagnation. This initial step towards changing the quantitative aspects of salary (mainly its neglected monetary part) was followed by other measures that affected its form and composition (differentiation of the wage system, revitalization of bonuses and piece-rate wages). But all these steps targeted only the issue of distribution, and did not take into consideration the reform of labour relations, both inside and outside the enterprise, for which a different economic environment and a more stable political situation were necessary.

The first serious step towards 'nonegalitarian' labour policies came in May 1978, some months before the plenum, at the climax of a wave of experiments targeting the redistribution mechanism of the Chinese *danwei* system. The revival of the practice of distributing bonuses and production rewards for outstanding performance was coupled with the re-establishment of piece-rate wages for 'above quota production.' The circular published by the State Council on 7 May corresponded with a central decision to implement a large-scale experiment with these two wage systems, involving 30 percent of the productive units in the new system.[9] This testifies to the experimental character of the new system and probably also to the difficulties in implementing it, which clearly appeared between the lines even of the text of this first major document on labour reform. The circular stressed the need to 'build conditions and set norms' for the functioning of the system, in order to avoid 'continuous rediscussion and reappraisal' of the distributive criteria. The experience of intra-unit conflicts during the 1977 adjustment was good reason to be cautious about the process and the criteria for assigning productivity bonuses (for quality as well as for quantity). At the same time, the re-introduction of piece-rates benefited from earlier experience which indicated that the major obstacles to a rational use of labour time at the production level were the relaxation of controls over labour attendance and production quality. Finally, to avoid the risks of a rapid increase in the income differentials, the circular set the maximum wage difference allowed within the enterprise at 20 percent.[10]

It is hard to assess the effectiveness of this first circular (immediately followed by others gradually enlarging the scope of the reform) from empirical data. However, the State Statistical Bureau estimates that the proportion of bonuses and above quota piece-rate wages of total wages was only 2.0 percent in 1978, but grew rapidly to a more significant 7.5 percent in 1979.[11] If we consider that the data is calculated on the basis of total wages of all SOEs, while the system was implemented in only a limited number of them,[12] we can infer that bonuses and piece-rate wages (paradoxically still grouped together in the statistics, despite their difference in both nature and form) were extremely popular and overused in the initial years after the plenum and the May 1978 circular.

This overheating is also demonstrated by a subsequent circular published in 1979, urging the control of waste in the process of implementation of the 'bonus and piece-rate wage system' (*jiangjin he jijian gongzi zhidu*).[13]

The target of this official document was some 'erroneous tendencies' (*pianxiang*), such as the 'arbitrary enlargement of the context of bonuses, the increase in bonus levels and bonus rates, the confusing distribution of subsidies, of additional wages (*fujia gongzi*) and commodities.'[14]

The circular critically argued that the bonus system was applied within the parameters of egalitarianism and not on the basis of DATL. No attention was paid to productivity, quality, performance, or skills; the funds allocated for bonuses were being distributed without serious attention to the necessary preconditions, and were generating an effect (further waste of materials, reduction of worker motivation, and lower productivity) contrary to that anticipated by the policymakers. In substance, the new step was probably having effects on the shop floor strikingly similar to those of a centralised wage adjustment, with all the same conflicts.

The reaction to implementation of the policy set down in the 1979 circular can be described as 'resistance.'[15] In fact, reform of a highly egalitarian and bureaucratically concentrated distributive system like that in China invariably faced opposition from both workers and cadres. The abolition, for example, of 'additional wages' (*fujia gongzi*) – that unlike bonuses and piece-rate wages had a long history of implementation and had become a fixed part of the labourers' incomes[16] – and the introduction of piece-rate wages, meant to favour younger and more skilled sectors of the working class, were harshly opposed by older and less skilled workers.

To make the situation even more difficult, the transitional stage of the political struggle added a third element to the twofold contradiction between improvements in livelihood and economic performance: the entire process was imposed over the heads of a disorientated cadre bureaucracy that was often unwilling to undertake initiatives that might become risky in the case of any change in the balance of power within the party. A 'wait-and-see' attitude that was not conducive to the changes in the system was reportedly adopted by many cadres, while some 'natural' or systemic resistance to the nonegalitarian distribution emerged, which largely influenced the pace of policy implementation as well as the extension of the new policy to all enterprises. According to Takahara:

> Some work groups distributed bonuses equally to all, while others went to restaurants and literally ate up the bonus from the same 'big pot.' In assessing staff and workers for bonus distribution, some units used only two or three categories with small differentials, while in others everybody took turns in receiving bonuses. All reports

criticized such egalitarian distribution because it nullified the policy objective of motivating the workforce.[17]

A second wage adjustment took place in 1979, placing more marked attention on the application of DATL, not only in shop floor distribution, but also in the assignment of funds to enterprises, de facto linking the ability of units to assign bonuses to an enterprise's overall performance. Although this can hardly be accepted by theorists as a proper application of DATL, it nevertheless increased the efficacy of the measures taken to stimulate productivity, as it was designed to favour workers with higher skills and most profitable enterprises.

3.2 Distribution and Wages: The First Focus of Labour Reform

While the measures introduced by the 1978 circular limited the incidence of bonuses and piece-rate wages to a maximum of 20 percent of salaries, the debate at the fourth DATL conference of October 1978, as mentioned in the previous chapter, went much further in discussing the issue of limited and unlimited bonuses, 'full' or extra-quota piece-rate wages and individual or collective production rewards. The objective of these initial steps of the reform was more the distribution of national wealth than the improvement of economic performance.

The reform of labour started with a step backward along a path leading to a restoration of the situation that had existed inside units prior to the Great Leap Forward (GLF) of 1958 to 1960, but it did not target any of the fundamental rights of state workers. The focus slowly changed from 'moral' to 'material' incentives, but the purpose remained 'motivating the workers.' The wage reform that started in an experimental way in 1978 could not rapidly change the close economic relationship between state and enterprise, nor could it modify the internal equilibrium of the unit. On the contrary, wage adjustments and reform were intended to reinforce the equilibrium by giving air 'to breath' (more money) to the micro social system of the unit, thereby favouring the idea of its economic and budgetary independence.

The 'rigid' structure of the Chinese wage system, which dated back to the nationalisation of Chinese industry in 1956 and the beginning of the 'low salary – full employment' distributive policy (also known as the 'rational low-wage system' – *heli di gongzi zhi*), remained basically unchanged during this initial phase. But a full correspondence between 'total wages funds' (that is, the total amount of money allocated by the state to pay wages) and 'total wages' (that is, the money actually distributed as salaries), which was evidence of the total central control by the state, was no longer possible. Elements of flexibility depending on specific situations and the behaviour of enterprises, as well as on 'local' bargaining, were introduced into the salary structure.

Nonetheless, it is significant to note that reliance on monetary wages as the sole lever to increase worker motivation in the local context, as well as labour productivity in the macro-economic context, was not borne out by economic results in the following years. Although monetary wages grew by a significant 25.5 percent between 1978 and 1981 (while the component of bonuses and piece-rate wages was already 11.3 percent in 1981), the labour productivity index officially marked a mere 6.5 percent increase over the same period, suggesting that productivity growth could not simply rely on reform of the wage system. Although it was wrong to expect that reforming wage distribution alone would be able to assure a major increase in productivity, as many other factors (technology level, organisation, know-how, infrastructure, etc.) are needed to raise productivity, the general conditions contributed to taking the initial steps of the labour reform in the direction of wages and distribution mechanisms.

First of all, the hardships experienced by the Chinese working class during the Cultural Revolution were strictly related to the 'political' nature of distributive criteria at that time.

The 'new' leadership ('new' in terms of strategy for economic development, but not new in terms of individuals and factions in the government) faced very serious threats of instability in urban areas. To cope with this situation, the leadership acted as would an employer who fears a further decrease in plant productivity, that is, by increasing wages and, only later, acting on the wage composition to increase internal competition and production. But, as we have seen, the Chinese state was *not* a normal or rational employer and these moves were far less effective than expected.

Second, the ideological legacy played a role in slowing down the practical implementation of labour policies that had already been outlined in the theoretical debates on the labour issue. The tendency towards greater independence of the enterprises and towards the transformation of the nature of labour in the context of production relations was therefore anticipated by a 'soft' attitude that gradually began to erode egalitarian practices through the application of the *correct* principle of 'distribution according to labour,' and by concentrating exclusively on the issues of distribution and productivity. Employment, labour relations, and the labour market were not dealt with at first. The reform of distribution was also the first step in the reorganisation of the *danwei* system and of the relationship between the unit and its owner, the state, but not yet of the relationship between the unit and the economic environment (market, property rights, legalisation, contractualisation) in which it was going to act.

Third, although the goal of modernisation stressed efficiency, the backwardness of the Chinese industrial sector, isolation from major technology providers, as well as a lack of infrastructure, dynamic light industry, and a consumer market, forced policy-makers to believe that the only factor China could realistically rely on for *visible* economic improvements in the short term was labour. Yet, although a major resource in the Chinese economy, labour could not achieve the immediate expected returns in productivity, as the composition of China's labour force was largely inadequate to support fast economic development, and the phenomena of hoarding and overstaffing were common in most of the state-owned sector which employed 78.4 percent of the total workforce in 1978.[18]

3.3 A New Contradiction: Employment and Efficiency

It was not until 1981 that a new set of regulations gave more precise shape and direction to the practice of labour reform and to the entire economic system. The regulations affected two different economic relationships. The first involved ownership, as an individual economy (*geti jingji*) was re-established after years of having been considered 'forbidden and illegal' during the Cultural Revolution.[19] For the first time this allowed the hiring of labour from outside the narrow boundaries set by central allocation plans, as several forms of non-state enterprises began to emerge. In particular, the Cultural Revolution practice of creating 'large collective units' (*da jiti*) by merging collective enterprises into state-type collectives became a target of criticism, and the founding of 'collectives run by the people' (*minban jiti*) was strongly encouraged as a means of increasing the number of available urban workplaces.

The second involved the relationship between enterprises and the state as a first step in decentralisation (the 'tax-for-profit' regime) and introduction of a mechanism to favour the autonomy of fund and labour management (the 'management responsibility system' – *guanli zerenzhi*), which largely influenced the subsequent direction of labour reform.

The two relationships featured a new contradiction between the need to solve the growing problem of unemployment in the urban areas and the systemic need for economic efficiency.

At the end of the 1970s, China was facing its first serious urban employment crisis of the reform period (two other crises – one in 1989 and the most recent beginning in the late 1990s – were to follow). As the structural causes were all related, Chinese policy-makers identified four major structural factors that would shape employment policies as a new component of labour reform.

The first was population growth and the increasing availability of a workforce, coupled with the urbanisation process. The statement that China is 'big' (*da*), the Chinese 'many' (*duo*), and the situation 'complex' (*fuza*) has often been a simple and reasonable way for Chinese policymakers to justify policy options and major slowdowns along the reform path. But, in fact, if we look at the population growth experienced by China in the radical years of its Communist history, we see that this assertion is something more than a mere excuse and, if coupled with the limited rate of industrial development, population growth was a significant factor in evaluating the country's performance.

It is well known, but nevertheless useful to remember, that China had a total population of 541.67 million in 1949, at the time of the Communist takeover, and that figure had grown to 962.59 million by 1978 (a net increase of over 77 percent[20]). The years immediately following the end of the Cultural Revolution were even more exceptional, not only for overall population growth (the one billion mark was reached in 1981, with a net increase of over 60 million within a four-year period), but also for urban population growth.[21] The forced rustication and anti-urbanisation policies (together with the development deficit suffered by the entire economic system) during the 1960s and 1970s had kept the figures for urban population low (18.4 percent in 1959, 17.9 percent in 1978), but the end of the Cultural Revolution re-ignited the urbanisation process. In the first six years after the Third Plenum (1978–1984), the urban population jumped to 23 percent of the total population (it was 28.6 percent in 1994).

These figures on urban population surely do not justify talk of a classic urbanisation process in early reform China. The particular configuration of management of the population through the *hukou* system, which tied residence and productive activity either to urban areas *or* to the countryside, does not allow for speculation on the global figures of the urban *vis-à-vis* rural population, as the phenomenon of unauthorized migration has not yet been seriously considered in the statistics. Nonetheless, there was a dramatic change of direction.

The second recognized structural cause of unemployment (the word still used is *daiye renyuan* – 'people waiting for employment') was indicated as being the predominance accorded to heavy industry and the relatively small quota of light production. The first Soviet-style Five-Year plan had given free rein to this bias, which was later stressed during the long leftist interlude.[22]

According to one estimate,[23] in the actual conditions of the industrial economy, each million yuan invested in fixed assets in state enterprises could create 257 new workplaces if invested in light industry, but only 94 new workplaces if invested in heavy industry.[24] It is neither a mystery nor a novelty that light industry and services have a much more effective employment/capital ratio, but the relation between labour and capital in the 'labour-intensive heavy industry' of the radical years of Maoism has been thoroughly discussed. Different opinions have emerged as to how the 'classic' Chinese system can be defined in terms of labour usage. Whyte and Parish[25] argue that it was 'capital intensive,' and that its low productivity was due to the 'egalitarian policies, combined with the official wage freeze and high job security,' as well as to the consequent 'problems of absenteeism, shoddy work, and simple laziness [that] mushroomed in work units.'

In contrast, another author sees the full usage of the labour force during the low wage-full employment policy period as necessary for the Chinese economic system and the only way to mobilize and develop an economy with scarce natural and financial resources.[26]

> One of the ways full employment has been achieved has been the utilization of cheap and inferior technologies and labour intensive methods of production. Naturally this results in levels of labour productivity that are lower than in nations that can afford capital- and knowledge-intensive technologies. The literature on appropriate technologies is full of convincing arguments as to why such a strategy is rational and efficient in a context of labour surplus and capital shortage.[27]

It should be argued here that the substitution of labour for capital and technology is a sort of *extrema ratio* that cannot generate long term development (as shown by development in other East Asian NICs that rapidly turned to capital and technology investments after the exploitation of their cheap labour force), as eventual technological advancements are in contrast with the major goal of full employment. But the issue is not whether it is appropriate to base the foundations of development on labour-intensive activities, but, rather, whether it makes sense to base *heavy* industrial development on labour intensity, as this appears to be a paradox, or at least an open contradiction that led China to the verge of collapse in the late 1950s and had consequences for later stages of development. The economic system of the years of the Great Leap Forward and the Cultural Revolution, in fact, can hardly be depicted as 'capital intensive.' I would prefer to use the Chinese expression 'large and collective' (*yi da er gong*), which better depicts the objectives of enlarging production, enlarging dimensions and hoarding labour that characterized the strategy of workunits at that time. Full employment was the final aim rather than a precondition or a production factor.

Furthermore, and this is the third structural cause, the predominance of heavy industry was coupled with that of SOEs and semi-SOEs (large collectives), seen as the result of industrial policies during the years of Maoist radicalism and the Cultural Revolution. Their effectiveness in reducing unemployment was challenged after the beginning of reform, since the cost of creating one new workplace in 1978 was much lower (2,000 yuan) in a collective enterprise than in an SOE (9–10,000 yuan).[28] The focus on national industry and on public ownership during the radical years also contributed to the dismantlement and decline of almost all economic activities of the lower middle class (petty commerce and craftsmanship in particular), thus further reducing the efficiency of labour allocation and increasing the concentration of labour in state industry.

The fourth structural cause lay in the rigidity of the allocation system, which still largely limited the possibility of finding alternative sources of employment. The system of mixed allocation that was to emerge as a response to this situation (partly from the state and partly through rational exchange and 'recommendation' – *jieshao*) was not at all new in the history of Chinese socialist labour, as it had been put into practice both before the Great Leap Forward and in 1963–64 when, for example, 'labour recommendation offices' (*laodong jieshaosuo*) were organised to tackle the dramatic increase in unemployment before the high tide of the Cultural Revolution initiated the central method of labour allocation which lasted until 1978.

In addition to these structural causes, at least one further contingent reason is to be found here, that is the waves of 'returned youth' from the countryside. The rusticated young students from the Cultural Revolution were demanding to return to the cities dramatically increasing the number of young people 'waiting for employment.' As just one example, in the city of Shenyang in Liaoning province, 25,000 of the 33,000 youths waiting for an assignment in 1981 were 'educated youth returned from the countryside.'[29] Whyte and Parish estimate that 'more than half of urban young people' were involved in the recruitment system during the high tide of the Cultural Revolution, implying both 'thought preparation' and 'up to the mountains and down to the countryside' (*shangshan xiaxiang*) experiences.[30] The percentage of the 'registered' urban population that had stagnated during the 1960s and 1970s grew significantly between 1977 (12.59 percent) and 1984 (16 percent), mainly as a result of the reallocation of urban youths that succeeded in officially recovering their urban status.[31]

Although the word 'educated' did not always correspond to a full education cycle (which was often cut short by the trip 'down to the countryside'), this segment of unemployed youth was particularly important for the Chinese economy, with its abundant reservoirs of unskilled labour but shortage of skilled workers and experts.

Indeed, the issues outlined in the foregoing analysis deeply influenced the results of the 1980 central conference on labour and employment sponsored by the Central Committee of the CCP.[32]

The major policy suggestion that emerged from the conference had to do with the structural problems of employment, the diversification of ownership and production activities, the progressive abandonment of unified allocation, and the encouragement of individual and cooperative economic activities; it also defined the parameters for a redefinition of the state-enterprise relationship. In order to solve the issue of labour efficiency and employment, an economic system that gave priority to labour-intensive activities instead of capital accumulation, as well as to services instead of direct production, was sketched. In particular, the following practical suggestions, which largely corresponded to contemporaneous or later policy decisions in this first period of readjustment, were formulated at the policy conference:

- Develop all types of 'cooperatives' (*hezuo she*) and 'small cooperatives' (*hezuo xiaozu*);
- Actively support the creation of small cooperatives of SOE young workers who are in a position to do so;
- Develop collective production units based on educated youth as well as 'agriculture-industry-trade' joint enterprises;
- Encourage and foster the development of the individual economy (*geti jingji*) in the cities;
- Diversify the employment system and the working time for some specific work positions and industries;
- Reform the system of middle schools and develop vocational and technical education;
- Create labour service companies (*laodong fuwu gongsi*);
- Solve the issue of allocation of employment funds.[33]

At this point, the attention of policymakers was focused on a re-establishment of economic institutions and policies that had already been part of the pre-Great Leap Forward labour system in socialist China. This had also been the case for the wage adjustments and reform in 1977–79 (bonuses, piece-rates, and material incentives) and was even more the case for this set of policy suggestions concerning employment. A positive model was formed, based on the more flexible and mixed (for ownership and forms of economic organisation) system of the early 1950s, rather than on the parameters of a market economy. Many direct references to that period, as opposed to the negative examples of the radical years, appeared in both official documents and academic discussions.

The years between 1949 and 1955, before state intervention in the economy was completed, were characterized by the existence of a labour market, by the co-existence of different forms of ownership, by the use of contracts in industry, by a flexible wage structure, and by an unusually high level of mobility. Many of the institutions that once again became familiar to young Chinese in search of employment during the eighties (such as the labour recommendation offices and talent exchange centres), were part of the labour system in the 1950s, as were mobility, contracts, and temporary labour.

During the transitional period up to the launch of the Great Leap Forward, the nationalisation of industrial plants featured a transition from a 'flexible to a rigid allocation system,' a progressive disruption of the labour market, and centralization of a scattered recruitment system to a system fully in the hands of labour bureaus.[34] The reform of the late 1970s was intended to restore the earlier flexibility, market relations, and decentralisation in labour relations.

The origins of the decentralisation scheme, as noted by Peter Lee, can be traced back to the policies suggested in 1957–58 to cope with excessive central control following the First Five-Year Plan.[35] In particular, four sets of policy recommendations were advocated that largely recall the schemes of the early reform stages: the first concerned the 'improvement of macro-managerial systems,' redefining roles and competencies between the central, local, and enterprise levels; the second established a 'profit retention policy'; the third concerned decentralisation of control over working capital (from departments to enterprises and banks); and the fourth outlined a responsibility system of capital investment.[36]

The fiscal reform of the 1980s re-established for enterprises and local authorities the 'right to the residual'[37] that was a first step in the reform of property rights and 'gave localities positive inducements to promote rapid economic growth, which became not only a necessary strategy for bureaucratic survival, but a viable strategy for getting ahead.'[38]

Thus, both at the level of economic and administrative reform and at that of labour institutions, the principles presented as new to Chinese reform in the crucial years between 1978 and 1983 had all already been present in the previous policy experiences of Chinese socialism.

In the field of labour institutions, among the novelties of the reform period was the creation of labour service companies (LSCs) (*laodong fuwu gongsi*), the main duty of which was to organise unemployed urban youth (later also workers dismissed from SOEs) into collective enterprises and production activity. Originally intended as mutual-help actions or temporary parking for youths 'waiting for employment,' they soon became important economic units able to create employment and profits independently.

LSCs were first described in the 1980 document on national employment. They could be run by local labour departments or, more frequently, by large state enterprises. Similar to small urban collective enterprises, they enjoyed several advantages, the most significant being substantial tax exemptions. This fostered their growth. They were further encouraged by the new profit-maximizing attitude of state enterprises, which often transferred profitable activities to such side-enterprises that enjoyed a preferential administrative and fiscal regime. In the first years, special benefits were also awarded to those LSCs that employed among their staff and workers at least 60 percent of 'returned educated youth.' LSCs were therefore the 'very embodiment of extra-plan economic activities within the ambit of the state-owned enterprises,'[39] and allowed a consistent transfer of production activities to privileged production centres; although under the control of mother enterprises, they were largely relieved of the burdens of welfare and services connected to permanent workers, while providing access to employment opportunities for the 'children of the unit' (*women danwei de erzi*), otherwise no longer entitled to 'substitute' (*dingti*)[40] for their mothers and fathers in the enterprise.

This urgency of the state sector to free sections of its productive activity partially explains the unexpected economic success that transformed LSCs into important elements in both the urban and rural economies.[41] According to official statistics, these centres, intended to be labour-oriented and only marginally profitable, achieved an impressive economic record in the 1990s: in 1994, 188,000 companies employed 8.7 million workers and produced an output value of nearly 172 billion yuan, with a profit of 5.8 billion, while only 20.4 percent of them faced deficit.[42] LSCs played a role which involves both employment/allocation policies and the revitalisation of the non-state sectors of the economy.

As of 1983, the idea of a 'rational flow' also suggested the implementation of new administrative and organisational measures and structures dealing more specifically with the distribution of highly skilled workers or technicians, a scarce commodity in the Chinese labour arena at that time. The State Council regulations on the rational flow of technical personnel,[43] the first of a series of such regulations focused on the planning activities of the State Council, the local administrations and the departments, as well as on the monitoring of technical human resources (*renxuan*) in order to improve the distribution of skilled technical personnel in both cities and the countryside.

The major problem to be tackled was the reluctance of state enterprises to allow the worker 'aristocracy' to leave the unit. This was coupled with the technicians' unwillingness to undertake major changes in their working and living situations, generally implying a radical reduction in status, especially when moving to less developed areas or the countryside. The regulation was therefore very careful to establish, on the one hand, the planning power of state departments and, on the other, the possibility of maintaining the same political and economic status in the new location or job.

After the departments singled out individuals eligible for talent exchange or transfer, the conditions (duration of transfer, conditions of payment, and benefits) resulted from the contracting (*shangding*) between the two enterprises were spelled out. From an administrative point of view, the state could confirm that *hukou* status (generally an urban *hukou* for the most skilled industrial workers or technicians), as well as related prerogatives, would not be jeopardized when moving to a rural or border area. Preferential treatment for talented workers moving to border or rural areas was also accorded.[44]

The regulation also introduced an 'experimental' measure that allowed for a so-called 'bi-directional choice.' For the first time (with all the administrative restrictions on hiring procedures, such as the *hukou*), enterprises were allowed to hire and fire technical or skilled workers independently (outside of the plan), while skilled workers could formally choose whatever enterprise they preferred, potentially the same way as they would in an open labour market.

The first contradiction mentioned at the beginning of this section (employment) was, therefore, tackled through initial reform of the allocation system and implementation of the 'three-in-one' (*sanjiehe*) scheme; the second contradiction (efficiency of the enterprise) was to be addressed after initial marginal adjustments in the wage system by means of reorganisation of the administrative relationship between state and enterprise and by the release of property rights to enterprises now able to retain part of the profits and resources they had produced.

3.4 Enterprises: Reforming the *Danwei* System

Before turning our attention to the situation created when the policies that radically changed the relationship between state and enterprise began to erode the importance of the 'micro societies' (work-units), thus opening a path for a remaking of labour relations in the context of Chinese urban societies, it is worthwhile to attempt a general assessment of the situation of Chinese urban labour institutions in the initial years of reform.

According to one famous definition, up until the reform period the Chinese socialist urban system consisted of two parts: neighbourhood organisations (in the form of resident committees or urban communes) and production units:[45]

For complete organization of the urban population, then, there has to be a production unit administrative system as well. In this second mode of organization we see the central stress in Chinese thinking on the work-unit (*danwei*), which is seen not simply as a place to punch a time clock and earn wages, but as an entity that plays a central role in organizing lives of those employed there.[46]

Many authors have devoted great attention to the overlapping roles of society and the work-unit in the urban administrative system in contemporary China.[47] The *danwei* has generally been understood as a particular feature of Chinese socialism, with an autonomy, independence, and self-reliance as a social organiser that contrasted with its high level of dependency (on the state and local branch departments) as a production, management, and financial unit. The two major social, economic, and political relationships (state-enterprise and enterprise-worker), which made the *danwei* system particular to the cell-structured socialist society, were both challenged at the beginning of the economic reforms. The attack on the soft-budget constraints in SOEs implied that the enterprises were going to lose the advantages of a secure balance of accounts, but also that they would be able to enjoy greater autonomy of decision making and to re-invest more of their profits, with the help of the local and more accessible bureaucracy. Worker families, for their part, would miss the security of life tenure and iron wages, but were able to exploit more fruitfully the possibilities offered by the individual economy, while still relying on state-unit sponsored welfare.

Work-units, and in particular large industrial units, were all-encompassing structures in which workers found almost all their needs met, from social services to education, housing, health care, and recreation. Work-units emerged from the years of radicalism as the major social reference point for workers: the very existence of a society outside of the *danwei* was beyond the perception of the Chinese urban worker.[48] The Chinese system was more immobile and rigid than the Soviet industrial employment system, as well as more extreme in terms of ties between workers and units than the Japanese, as it did not properly hire employees, who were mainly assigned by administrative offices according to plans and skills.[49]

As the work of Andrew Walder, among others, has revealed, the importance of the traditional work-unit in Chinese society and the role of its authority system can be understood through the degree of dependency experienced by the workers. This was contingent not only on the nature of the work-unit's organisation, but also, for example, on the external environment.

'Organized dependency,' as Walder calls authority relations inside the work unit system, is measured by two major parameters: the ability of the organisation to cope with the workers' needs and the availability of alternatives.

> Organized dependency ... refers to the institutional positions of subordinates with regard to superiors in organization. The greater proportion of the subordinates' needs that is satisfied by the organization, the greater is the subordinate's dependence on the organization. The fewer the alternative sources for satisfying these needs, the more dependent are subordinates. To the extent that subordinates are unable to organize themselves collectively to resist the demands of superiors and to the extent that they are unable to develop and protect a competent leadership of their own, the more dependent they are on superiors.[50]

Walder uses 'organized dependency' to investigate the patterns of 'institutional culture of authority,' in Chinese industry, while the issue of dependency and its twofold parameter is useful here in understanding the administrative changes in the work-unit system and the direction taken by the reform process. In the initial phase of labour reform, in fact, it was the *internal* ability of the enterprise to satisfy the workers' needs (the so-called 'three irons system')[51] that was challenged, while in the following phases (what are called *contractualisation* and *marketisation* here), the choices and the existence of alternatives (and of an *external* economic reference, both for the enterprise as an administrative and economic entity and for the individual), were the major focus. The entire issue of dependency was then challenged by the growing complexity of labour market relations and by the emergence of what has recently been labelled the 'disorganized despotism'[52] of labour relations.

In the years immediately following the 1978 takeover by the new reformist leadership, however, the administrative measures to increase enterprise autonomy, diversify the economic structure, and link rewards to objective economic performance made the traditional paths of status attainment and upward social mobility slightly more difficult, while the role of the *danwei* was challenged in these areas. In fact, the social status of the workers was strictly related to the type of enterprise they worked in,[53] while upward mobility patterns were a major consequence of the clientelist structure of authority systems inside the enterprise. Both these parameters were stable when the enterprise could rely on secure resources, the amount of which was almost independent of external variables, as well as of the quality of internal performance.

As a result of the initial reforms, the units progressively lost their security *vis-à-vis* the outside world and this increased their need to pay attention to previously neglected efficiency parameters.

Efficiency meant work-unit efficiency and work-unit efficiency meant labour efficiency. In the framework of the reform policy, the main path to achieving efficiency was decentralisation; decentralisation had several important implications for enterprises, namely:

- participation of the enterprise in the direct management of resources and production factors;
- participation of the enterprise in the redistribution of its profits under different forms (profit retention, then taxation);
- emergence of budget constraints related to production efficiency (still constraints set by the government and not by the market);
- increase of managerial responsibility and pressure over the economic results of the enterprise (both upward to the state economic plan and downward to the workers' economic expectations).

Among the major consequences of the cell-type organisation of China's urban society was the extremely low level of labour mobility beginning in the years following the Great Leap Forward. Geographic mobility from the countryside to urban areas was discouraged and strongly opposed with the help of administrative barriers, such as the *hukou* system. Access to employing units was also restricted by the unified allocation system and by the virtual absence of labour recruitment paths other than administrative paths. At the same time, administrative limits to labour force movements were also applied to inter-unit mobility, which remained a centrally controlled adjustment (authorisation from the labour bureau was necessary) in the labour allocation system.

The *danwei* became the watchdog of this *status quo* in the aftermath of the food crisis of the Great Leap Forward when an uncontrolled flow of enthusiastic or desperate workers largely increased the economic pressure on urban centres. As a consequence, the 1958 *hukou* regulations were implemented much more strictly after the Leap contributing to further protection of the privileged working class from social and economic competition from in-migrants.

At the beginning of the reform, the mobility rate of Chinese workers was close to zero. As noted by Naughton, in 1978 'death was four times as important a cause of job leaving as were resignation and being fired.'[54] In that year only 37,000 of the 63 million state workers quit their jobs or were dismissed. The immobility of the Chinese workforce, so strictly intertwined with the social role of the *danwei*, was a political as much as an economic option, resulting from steps taken under the pressure of major social crises, later deepened and upheld under the policy arms of radical politics.

As we saw earlier, although mobility soon became a subject of discussion among economists, the initial steps of reform targeted enterprise efficiency as well as wealth distribution as factors in the people's well being.

To achieve the goal of efficiency, therefore, decentralisation and managerial autonomy were needed. Reform of the *danwei* system began by tackling the problems related to the state-enterprise relationship, which mainly concerned financial issues and responsibility for the management of resources.

The very first decision in this direction was the re-creation of enterprise funds for the payment of bonuses and rewards. The State Council re-established this practice in November 1978, when enterprises were again allowed to keep part of their profits, provided that they exceeded the established yearly quota. The decision allowed for the retention of a maximum of 5 percent of the total payroll. At the same time, in this initial formulation, the new policy gave the industrial branch departments the right to retain between 5 and 15 percent of the above-quota profits[55] and to redistribute them as bonus funds to profitable enterprises, thereby turning the profit retention policy into a tool of 'autonomy *vis-à-vis* the central controllers not only at the national level but also at the local level.'[56] Later on, following opposition by the enterprises and policy adjustments, the above-quota profits were retained directly by the enterprises.

The 'profit retention' policy (*lirun liucheng*) was fully implemented in March 1979 with the Ministry of Trade and Ministry of

Finance Circular on Systematically Experimenting the Profit Retention System.[57] This regulation nevertheless contained a major redefining of the previous 'enterprise funds,' and the new fund – managed directly by the enterprise – was not intended for bonuses and rewards or for worker welfare, but exclusively for expenses for equipment and 'simple construction works,' for technical improvements and for a 'management fund' (*jingli jijin*).

The 'profit retention' policy was soon accompanied by a deepening of the administrative reform, with the extension of the economic responsibility system – already in effect in the agricultural sector – to industrial units. Rather than simply assigning the responsibility for management of the enterprise to the factory director, this system sought to clarify the division of tasks among state, branch departments and units, in a process of redistributing financial resources and production factors, and establishing a formal link between funds allocated by the state and work-unit performance. Thus, DATL's double track (that is the evaluation of both individual and enterprise performance) was recognized in policy implementation as a necessary path leading to greater autonomy and efficiency.

The economic responsibility system was first mentioned and discussed in a long document published after the Conference on the Reform of the Industrial Management System held in March 1981,[58] and it was later implemented with some substantial corrections in November of the same year.[59]

As with most of the policies of those years, the major problem acknowledged by the circulars was the overheating from the effects of the experimental regulations. The autonomy enjoyed and requested by the enterprises was, in fact, so high as to endanger the fulfilment of overall production objectives. Many units engaged in unsound practices, such as the distribution of bonuses without reference to standards of efficiency or productivity, or they turned to more profitable production than that required by the state plan. The practice of *li da da gan, li xiao bu gan*[60] (engaging in profitable, and abandoning less profitable, activities) must have been extremely common, as the November circular explicitly stated that it was to be rejected by managers and local authorities.

The implementation of bonuses and piece-rate wages as well as other material incentives, was also a way of undermining the internal clientelistic structure of the work-unit, as it fostered conflicts not only between cadres and workers for the distribution of bonus quotas, but also among the workers themselves. For example, the latter concerned the criteria for assignment of individual bonuses or material rewards of model workers, who became the targets of unofficial criticism, as their outstanding performance contributed to raising production norms and productivity standards.[61] Although the *danwei* system was still far from dismantled, the emergence of uneven distribution practices, coupled with the limitations imposed on internal recruitment, caused a steady decline – with respect to the expectations created by reform during these years – in the levels of satisfaction of workers' growing needs inside the enterprise and the importance of the unit in the process of attainment of individual status.

Although the structure of the unit was about to change, the major direct effect on workers and the organisation of labour was still exerted by the wage system, which was continuously adjusted and reformed in the years up to 1985.

In particular, praise for the experimental application of 'floating wages' (*fudong gongzi*) since late 1982 led to large-scale implementation of this system in 1983. The expression 'floating wages' identified a system linking the distribution of individual wages more directly and systematically to the performance and productivity of individuals and their units. The concept of floating wages was flexible as it could be applied by the enterprise to the total amount of the salary, or to the part exceeding the standard wage; it could be related to individual, group, or collective performances or to general indices, such as profit-making, productivity, or sales.

Floating wages were a direct consequence of the new policy of 'tax for profit' which, as of 1982, favoured the transformation of enterprises into independent economic units (not yet independent accounting units, though), that is, enterprises whose agent-principal relationship with the state was expressed, albeit partially, in tax remittances and no longer in contracted profit quotas.

Tax for profit strengthened the independence of work-units from their owner, and radically separated the internal management of production factors and of labour.

The factory director responsibility system adopted in 1984 was the last step in the formalisation of this independence. The director was given the power to manage personnel according to productivity factors and to act as a de facto capitalist, able to take part in economic benefits and to act on behalf of the government but within limits increasingly set by his own interest or by that of his enterprise. The responsibility system, that assigned to the factory director much greater decision-making power and (at least on paper) the discretion to decide on all labour-related issues, became, with the deepening of the reform, a powerful tool for production despotism. This later became evident when the market was intended to act as the principal regulator of labour relations.

The economic independence of the unit was thus a necessary precondition for a market-driven and contract-regulated recruitment process, that is, for enterprises to become employing units (*yongren danwei*) and for what we have called the practice of *contractualisation* of labour relations.

For the moment, however, all decisions remained strictly contained inside the logic of policy accommodation; they were all 'old tricks' of a more pragmatic approach to labour and workers; and they were all aimed at 'damage containment.' This approach proved insufficient once the opening up of the Chinese economy progressed and both enterprises and workers discovered to their own expense that the rigidity of central allocations no longer fitted into the picture.

4

WHAT IS LABOUR?

Towards the Marketisation of Labour Relations (1984–1991)

4.1 From Distribution to Employment: Labour Relations and Social Constraints

The second turning point in the reform period was another 'Third Plenum,' this time the October 1984 Third Plenum of the Twelfth CCP Congress. The comprehensive decision on the structure of Chinese economic reform adopted at this plenum changed the definition of the national economy from a *'planned* economy' (*jihua jingji*) to a 'planned *commodity* economy' (*you jihua de shangpin jingji*).

As already argued, this change corresponded with some major shifts in policy orientation, theoretical understanding, and justification, as well as changes in the process of restructuring production and social relations.

Although the period beginning with the 1984 decision and lasting until the beginning of the 1990s cannot be considered homogeneous or without contradictions from the point of view of policy implementation and political struggle, a visible trend in the development of social and economic relationships convinces me that this period can be identified by the process of *contractualisation* of the labour economy.

The process that I label contractualisation can be summarized by the following points:

(a) The diversification of the economic structure and the emergence of greater geographic mobility despite still limited official labour mobility (both horizontal and vertical) contributed to a much more hostile labour environment, whose social demands for labour opportunities were progressively addressed less to the state and more and more directly to the newly formed economic players (economic units, enterprise management, labour service companies, labour agencies), which were inclined to behave in consideration of economic profitability;

(b) At the same time the state's role in the labour economy increasingly became one of supervision, not only over redistribution, as had been the case until then, but also over allocation, mobility control, and social welfare functions;

(c) Formal recognition of a decentralised structure of the economy, extended application of a responsibility system (comprising the industrial as well as the agricultural sector), and initial changes in the property rights structure and in the economic relationship between state and localities and between government and enterprises helped to formalise the labour contract as a major control device of labour relations, thus expanding the 'contract' system from the level of state/enterprise relations to that of enterprise/worker relations;

(d) Diversification and the growth of external opportunities made it essential for traditional productive units to deal with insider/outsider relations, integrating paternalism as a typical feature of the internally productive and protective *danwei*, as well as clientelism towards the state and its bureaucracy. The smashing of the 'iron rice bowl' (*dapo tiefanwan*) consequently brought about the crisis of the *danwei* as a model unit of productive organisation, while more complex labour relations and conflicts emerged in the new situation.

(e) While China was heading towards a commodity economy with a diminished role for planning, the declining role of central planners made it possible for theoretical efforts and related policy processes to enter more thoroughly the discussions of whether or not 'labour is a commodity,' that is, of the contradictory nature of labour relations under a socialist system. It was not a coincidence that these discussions began and steadily developed from 1984 to 1987 when labour contracts were first advocated and later implemented as a guiding hiring principle.

Although a main feature in the field of labour policy of this period was the implementation of contract labour regulations for state-owned enterprises, the term contractualisation must be understood in a wider sense, that is in the broader context of the economic, ideological, and political transformations that were modifying economic relations inside the Chinese productive system and that involved not only state enterprises but also many other fields of the economic and labour society.

Although Chinese analysts prefer to see contract regulations as a consciously implemented component of a longer process of building a labour market in socialist China, and while there can be no doubt that labour reform was moving in the direction of a marketisation of labour relations, deregulation was not yet complete and many of the theoretical and economic conditions for the development of a labour market were still absent during this phase.

First of all, the role played by the state sector was still overwhelming and the restructuring of industrial state-owned enterprises still had a long way to go. The attitudes of workers, enterprises, and the state towards the labour issue were still very much influenced by social stability, worries about social conflicts and, lastly, the economic interests of social groups and economic elites. While opposition to the reform by different players has sometimes been overestimated, resistance and intra-unit conflicts were the major reasons why the system was only partially implemented in the initial years and did not obtain the expected results in terms of an increase in labour mobility.

Second, when the regulations were introduced, China had a large number, but not a large variety, of workers willing to participate in the labour 'market.' The most skilled among them were still generally attracted to secure positions inside state enterprises, while the available workforce was mainly made up of low-level, non-specialized workers of rural origins, who entered the urban labour arena as migrants and were difficult to employ in industrial state enterprises because of administrative and residence barriers that were still in force in the field of geographic and labour mobility.

Third, while structures such as the labour service companies (*laodong fuwu gongsi*) and talent exchange centres (*rencai jiaoliu zhongxin*) were already active in contributing to a 'rational flow' of the labour force, the supply and demand relationship remained as unbalanced as it had been under the classic socialist system: an excess of supply of unskilled labour still corresponded to a short-age in other segments of demand (trained, specialized, and skilled labour).

The introduction of the contract system, therefore, was likely to be a further important move along a path leading to the greater independence of the enterprise, rather than towards a conscious decision to implement a labour market.

I will try to justify this assumption both in this chapter, by discussing the labour debate, and in the next chapter, by taking into account labour contract policies.

4.2 A Changing Policy Strategy: Labour Relations Discussed

At the time of the fifth conference on distribution according to labour (1983) the discussion on labour had already changed directions to a thorough economic analysis of the labour factor in the rapidly changing social environment, with the principle of DATL definitively accepted after the long ideological discussions of the previous years. Actually, the need even to hold such a discussion in 1983 can be traced back to the emergence in those months of some residual 'leftist' positions 'arguing the dangerous emergence of individualism, while in reality a high degree of egalitarianism still existed.'[1]

The conference eventually paved the way for an expression of the correctness of the DATL principle, which, from that time on, became an *accessory* tool of the theoretical interpretation of labour, as much greater attention was placed on the interaction of economic and productive factors.

The communiqué on 'Actively Implementing a Labour Contract System,'[2] published by the Ministry of Labour and Personnel (MoLP) in February 1983, together with the new instructions on worker selection,[3] were yet another recovery of earlier policy steps in China's socialist labour history: in the 1950s, before the egalitarian attitude of the Cultural Revolution changed both practice and rules, contract labour, as well as temporary labour (mainly from the countryside), were widely employed in the urban industrial sector, and were never really eradicated despite the high tide of radicalism. Furthermore, at the time of the publication of the communiqué, experiments on contract labour had already been carried out, mainly in Shenzhen where a 'special economic zone' (SEZ, *jingji tequ*) was established in 1979.[4] As a provisional regulation, the communiqué represented no more than an endorsement of the political correctness of an experimental practice that had already been going on for some time in many enterprises, and it was not yet a sign of its adoption as a guiding policy principle.

The low *mobility* of the Chinese workforce was one of the principal results of the traditional Chinese egalitarian policy, and it soon became clear that immobility was the main target of the campaign in favour of a contract system. Initially, the attack on low mobility was aimed at opening the 'closed (internal) system' of recruitment in the Chinese *danwei*, in order to allow for a rational (*heli*) exchange of labour inside and outside of the factory, testifying to the emergence of an 'outer' dimension (in theory as well as in practice) of the labour force, as necessary prerequisite for the emergence of a labour market.

One example of this strategy was the attitude towards 'internal recruitment' (*neizhao*). While the 1979 regulations on worker selection[5] implicitly accepted that the characteristics of virtue (*de*), knowledge (*zhi*) and health (*ti*) had to be respected for *all* workers hired by 'state and collective enterprises at district and county level, *including the sons and daughters of the staff and workers already working in the unit*,'[6] the 1983 regulations explicitly stated that 'unless otherwise decided by the central authority, enterprises are *not* allowed to *hire from inside*'.

The practices of *neizhao* and *dingti* (substitution) were definitely not among the most important economic factors affecting labour mobility, but the specificity of the integrated social-productive system built around the Chinese *danwei* contributed to making 'internal recruitment' an accepted worker benefit, while the popularity of this custom created major implementation problems when direct relations (not mediated by state intervention) between enterprise (demand) and worker (supply) became a theoretical imperative, under the label of 'bi-directional choice' (*shuangxiang xuanze*).

The traditional employment system[7] in socialist China was based on the principle of central and unified allocation of the labour force and was justified by the rationale of state control of economic policies. The decentralisation of responsibility and the emergence of the principle of independence in enterprise management resulted in the units deciding on the allocation of a progressively larger part of their profits, as well as their being in a position (at least on paper) to hire labour according to effective productive needs rather than according to general policies or balances of power.

Experiments with this new system of recruitment of the labour force were the result partly of the new economic ideology and partly of a widespread dissatisfaction among workers, mainly skilled workers, whose position and compensation had largely been eroded during the egalitarian years.

The contract system was also a cautious 'second step' (after that of wage reform and diversification through DATL) towards the independence of the labour policy of enterprises. Once enterprises were able to allocate economic resources in a slightly more autonomous way, they had to be given the opportunity to act to alleviate the heaviest of their economic burdens, that is, redundant (*fuyu*) labour.

Caused by the 'hoarding' of the labour force – a practice connected to the accumulation of resources permitted by the central allocation system during the hiring of new personnel – the excess mainly involved non-trained personnel while the shortage of skilled labour remained unchanged or was even aggravated by technological upgrades and by the changing demand structure of 'modernised' enterprises. This testifies to the legacy of irrational labour policies at the unit level which, although constituting a financial advantage during the years of central allocation, often became an unbearable burden after decentralisation was under way.

Criticism of the immobility of the labour force in state enterprises appeared after 1984 as a result of the acknowledgement in 1983 of contract labour experiments in nine provinces. As with many other policy measures in those years, contract labour had been intensively experimented with before any official announcement on the issue. The policy option described by analysts consisted of a three-stage process, that is, 'an intense propaganda and overall discussion of the issue of contract labour, an experimental phase in which the new system is introduced together with the old system, and final implementation in all enterprises.'[8] This is what was to occur between 1983 and 1986, that is, during the period when new regulations were approved that required all enterprises to hire exclusively under the contract labour system regulations.

Meanwhile, at the theoretical level, two different discussions were taking place: one concerning the economic and social significance of the transformation of labour allocation systems, and the issue of labour mobility in particular, and the other regarding, more specifically, the theoretical implications of the 'contracting' of the labour force, that is, the question of the commoditisation of the labour force.

Discussing Labour as an Economic Factor

As of 1984, the issue of DATL was suddenly no longer problematic. Significantly, the major journal for economic research in China (*Jingji Yanjiu* – Economic Research) published only four articles on the general issue of labour (*lao*) and wages (*gongzi*) during the whole of 1984, only one of which concerned DATL.

The starting point of the renewed debate on labour was the acknowledgement of the immobility of labour in the Chinese industrial system. The 'iron rice bowl' system had turned out to be a constraint on economic development in the initial years of reform, both at the enterprise level, where the attention on 'internal' pressure was often greater than on economic rationality, and at the macroeconomic level, where China was now facing the contradiction of joint pressure from industrial growth and increased rural-urban mobility on the one hand, and administrative inadequacy and mammoth-like systems for the central allocation of economic factors, on the other.

Thus, reform in this field called for workers to be considered 'production factors' (*shengchanli yinsu*), that is, not persons 'born in worker families,' but individuals who, potentially or concretely, contribute their working capability to the productive process. The boundary of the category of worker (*gongren*) is his possession of a labour force in relation to the social reproduction process.'[9]

The immobility of the labour force was largely discussed with reference to the theory of production factors. A need was felt for a functional link between the general debate on labour, the issue of mobility, and reform of the employment system in the direction of contractualisation. 'Labour mobility,' it was argued in an essay of 1984, 'is not a component of the direct production process, but an important precondition for it.'[10] The theory of production factors and the mobility of labour were both constituents of the new interpretation of industrial production. This was now considered a result of the 'rational behaviour' of economic players (enterprises and the state) and of the influence of economic levers on social development and individual as well as social aspirations, to the point that mobility 'reflects the objective economic needs' of the reforming Chinese system.

Mobility was not only seen as necessary for industrial development but also as a consequence of the unequal distribution of economic factors, such as a different natural population growth in different regions, uneven levels of technical development, an unequal geographic distribution of productive forces, and, finally, a different quality of labour.[12]

There were three major positions regarding reform of the permanent employment system. As with many other issues in the dialectic of reform, various contending positions were raised against the 'conservative' idea viewing the system based on life tenure as the only way to safeguard the 'right to work' of socialist labourers and to protect workers from instability, risks of unemployment, and privileges.[13] Counterarguments generally supported the temporary implementation of a double-track employment system, maintaining both permanent workers and contract and temporary workers on the one hand, while gradually abolishing the permanent employment that had become 'an unconditioned life-long system' on the other.[14]

Both arguments supported the setting up of a more flexible and diversified system, the superiority of which was described by Liu Qintang as follows:

1. It is advantageous for the development of the virtue, knowledge and health of workers and to increase the quality of labour. Due to the implementation of a contract system of employment, a hiring method based on selection, as well as a policy of 'training before employment' (*xian peixun, hou jiuye*), the basic malfunctioning of the employment system will end, and the quality of the hiring mechanism will be greatly improved.

2. The possibility of a rational flow of employees from and to the enterprise establishes conditions for development of scientific labour management. The duration of the contract as well as the number of hired workers can be decided by the enterprises according to their production needs, contributing to the solution of the concrete problem of 'hoarding' of labour....

3. It has a positive influence on the strengthening of socialist discipline and on decreasing absenteeism....

4. By increasing the enthusiasm of both workers and employing units, it greatly contributes to increasing productivity. The implementation of contract labour allows enterprises to expand their hiring independence,

as well as their choice of the labour force needed for production, while individual workers will be able to choose their enterprise and position according to their skills, qualifications, capabilities, and interests.[15]

This short description (one of many which could be quoted here) gives an idea of how the parameters of the labour arena were outlined. First of all, the *actors* were now the worker and the enterprise, while decreasing importance was assigned to the role of the state. Second, *labour society* was described by relations based on 'choices' in an open economic situation involving the 'outside world' and 'individuals.' Third, the final *aim* was now the efficiency of management, and the modernisation of bureaucratic/economic mechanisms.

In the initial months of contract experimentation, a major supporting argument was that the system maintained its feature of 'security' while granting greater 'flexibility' to the labour factor. As mentioned, the security factor was still a highly regarded concern for individual behaviour, while a flexible method for hiring and firing was an economic necessity for the rapidly growing industrial units.

Tools of labour flexibility were still of a bureaucratic nature at this stage, while flexibility itself was related to 'rationality' in labour mobility. This means that the flow of labour, which was the final aim of the entire reform process, was at this point still considered a top-down decision and that the field of intervention of the bureaucracy in labour allocation had been shifted from the school/unit relationship of the *unified allocation system* to the larger field of labour society. Public employment agencies such as 'labour service companies' or 'talent exchange centres' (TECs) were still visible signs of state intervention created to deal with phenomena that were growing (unemployment) or had simply not been acknowledged previously (shortages of skilled labour); in the initial years, these institutions dealt mainly with the transfer of the labour force from unit to unit, rather than with the accession of new workers to the economic system.

The following is an example of how the intermediary role of LSCs was described:

Labour service companies became a form of organisation of social labour and have the function of a 'reservoir' of the labour force redistributed by the enterprises. LSCs can organise the social labour force and, through planning, proceed to dispatch and redistribute labour, thereby contributing to a rational use and to the saving of the labour force. They can also become 'transfer stations' (*zhongzhuan zhan*) for excess workers in those enterprises undergoing restructuring, who can be organised by LSCs to be trained, re-introduced into other units, and employed to open up further opportunities.[16]

Although we shall see the greater, autonomous economic relevance of LSCs become an important component of the contradictions between the state and nonstate sectors in a later phase, at this point these intermediate bureaucratic bodies still represented the will of the state to control the 'rational flow' of the labour force within the framework of a planned economic environment.

This attitude was also clear around 1986 when the phrase 'labour force market' first appeared, accompanied by a deepening of the labour reform. There were two types of labour force markets: the 'divided and unorganised labour force market,' that is, a market made up of self-organised (mainly rural) labour suppliers seeking jobs in the cities (an often-quoted example is the 'nannies market'[17]); and the 'concentrated and organised labour market':

> As information about supply and demand of labour does not flow easily between workers and enterprises, units often have difficulty in finding workers that fit their needs, while workers have no way of finding a job in the desired position. To solve this situation we need to create a concentrated and organised labour market that fosters the exchange of relevant information about labour supply and demand, and that can become a place for them to meet.[18]

In the beginning, these *places* were such formal organisations as LSCs and TECs in the form set up by the local (generally municipal) labour bureaus.[19]

The Chinese expression for 'labour market' still evoked a physical place in which two sides meet under the precondition of a planned, rational distribution of the labour force. The socialist labour market, at this point, was not only still a market of non-commodities, but also a 'planned market.'[20]

The labour market was therefore intended to serve as the marketplace for something which flows but cannot be purchased (as it is not a commodity), nor sold (as it is not individual property). In this way, it remained no more than a tool of the rationalisation of the productive process.

At a seminar convened by the Beijing Municipal Labour Academic Association, and held at the end of 1985, this organisational and institutional role of the 'labour market' was outlined. Three main opinions emerged. The first argued that the labour market is 'a mechanism and a means for the social distribution and regulation of labour power.' This was the so-called 'labour market under leadership' and stressed the existence of a joint organisation of job seekers (be they self-organised, individuals, or LSCs). The second opinion also intended the labour market to serve as a mechanism, but aimed at objectively regulating the labour flow. This meant that attention had to be focused on both sides of the hypothetical labour market (supply and demand) and that 'both recruiting units and labourers have the freedom to choose,' while labour mobility is a 'non-commodity exchange.'

The third opinion which emerged at the conference claimed that the term 'labour market' did not fit the reality of the mechanism required for restructuring the labour system and that instead such terms as 'appropriate labour allocation' or 'rational labour flow' should be used.[21]

As we can see, all three opinions stressed the role of the labour market as a *mechanism* (a tool to be used by the state according to general needs), the main purpose of which was the resolution of irrational behaviour on the part of labour supply and demand in the new economic situation. However, it was still an idea related to the inter-unit exchange of labour, whereas the term mobility 'refers to the transfer of the labourer between work-units.' While the use of the term 'labour market' had great ideological appeal in a period in which the 'market' was the main objective of economic reform, no market-related economic principle lay behind the concept, as price, opportunity, or supply and demand were not allowed to act freely in a commoditised environment and mobility was still the result of rational (that is, policy-driven) choices and not of the interaction of economic forces.

This discussion, which corresponded to some relevant steps forward in the process of ideological reform, was accompanied by an enlargement and further opening of the debate about labour and reforming socialist economies. After 1986, the structural difficulties of a 'classic' socialist economy were openly discussed, and works by foreign economists introducing the implications of reforming socialist systems were studied and sometimes translated into Chinese.

This shift in theoretical strategy appeared clearly in a number of academic publications in which the influence, in particular, of Janos Kornai's[22] view of the reform of socialist systems was directly reported.

As an example, let us look at an influential article by Luo Shouchu on Labour mobility and reform of the labour system, published in spring 1986.[23] Luo's analysis begins with the question of labour immobility in the traditional system and the conclusions she draws are strikingly similar to those of Kornai in describing the 'classical socialist economy':

> Under the traditional system, enterprise input and output are decided by the state, cost and profit are exogenous quantities, gains and losses are taken over by the state, capital is utilised free of charge, personal incomes, unrelated to enterprises gains or losses, are determined by uniform state standards.... [In some cases] the enterprises are forced to adopt the easiest fulfilment of plan indicators as the goal of their behaviour and they subsequently develop a 'capital hunger' (*touzi jike*) and a 'means of production hunger' (*shengchan ziliao jike*) at the same time as they become 'labour hungry' (*laodongli jike*)....
>
> The 'big pot' causes labour to lack initiative and enthusiasm. All this makes it difficult for labour productivity to rise. Those enterprises that do not obtain requested equipment increments must request an increase in labour to fulfil quotas. When requested labour increments are obtained, they become an excuse for raising the enterprise's grade and requesting new equipment and other advantages.[24]

This analysis, assigning structural economic significance to the phenomenon of 'labour hoarding,' earlier identified as an irrational trend of enterprise management, draws heavily from Kornai's 'soft-budget constraint' in traditional socialist economies affecting the rationale of labour management.[25]

Luo takes a halfway position: the softness of the budget constraint, on one hand, and the restriction of planning to industrial labour allocation, on the other, both contribute (from diametrically opposed perspectives) to the 'lack of a selection mechanism which should function to promote excellence and eliminate the inferior.'

> In China, constraints on the increase in labour in large industry come from economic (funds and planning) factors, rather than from natural ones. The after-effects of 'labour starvation,' rather than being reflected in labour shortage show up in other forms, such as labour immobility, more employees in enterprises than there are jobs, under-utilization or nonutilisation of skills, and indifference everywhere.[26]

While the existence of such structural problems in labour allocation and utilization had already been pointed out in an earlier phase of the debate,[27] the systemic interpretation that emerges from Luo's article was rather new and reflected the growing importance assigned to economic constraints in the analysis of labour allocation and organisation.

Evaluation of the poorly performing allocation system led to the conclusion that 'the traditional labour management structure cannot achieve optimal results in labour allocation' and that an 'organic combination of plan and market is necessary.'

The novelty of this point in the debate and in this emerging interpretation was less the recognition that market relations must also be admitted in the realm of labour allocation than the understanding of structural problems such as unemployment (people waiting for employment) as a result of both labour overflow (due to units seeking efficiency in their production process) and friction or disequilibria when supply and demand are met ('outside of production').

From this point on, the debate entered a phase in which the word *rationality* was applied to the sustainability of economic factors rather than to adherence to rational Marxist principles.

Is Labour a Commodity?[28]

Although a more pragmatic attitude towards labour emerged at this stage, the greater part of the theoretical debate was still devoted to an issue of pure socialist theory, that is, the question of the commoditisation of labour in the changing economy of Chinese socialism.

The particular intensity with which this topic was debated during the years of labour reform and contractualisation is logically related to the issue of marketisation of labour relations being discussed here. While the rationality of market mechanisms was advocated, it was impossible to find justification for the application of market relations in the traditional understanding of labour as a noncommodity economic factor.

In accordance with the tradition of Chinese theoretical debates under socialism, the two categorical answers to the question put at the beginning of this paragraph were not related to different policy options and both supported the current policy of labour reform. There is probably one major reason for this: the question of commoditisation of labour was not related to the specific policy of mere labour reform (although this was the most visible among the recent changes in the Chinese social and economic system) but more broadly related to the economic reform path as a whole. For all commentators, reform of the traditional allocation system, as well as an extension of the contract system, were essential for China's modernisation. But the creation of a labour market (for which the main precondition is a recognition of the commodity nature of labour – *laodong li shangpin xingzhi*) would lead to the question of what kind of economy China was to have – whether a 'planned commodity economy' or a 'socialist market economy' – and what the relationship between labour and other production factors (such as the means of production and a growing variety of capital) would be.

Seen from the perspective of this final goal, this otherwise uninteresting, redundant, highly ideologised discussion can probably be better understood as a part of the process leading to the following stage of the reform, that is, the 'socialist market economy' of the 1990s.

The discussion gave rise to some arguments in favour of a positive answer to the question. These points are what we will associate with support for a 'market socialism' solution of the reform: first, while labour and the means of production are (by definition) jointly owned by labourers in the general economic system, during the production process the quantitative and qualitative combination of labour and the means of production turns labour into 'something with measurable value circulating on the market.'[29]

Second, the existence of a labour market is conditioned by a recognition of the commodity nature of labour. In order for a market to exist, there must be a commodity to be marketed.

Third, as the mobility of labour increases, the intersection of supply and demand creates a difference between the value and use-value of the labour force, which is a main characteristic of a commodity.

While advocates of 'labour as a commodity' generally found it very easy to support their stance once the precondition of a labour market had been accepted, it was more difficult to justify such a position in the context of a socialist economy, in which workers are both suppliers and owners of the means of production.

On the other hand, those who supported the principle that labour can *never* be considered a commodity under socialism had to find a different definition for a labour market, which they accepted as a mechanism but not as a principle.

Tortuous and partial reformulations of the unacceptable principle of wage-labour markets were therefore a clear sign of how hard it was to overcome these difficulties and how intense the need was to be consistent with the leading ideology: such concepts as 'labour service market,' 'live labour market,' 'manpower resource market,' and 'job market,' (strangely enough, the controversy was not about the term 'market') were all used to describe the actual relationships (between enterprise and workers, inside the production process, between the two roles of the worker as supplier of labour and owner of the enterprise, etc.) in terms of a rationalisation of the allocation process.[30]

As an arena for the debate in those years, the journal *Zhongguo shehui kexue* (Social Sciences in China) was particularly active in hosting open discussions in which the different positions challenged each other directly. Both positions expressed supportive views for the new policy of contractualisation, but were sharply opposed in terms of their definition of labour.

I will report some parts of this debate in the following pages, not because I consider them essential to the evolution of the labour debate but simply to show how instrumental these positions were to the struggle over the future of the Chinese economy, and how quickly 'conservative' positions were abandoned once the political struggle had been resolved in favour of a further deepening of reform.

Socialist market economists (SMEs) often based their analysis on a pragmatic re-consideration of labour mobility and of the role of workers as owners of the means of production.

> One collective expression of the worker's position as owner [of the means of production] is that he can move freely, and autonomously decide his productive and

administrative unit, while realising the unity of labour and means of production *in the social environment.* Without a labour market, without the chance for the worker to move his labour freely as if it were a commodity, the position of a worker would be that of a passive allocated and adjusted factor, therefore becoming dependent on only one part of the means of production.[31]

For those opposed to this position (to simplify, we shall call them Planned commodity economists, PCEs), the problem lay elsewhere. In an article in response to the above, which appeared in the same journal, Ma Conglin does not accept that 'the free movement of labour force implies that labour is exchanged on a trading (*maimai*) basis,' and he argues that mobility and commoditisation do not necessarily go together.[32]

Similarly, in the same issue of the journal, Wei Xinghua quotes the contrasting examples of life tenure in Japanese (capitalist) enterprises and of the high mobility rates in the Soviet (socialist) labour system to demonstrate that the nature of labour in fact has nothing to do with the issue of mobility.[33]

The basic difference therefore is in the final aim of mobility. While SMEs consider 'free mobility' (*ziyou liudong*) as the general rule, PCEs advocate mainly a 'rational flow' (*heli liudong*) of the labour force.

While the former concept implies that the rationality of the system lies in individual behaviour (and regulation is a result of market forces), the latter assigns superiority to the (public) mechanism. This is clearly a difference that is not limited solely to the labour allocation system but extends to all fields of the economy.

> Firstly, the labour flow we discuss here and the free flow of commodities in all markets are not the same thing. Still people are not encouraged to seek jobs as they please, in disregard of the requirements of the state plan and overall arrangements, and exclusively out of personal considerations. While a rational flow of labour is encouraged, labour should be relatively stable.... Secondly, by labour flow we mean chiefly the flow of *qualified* personnel rather than the sale of labour as a commodity on the market. We should not regard the flow of qualified personnel exclusively as a relationship of exchange between labour as a commodity and money.[34]

A similar dispute, in fact, emerged in connection with the principle of DATL. Can the principle of DATL (that is, remuneration based on equal quantity and quality of labour) be used when labour is a commodity or does the principle of labour pricing (implying different remunerations for equivalent labour because of different economic conditions) 'naturally' emerge?

PCEs stressed the contradiction between the two principles, while SMEs attempted to keep the contradictions within the framework of socialist theory.

> The commodity nature of social labour under socialism is the starting point for individual commodity distribution, and the recognition that the labour force is a commodity helps the implementation of DATL. As labour exchange is based on equal value, to accept the principle of labour-commodity can guarantee that an equal quantity of labour receives equal remuneration; if the labour cost is not based on an equal-value exchange, it will be very difficult to implement DATL.
>
> Owing to limited competition among labour suppliers and too little possibility for choice on the demand side, demand-supply joint regulation of the market does not emerge.[35]

Compared with the debates in the initial years of the reform, this was a very different interpretation of DATL, mainly based on the superiority of the regulatory power of market relations over the redistributive principle for which the problem lay in the *measurement* of labour quantity and quality.

This contradictory position, which tried to combine the equity of central distribution with the advantage of market relations, was stigmatised by the opposing view that 'if labour is a commodity, DATL cannot succeed.'

> ... if distribution is carried out according to the value of labour, the income of labourers will have nothing to do with surplus products and their value. The latter is owned by others. However, distribution according to labour means distribution of products owned collectively by labourers as well as of the national wealth. Apart from the portion of the products distributed among labourers as consumer goods according to work done, the remaining

products and their value will go directly or indirectly to labourers in the form of social deductions. The higher the development level of socialist production, the more social wealth and the greater the disparity between the income earned in accordance with the principle of distribution according to labour and the 'value of labour.' This is because distribution according to work is not restricted by the 'value of labour.'[36]

As we can see, the contenders in this ongoing debate expressed two well-defined positions that were probably more important for the consequences they had on the general discussion of socialism than in the field of labour policymaking where, instead, a pragmatic attitude dominated.[37] The extension of the mechanism of labour contracting was surely one of the reasons for the explosion of this debate from 1985 to 1987, but this policy and the process of its evaluation also brought some new issues to the main table of the labour debate.

4.3 Labour Contracts and the Nature of Labour Relations

On 1 October 1986 the newly promulgated 'Regulations for the Recruitment of Workers in State-Owned Enterprises' and 'Regulations on Dismissal of State-Owned Enterprise Workers' became effective. SOEs were thereafter required by law to 'practice the labour contract system' while 'openly recruiting workers from society.'

The introduction of a contract system for labour partially elim- inated the long-established and dominant practice of bureaucratic allocation. This was a much longer process than that first sanctioned by the 1986 regulations and it did not end such pater- nalistic and clientelistic practices as 'internal' recruitment, or the important role of administrative allocation.

Contracts changed, if not in theory at least in the individuals' perception of their labour, the role of workers inside the pro- duction unit, and consequently fostered the transformation of the work-unit from the all-encompassing organiser of life and produc- tion to the employer.

The new system also acknowledged a division of workers into different types, namely permanent, contract, and temporary workers. While the three categories were not new to Chinese labour organisation, a recognition of different statuses became a foundation for an economic division between workers who were occasionally assigned similar tasks with different monetary incomes and non-monetary benefits.

The reform also introduced elements of a legalisation of labour relations; the existence of an agreement underwritten by both parties allowed (mainly in theory) workers to act against the enterprise and, consequently, to turn to the state to safeguard their legal 'labour rights.'

Finally, the emergence of the new system diminished the incidence of social benefits and social security, which were the major features of the traditional social contract between workers and the state. This was soon targeted as the principal reason for the deterioration of labour conditions. The emphasis on this feature is also very important in our discussion of the labour issue in Chinese debates during the 1980s as it contributed to turning attention from distribution and allocation to the labour process and individual attitudes and behaviour.

This further step is also partly a legacy of the re-emergence of the social sciences (other than economics) as an element in Chinese theoretical debate. With the relative 'relaxation' of central control over discussion of theoretical issues, which lasted until 1988–89 and was partly due to the transitional nature of reform theory (that is, to the generally shared impression that the reforms need experimentation and options from which to choose), some considerations arising from sociological experiences and field research were introduced. Therefore, labour became an issue that involved not only the economic performance of the system but also individual satisfaction, social development, and security.

This new way of presenting labour is well described in an article published shortly after the 1986 contract regulations went into effect; in addition to the 'many merits' (mainly those linked to the efficiency of production and of economic mechanisms) of the new system, the essay also found several difficulties in implementation, mainly related to contradictions at the level of production and individual attitudes.[38]

Of particular interest is the section of the article devoted to workers' 'concerns' in the two factories surveyed:

> For the time being, since society and family cannot understand the labour contract system, they thus view contract workers in an unfavourable light. Some people say: 'Contract work is temporary work for which there is no

guarantee at all. Those who take on such work have to suffer throughout their lives.'

Contract workers also consider themselves 'inferior' to others and some of them say: 'We are second-class citizens in that people prefer not to choose us for husbands or wives and in that we have to worry about questions like health and livelihood after retirement.' As reflected in actual situations, they are not entrusted with important tasks and very often are dismissed from their jobs if a mistake is made.[39]

While this early investigation anticipates one of the problems in the implementation of labour contracts, what is more interesting is that a new sociology of labour (the scientific method of which is still very questionable) was emerging as an important tool of interpretation and a consistent part of the labour debate.

As seen, the arguments in the debate on the nature of labour have to be understood within the general context of economic changes; however, statements of the official line on the labour system took over and summarized some of the arguments (mainly the ones used by those whom we called SMEs) to justify the marketisation of labour relations.

In a June 1986 speech, for example, Hu Qili assured that the reform of the labour system and the introduction and wide implementation of labour contracting was aimed at 'improving the quality of workers and staff,' responding to the needs of *stability* as well as *mobility* and conforming to the demands of modernized *planned* production and development of a *commodity* economy.'[40] Labour contracts according to this official statement *do not harm the position of workers as owners of the enterprise* and the nature of the socialist contract remains *opposed to that of wage-labour under capitalist conditions.*

But behind the emergence of the contract labour system, which the Chinese leadership dealt with as another political campaign to be 'enthusiastically supported,' some related macroeconomic problems were appearing and were already being pointed out by analysts.

One problem was the increase in hiring costs and the relative contraction of employment. This was understood to be a result of one of the principal goals of socialist enterprises, that is, the growth of per capita income rather than overall profits.

The current reform generally induces enterprise goals to turn toward the increase of per capita income. Thus their hiring standards differ from those of enterprises pursuing overall profits. As a result, while there is a slackening of enterprise hunger for labour and a hoarding tendency, there are also trends towards an increase in the cost of using workers and a relative decline in the number of placements. ...

Despite the fact that the cost[41] to the enterprise of the use of workers on the accounting books is wages, the goal of the enterprise and the rigidity of income compels it to view the proportion of profits set aside for bonuses and the welfare fund as personal income, as an actual cost which has to be guaranteed.[42]

This situation opened up contradictions within enterprises, that required greater autonomy to become effective economically, but whose 'rational economic behaviour' meant the risk of increasing unemployment. This situation was further exacerbated by the unbalanced nature of China's labour supply: abundant in unskilled labourers, the pressure of which reduces wages, but comparatively poor in highly sought skilled workers, whom the enterprises are generally ready to compensate in a more attractive way.

But the Chinese *danwei*, it was recognized, was still a 'community' and its egalitarian mechanism tended to respond to the expectations of unskilled workers for higher income, thereby entering into a spiral of increasing labour costs. Only the deepening of reform and growing of economic constraints would later overcome this limitation.

Another macroeconomic problem to which attention was turned was rising unemployment in the industrial sector (coupled with growing concern for the increasing number of displaced agricultural workers). The consequence of contract labour and independence in hiring and firing was an increase in the dismissal of redundant workers, as they became a burden for the enterprises rather than being the financial advantage they had been under the traditional system.

The problem of large-scale unemployment (a central concern in the late 1990s) was already clear in the eyes of observers at that time, not only as a result of changes in enterprise behaviour, but also as a macro social factor, the consequence of the growth of the working population, of the decrease in the percentage of the population employed in agriculture, and of a general disequilibrium in both the sectoral and geographic distribution of labour supply and demand.[43]

What may be concluded about the debate on contractualisation is that it evolved radically from 1983 to 1988 in at least three major respects: it became more pragmatic, wide and rich in economic considerations, in particular after the labour reform went into effect. The question of the commodity nature of labour came to be understood as a component of the larger debate on economic development, but insofar as the specific issue of labour is concerned, the traditional unanimity of consent accompanied the birth of the new system. As of 1987, finally, some critical and worried analyses of the future labour society appeared, probably corresponding to the re-emergence of a scientific attitude towards field research which exposed the crisis of China's work-unit identity and the growth of a desire for mobility which (coupled with the administrative crisis) was the problem at the centre of the debate on labour markets in the following years.

The end of the monolithic *danwei* system, ushered in by the emergence of diversified workers' identities, accompanied the end of a privileged society built inside the closed gates of industrial enterprises. The traditional (rural/urban, industrial/agricultural) divide, the origin of this privilege, was further complicated by labour policy reform, and by the progressive decline of administrative control over society and mobility.

The process of policy formulation, in the years leading to the implementation of the contract system, more than at other times, enjoyed the possibility to investigate and evaluate experiments of a different nature, and was not forced to apply only rigid ideological schemes, thus resulting in a more complex set of policies that set the tone for the reforms to come. Contracts penetration of Chinese enterprises was slow, difficult, and driven by economic and political considerations, as well as by market opportunities. Nonetheless it was a massive and dramatic change in the management culture and in social organisation. Despite social and political resistance, contracts did change the labour arena for good, although this was still questionable in the years when the policies were first formulated.

5

THE CONTRACTUALISATION OF LABOUR RELATIONS

5.1 A 'Structural' Economic Reform

Towards the end of 1984, the set of experimental policies of economic reform implemented during the initial years of readjustment resulted in major official recognition of the new nature of the Chinese economic system. The 'Decision on Economic Structural Reform' adopted by the Third Plenary Session of the twelfth Central Committee in October 'summed up,' in the official words of Hu Sheng,

> the experience of economic structural reform since the third plenary session of the 11th Central Committee, put forward and elaborated *more systematically* a series of important questions, both theoretical and practical, concerning this issue. It is a programmatic document for carrying out overall economic structural reform.[1]

This document marked the end of the experimental phase of economic reform, and 'shattered the traditional concept of setting planned economy against commodity economy' [sic].[2]

The planned commodity economy (PCE) was the name given to the new framework for the Chinese economy which opened the path for a more structured reform of labour relations. In the 'Decision on Economic Structural Reform', the PCE was seen as involving: further development of the nonstate sector, while maintaining the leading role of the state sector; further devolution of autonomy to enterprises through expansion of the tax-for-profit system; reduction in the control function of state organs and transition from state control to state supervision of the economic system.

All measures proposed in the document signalled an intention to proceed along the path to decentralisation of state prerogatives in the economic system. The effectiveness of the principal means of state control of the industrial sector (mandatory production plans, distribution of materials and production factors, and distribution of funds) steadily and consciously decreased in the years following 1984.

In 1987, for example, the number of industrial products controlled by mandatory plans of the State Planning Commission decreased from 120 to 60 (17 percent of total industrial output), while only 26 production materials were still distributed by the state (as compared to 259 before the reforms). In addition, state funds had largely been replaced by bank loans (76.6 percent and 23.4 percent in 1978, respectively and 31.2 percent and 68.8 percent in 1987, respectively).

The decreasing role of state planning had major consequences for the enterprises as they acquired an increasingly greater degree of autonomy through an enlargement of the scope of the responsibility system and implementation of the factory manager responsibility system in 1985. This new autonomy, as well as the dismantling of the previous system for state financial and productive supply, forced enterprises and their managers to adopt an active and aggressive attitude towards production factor markets, including the labour market.

At the same time, the new 'economicism' in enterprise behaviour caused disorientation among workers, who faced new complex and alternative choices as full-scale contract employment was introduced into the state sector (1986). Although the number of workers under contract was still very low with respect to permanent workers until the late 1980s (about 10 percent in 1988), almost all working families were confronted with choices, at least for the new members of the family who were entering the labour arena. As of 1986, life tenure in SOEs, with all its advantages and high levels of individual and family dependence, was de facto abolished for all new recruits. Worker families, the backbone of the *danwei* system, took on a new attitude which has been called 'one family, two systems' (*yijia liangzhi*),[3] that is, maintaining the family position in the state unit, while dispatching sons to run individual enterprises or to find employment in the more profitable though more insecure private sector.

This chapter will focus on three aspects of the implementation of contracts in the Chinese labour system: the institutional arrangements and policy derived from the new basis for economic policy set by the 1984 decision on economic reform; workers' reactions and adaptation to the new regulations; the impact on enterprise management and on the nature of work-units.

5.2 The Labour Contract

Labour contracts were first mentioned in 1980 in the regulations on labour management in Sino-foreign joint ventures.[4] In this case, contracts were the only way to regulate employment relations in enterprises. Contracts were signed by management and trade union representatives and confirmed (*pizhun*) by local labour departments. Revival of and experiments with contract labour were thus fostered and accelerated by the emergence of private and foreign investment, in areas such as Shenzhen special economic zone.

Only later did the idea of contracts in labour and employment relations become associated with the reform of SOEs. The first experimental regulations involving recognition of a direct and contractable relationship between worker and enterprise were more concerned with the quality of recruitment and the selection of recruits than with the conditions and competitive advantages offered to the economic unit by the abolition of life tenure and related commitments.

In February 1983 the Ministry of Labour and Personnel issued a circular calling for a large-scale experiment with labour contracts in SOEs as a means of eliminating 'iron rice bowl' and of definitively applying the principle of 'from each according to his ability, to each according to his labour' (*gejin suoneng, anlao fenpei*).[5] The circular targeted both state and collective units and called upon 'provinces that have not yet tried out this system to choose one or two cities or counties to implement this experimental reform before the end of the present year.'[6] The contract described in this circular could be long-term (without specified duration) or short-term (three to five years), with wages calculated 'according to labour,' including (at least for workers holding urban *hukou*) all major social security items (such as old age pensions); no mention was made of the welfare items generally issued to life-tenure workers (such as housing, schooling, etc.).

Shortly after this circular was issued, provisional regulations for the 'recruiting, testing, and selection of workers' were issued and made public.[7] This second circular talked explicitly of open recruitment, officially putting an end to the practice of *neizhao* (internal recruitment) of 'children of the unit's workers,' one of the most obvious clientelist forms of family protection in industrial units.[8]

Both documents intended therefore to introduce rational practices into hiring procedures, keeping the labour contract and labour management (*laodong guanli*) separate from recruitment and from the broader issue of employment (*jiuye*). Judging from the time it took for the system to go into effect and become compulsory for all state and collective enterprises (1986), and then to be popularised, the experiments must have met with numerous difficulties. In 1987, the number of contract workers reached six million, slightly more than 5 percent of the total industrial workforce (including the private and foreign investment sector), of which 61.5 percent were new recruits. A significant trend towards substitution of fixed workers with contract workers did not take place until the beginning of the 1990s: it is only since 1992 that the number of contracts stipulated yearly has begun to exceed the number of new recruits in the state sector, meaning that some of the fixed workers were slowly turning to contract labour.[9]

There were 13.7 million contract workers in SOEs in 1990 (13.3 percent of total SOEs staff and workers), but their numerical growth was much more evident in the following years, reaching 26.2 percent of the state industrial workforce in 1994 and 52 percent in 1997. This contributed to the optimism of the Chinese government regarding conversion of the entire industrial labour force into contract workers by the year 2000.

While it should be noted that implementation of the labour contract system progressed at a slower pace than expected, it is reasonable to assume that this change was probably the most significant of all changes imposed by the reform and the one with the deepest impact on Chinese labour society. Rapid, straightforward, and painless development could not be expected.

As mentioned above, employment and labour management (wages and organisation) had been kept separate in labour policy-making during the early reform period. The extension in the use of contracts became the first tool to integrate the two issues within a framework that would eventually lead to the emergence of a labour market. Enterprises were encouraged to be actively involved in the demand side of selection. However, they lacked not only administrative support from public structures (labour service markets and talent exchange centres run by local labour bureaus developed rapidly only after the beginning of the 1990s), but sometimes it was difficult for them to be selective as their hunger for labour and for new recruits was very limited.

The previous practice of hoarding the labour force and the structural difficulties in laying off workers, for both internal and macroeconomic reasons, put the force already on the books to a more rational use, instead of hiring new workers. As the new system was compulsory only for new recruits in the initial years of contract work, workforce growth inside the state sector remained limited to this category, while the largest proportion of new entries in the arena of labour relations was in the private or collective sector and in the state-led (or collective) 'out of plan' production units of various types, such as labour service companies or township and village enterprises. The ability and willingness of SOEs to absorb new workers decreased continuously after 1986. In that year, before the full-scale implementation of the labour contract regulations, new urban employment entering the state sector was still 67.6 percent of the total (5.36 million); in 1991 it reached a negative peak of 47.4 percent (3.63 million), with a significant increase in collective (35.6 percent), individual (7.9 percent), and other kinds of enterprises (private and foreign, 9.1 percent).[10]

The set of labour reforms issued in 1986 included four major documents: one concerning the institution of labour contracts, one on hiring procedures for SOEs, one on the dismissal of workers violating labour discipline, and finally one on the institution of an unemployment fund. Once again, these four issues (labour rights, recruitment, industrial relations, and welfare), structurally a part of the same chapter of labour reform, were kept separate, as was the case in 1983.

The 'Provisional Regulations on the Establishment of the Labour Contract System in State-Run Enterprises' were published in July 1986.[11] According to this document, 'full year workers' (*changnianxing gongren*) have to be hired on a contractual basis. The document also establishes a difference between contract workers and seasonal (*jijie*) and temporary (*lingshi*) workers, that is, those hired (also on a contract basis) for periods shorter than one year.

Contracts could be short-term (*duanqi* – one to five years) or long-term (*changqi* – more than five years), and could be extended after expiry 'according to production needs' and with the agreement of the worker.[12] Recruitment was described as an open process directed by the enterprises under the leadership of local labour departments, on the basis of voluntary application by individual workers undergoing selection based on 'virtue (*de*), knowledge (*zhi*), and physical conditions (*ti*).' The workers, at the end of this process, were hired on a trial basis for a period of between three and six months.

The contract signed by the two parties included some regular items, such as quality and quantity standards (*zhiliang he shuliang zhibiao*) to be achieved by the worker; his/her duties; duration of the contract and of the trial period; production and working conditions; salary, social insurance and benefits; regulations concerning labour discipline; penalties for violating the labour contract; and all other items agreed upon by both worker and enterprise.[13]

The rights of the workers to terminate the contract and the duties of the enterprise *not* to dismiss the worker were also clearly stipulated, whereas the norms under which the enterprise could fire the worker were specified in another document regarding both contract and fixed workers.[14]

There were also provisions concerning the regulation of labour relations and the treatment of contract workers *vis-à-vis* permanent workers. There was the possibility for contract workers to receive fewer material benefits (*fuli*), with their lower income being compensated for by 'wage-type' monetary benefits that in any case could not amount to more than 15 percent of the standard wages. Material incentives (bonuses, rewards) and basic contributions for health, food, work security, and tools were to be calculated on the basis of the standard for fixed workers with the same productive duties.

On many other issues the position of contract workers was equal to that of fixed workers. For holiday and wedding leave, sick or maternity treatment, work-related accidents or illness, the conditions were the same as for other workers, although a limit was set, for example, on the maximum duration of leave for non work-related illnesses or accidents (three months to one year according to the overall duration of the contract, extendable for those already working in the unit for more than two years). When leaving a unit, contract workers were entitled to a severance allowance (the so-called 'life allowance' *shenghuo buzhu fei*), calculated as one monthly standard wage for each year of work completed in the unit (but not more than twelve). There was no payment if the worker had chosen to resign (*zixing cizhi*) voluntarily, nor after the expiry of the term or dismissal by the enterprise.

Finally, the document established a security system for retired workers: enterprises were to create retirement funds by allocating 15 percent of the yearly total contract wage bill, whereas workers were to pay 3 percent of their standard wage for the same purpose.

An earlier document had created the first public unemployment fund.[15] This fund – intended to protect workers dismissed by bankrupt or near-bankrupt enterprises, workers whose contract terms had expired, or workers who had simply been 'laid off' by enterprises – was put under the control and management of local government. Enterprises made contributions (1 percent of the total payroll before taxation) and local treasuries subsidized it and intervened when resources ran low. The fund was to be used not only to pay subsidies to dismissed workers but also, for example, to organise training activities, to cover early retirements (in the case of enterprises undergoing restructuring), medical expenses, and 'expenses that help unemployed workers provide for themselves by engaging in production.'[16] The latter could refer to the creation of labour service companies managed by local governments.

Workers with a standing of more than five years received payments from the unemployment fund for two years; others were paid for twelve months. During the first year, the unemployed were provided with 60–75 percent of their standard wage (as we saw, a small part of the total wage, at least for permanent workers), and with 50 percent during the second year.

Contracts and temporary labour were largely used in the late 1950s and early 1960s. Contract workers, mainly recruited from the countryside to increase productivity of low-tech productions, constituted an extra army of industrial workers who could be used in addition to permanent labour and who could be dismissed almost at will (sometimes in a rather harsh and uncontrolled manner by the urban bureaucracies), to be sent back to their original rural brigades, as was the case once the policies on labour mobility changed at the beginning of the 60s. The use of contracts, however, was never extensively used to undermine the prerogative of the urban worker elite.

Unlike the 1950s and 1960s, it was already clear in 1983 that the new contract system (*hetongzhi*) was expected to become *the* substitute for the 'iron rice bowl,' and involve also all those workers who had until then enjoyed the advantages of higher status and higher levels of security embedded in the life-tenure system of urban SOEs.

Labour contract workers are considered 'regular enterprise workers' and their wages fall within the national labour wage plan. They are formally entitled to the same economic and civil rights as permanent workers (work, study, participation, political rights,[17] and material incentives). In the optimistic official view, they differ from permanent workers only with regard to their insurance and welfare benefits which are charged partly to the enterprise and partly to the worker: 'the advantages of the permanent labour system have been retained while the iron rice bowl has been eliminated.'[18]

The use of contracts was made compulsory not by these regulations (which were concerned with establishing contract workers' rights, duties, and position inside enterprises) but by another document issued on the same date concerning recruitment of workers.[19] The two documents were kept separate in order to link contracts to the recruitment process rather than to SOEs' management. The second document also affirmed the need for open recruitment to 'respect the national employment plans.' Enterprises were, in fact, enjoying much greater freedom in resource management and managerial decisions, even though the constraints on their budgets were not hard. Acting 'outside of the plan' (*jihua wai*) was becoming a major source of revenue for SOEs.

Despite the breakthrough, contracts appeared to 'remain within the cultural tradition of reciprocity, with rights balanced by obligations,'[20] while they became a tool to establish new labour relations in both SOEs and foreign-invested and private enterprises as well as a way for enterprises to practice 'open recruitment' (*gongkai zhaogong*). However, the new tool was expected to lessen central level control of employment dynamics.

5.3 Contracts and Labour Mobility: Moving the Dual Market to the Cities

The provisional regulations also contained one strange article specifying the possibility of terminating a contract and signing a new one with a different unit in case of 'production necessities or of national regulations requiring cross-county (*kuo diqu*) movement of the labour force.' This was the first recognition of the potential for labour mobility under the contract system, although the regulation clarifies that the movement of contract workers is conditioned by 'the approval of labour offices and the fulfilment of *hukou* and pension fund formalities.'[21]

The 'mobility' incorporated in the contract system was probably intended to contribute to solving the economic and geographic contradictions between the developed urban labour demand and mainly rural labour supply; a solution to this dilemma had been obstructed largely by administrative measures such as the family registration system.

The work-units that had been involved in the decentralisation and independence schemes of the early reform years were changing their administrative and economic agency relationship to the state, but their internal structures had not yet been questioned. Clientelism and paternalism remained dominant in the unit-worker relationship, while the new responsibility system made it more evident that managers were directly responsible for choices and policies related to workers' well being. The contract system challenged existing interpersonal networks and increased competitiveness as well as intra-unit conflicts: labour contracts are generally individual agreements (not household-based as they are in the countryside) and are linked to individual and collective productivity, as well as being deprived of most of the acquired welfare benefits previously attached to labour. This new relationship largely reduces the political and social role implicit in the work-unit system and exposes the worker to different varieties of management despotism, rather than being dependent on the enterprise.

Newcomers were often convinced that a contract was the first step towards life tenure in an enterprise, while permanent workers were frequently reluctant to abandon their privileges as 'masters of the enterprise' to undertake a new and uncertain status. Not surprisingly, the labour contract contradicted the unit system and this factor affected the rapidity of its implementation. Only later, when the advantages (and sometimes the necessity) of *xiahai*[22] became more evident, mainly in the urban developing economy which could grant a higher – albeit risky – income, did the voluntary mobility of workers become more marked.

The demand for workers in the booming urban enterprises in those years and the difficulties of recruiting among urban *hukou* holders forced the authorities to shift from control to encouragement of labour movements from the localities towards the cities, and to facilitate the so-called *hukou* migration, that is, the formal and bureaucratically driven transfer of workers, associated with the transformation of their *hukou* from rural to urban status. This policy lasted only until the end of the 1980s when the new economic crisis and the relatively lower demand for labour forced the authorities to bring *hukou* migration under control again.[23]

It is no coincidence that the major experiments with reforming the contradictory nature of the *hukou* system were carried out during this period of significant administrative reorganisation of the allocation system. In 1985, new regulations were issued concerning temporary residence for non-*hukou* holders, extending the possibility of registering for temporary residence in small towns.[24]

The reasons for and structure of rural-urban migration in the second half of the 1980s strongly indicate that the distinction between *hukou* and non-*hukou* migration is still very effective in shaping migration patterns. Non-*hukou* mobility, an expression referring to self-initiated rural-urban migration, is predominantly work-related: 49.3 percent of these migrants leave the countryside for jobs in industry or the self-employed sector. But due to the high incidence among non-*hukou* (informal) migrants of self-employment and family businesses in the residual niches of the developing urban economy, a further 33 percent of them who may actually consider migration for 'family reasons' (migration with the family, marriage, or to rejoin family and friends) should probably be included in the total number of work migrants.

The employment structure of migrants revealed by the 1990 census shows that the non-*hukou* migrants were principally employed in the industrial workforce, and that a significant percentage (73.6 percent) were employed in privately-owned enterprises or in the self-employed sector.[26]

By contrast, *hukou* migrants are almost entirely the result of state-led job transfers, assignments, marriage migration, or other reasons (such as study or training) and only an insignificant percentage (1.8 percent) entered the labour market without being assigned by the relevant administrative units.

The demand for temporary labour has been very high since the beginning of the 1980s. The special economic zones that have enjoyed a special status in employment practices since 1980 have been the leading areas in the recruitment of temporary workers. According to official data, permanent labour only accounted for 44 percent of the total workforce in the Shenzhen SEZ in 1987, while contract workers amounted to 14.1 percent and temporary workers 41.9 percent.[27] Also, in the case of temporary workers, massive transfers of the labour force under the auspices of local authorities lasted into the 1990s, as demonstrated by the existence of special model collective contracts signed between mine plants or other labour intensive state-owned plants and local governments for the hiring of 'rural rotation workers' (*nongmin lunhuan gongren*).[28]

Employment 'out of the plan' (*jihua wai*) in SOEs also grew steadily in the reform years, principally in the fast growing coastal provinces, whose economy required a large pool of cheap labour. However, state-owned enterprises also preferred to hire temporary workers when needed because: they cost less than contract or permanent workers[29] as there was no need for the enterprises to grant welfare or to pay insurance costs; wage labourers from the countryside (*nongmin gong*) were considered simple-minded persons (*laoshi*) and therefore easier to manage; they were 'easy to hire and fire' (*zhao zhi ji lai huizhi jiqu*). Furthermore, workers coming to the city from the countryside to seek labour were ready to take on positions and to do the dirty work that the urban population now refused to engage in.[30] It was not the exception that temporary workers were hired outside of the official recruitment channels without being given formal contracts. This was especially true for the bearers of rural *hukou*, whose chances to find jobs in the cities remained limited to those in construction or in the lowest echelons of industrial production.

In 1988, the number of 'out of plan' workers in SOEs had already reached 10.49 million. About 21 percent of the excess total rural workforce that left the countryside between 1977 and 1988 (134 million officially) was hired by SOEs, although 90 percent of them had the status of temporary or seasonal workers. Later, in 1995, a survey revealed that around one-third of Shanghai's workers in foreign funded enterprises had either never signed a contract or were illegally employed.[31]

As on other occasions, the regulations on contracts contributed to the recognition of a situation that was already widespread in state industrial enterprises and the emergence of some major and latent contradictions.

The need to implement a labour market faced the existence and social importance of administrative barriers still largely active, though subjectively ignored by labour suppliers, moving towards areas with greater and more flexible demand for labour. At the same time, the ability of enterprises to maintain their role as the urban organisers of life and production faced structural problems, and while the interest of managerial activity turned towards economic goals, the policy towards workers led to the use of temporary rather than long or medium-term contracts.

The channels for recruitment were still largely conditioned by the lack of administrative and official recognition of the market mechanisms in allocation of the labour force. State enterprises were forced to use the labour force market inside the framework of the state plan; yet, due to their increased economic autonomy, they no longer had the advantages they had enjoyed earlier when they hoarded the 'in the plan' labour force to increase their total wage bill.

Finally, the contract remained an administrative means to control recruitment while allowing for greater mobility. The state attempted to regulate the situation by trying to reduce its direct intervention, and depicting itself in the role of 'arbitrator as well as a regulator, as is often the case in many countries in East and South East Asia.'[32]

5.4 From Work-Unit to Employer

It is a widespread impression among commentators on labour reform that – with respect to the original objectives – the process remained largely incomplete and labour relations were far more extensively influenced by changes in external conditions and the deregulation of the market than by new regulatory efforts.

However, looking at the entire process of implementation from an historical perspective, and considering both continuity and change in the system, contract regulations – as a major element in the labour reform – seem to have been quite helpful in transforming the macro and micro structure of Chinese labour society into its present configuration.

Contracts, based on mobility, were not simply intended to overcome laziness and low efficiency in production but also to rationalise the relationship between state and unit worker. They were issued outside of direct state control and contributed to making state employment less attractive and raising the competitiveness of nonstate and small business employment inside the labour market.

Contracts contributed to the segmentation[33] of the working class as recruitment replaced assignment. Skilled workers, scarce and in high demand, and young urban dwellers were able to obtain much better conditions and jobs in the market than were unskilled temporary workers, not so much in terms of wages as in other perks and benefits. Despite widespread opposition from the media and 'public opinion' to the increase in floating workers in the cities, because it was claimed they stole job opportunities from local youth, these two segments of the labour market apparently never really competed for the same jobs, as only migrant or rural workers would accept second-rate, dirty or unprotected jobs in the marginal manufacturing factories, since they were excluded from access to the privileged segments of the market.[34]

Korzec describes 'resistance' from workers and managers to full-fledged implementation of the major features of labour contracts, such as limited duration and the de-linking of wages and perks, and points out the difficulties of dismissals and the reproduction of 'iron security' among contract workers in SOEs.[35] While dismissals are not happily accepted by workers in any economic system, they were a completely new individual and collective experience for workers who had been accustomed to high levels of dependency and who were not willing or not prepared to face the market. Although still entitled to basic services unavailable to non-urban workers, the bulk of industrial workers began – with the gradual contractualisation of their prerogatives – to feel the anxieties of market insecurity. Resistance to the dismantling of the iron rice bowl became more and more prevalent as the reform progressed; strategies by workers' family, while 'avoiding open confrontation and open bargaining with the authorities,' – as another author puts it – 'may at least bring a modicum of mundane benefits and respite from abuse.'[36]

Together with the problem of dismissing excess workers, the new units had to deal with the increased mobility of skilled workers, as the privileged segment of the working class enjoyed more employment opportunities. Before the implementation of contracts, the mobility of technical and skilled personnel was very low. According to one report issued in Shanghai in 1986, at least 60 percent of the professional and technical personnel working in the city's enterprises had never been transferred after they started work, and about one-fifth of the 553,000 trained personnel were not working 'with what they learned and in what they are good at.'[37] In 1987 articles noted the 'scarce success' of the system established to exchange talent based on talent exchange centres (TEC). Only 14 percent of the over one million applicants for job exchange with professional or technical knowledge were transferred after 1983. In one TEC in Beijing, applicants willing to change jobs were said to have to wait at least three months, although it usually took more time – even a year – and then only 10 percent were said to have succeeded in obtaining a different position.[38]

Nonetheless, the natural force of attraction of state units began to decrease after the contracts were implemented, and the 'iron rice bowl' was challenged by the steady reduction in the dependency rate and the increase in alternatives. The contracts, the result of a bi-directional choice and not an administrative act,[39] theoretically could be easily terminated by the workers if they found better opportunities. The relatively high number of applications for the urban job exchange was a sign of a supply on the move, facing rigid demand from industrial enterprises that resorted heavily to administrative means to retain skilled workers.

The short duration and easy cancellation of contracts were an advantage for the enterprise only with respect to unskilled labourers, a workforce that (due to the greater pressures they generally face in the market) is more willing and ready to accept the despotism of hard labour and the instability of short-term employment, for example, in the construction industry, or to some extent the textile industry. In most other cases, and mainly for those positions where training is a necessary prerequisite and skilled labour is scarce, the situation differs and the managerial principle of workforce stability can be applied to reformed Chinese SOEs as it can to Western capitalist enterprises.

Yet the privileged use of long-term contracts has sometimes been seen as a failure of the labour contract system to eliminate the 'iron rice bowl,' and observers of the labour arena in the late 1980s were sometimes induced to conclude that 'labour contracts are actually not terminable' and that 'the specific relationship of the state, the management, and the workforce, institutionalised in the 'iron rice bowl', still exists in the newly created work relationship.'[40]

This view was partly contradicted not only by later developments towards a full contractualisation of labour relations, but also by the relatively broad use of temporary workers in urban enterprises. Resistance to an extension of marketised labour relations was unavoidable in such an all-encompassing structure as the Chinese *danwei*.

The conflicts originating in the contract system (as well as in such other sensitive issues as disparities in distribution according to labour) and the demise of the 'iron rice bowl' safety net were mainly intra-unit, as the workers initially widely perceived them as an attempt to reform, rather than to dismantle, the *danwei* system at their expense. The dismantlement clearly became the objective only as the contracts failed to offer a valid alternative to the old system, and when the workers' position inside the unit continued to decline in favour of the growing importance of managers and of their economic rationale. Opposition by workers to the widening gap between employees with different tasks, and even more to the growing income of the managerial elite went along with the clear perception of a decreasing level of security enjoyed inside the unit, that was not at all compensated for by the wider employment opportunities offered by the market at large only to the skilled, the young, and the educated. Cases of a de facto egalitarian distribution of bonuses or rewards under 'social' pressure from the workers, of resistance to the execution of central regulations, and of more active family strategies to preserve the accumulated advantages of the worker elite are widely reported in the literature.[41] In many ways, following the contract system, resistance inside the enterprises began to take the shape of disorganised collective action, or of 'ruses insinuated in the interstices of everyday life.'[42]

Contract regulations, together with a slowdown in the expected growth of workers' salaries and real wages (the latter decreased 0.8 percent and 4.2 percent in 1988 and 1989 respectively,[43] also because of the increasing inflation in those years), contributed to the mounting discontent that probably was one of the reasons for the participation of workers in the 1989 student protests in Beijing and other cities.[44]

The main change introduced by contracts was a direct and hierarchical relationship (despite an official denial) between employee and employer (rapidly identified with the increasingly despotic manager), in which neither could rely any longer on the unconditioned umbrella of state intervention. The unit became an enterprise, with all the constraints imposed on it by the new economic environment, but in the initial period it was probably easier for management to cope with external and macroeconomic limits than to cope with the social constraints imposed by a socialist ideology and a socialist community within the enterprise, from which workers still had great expectations.

Analysis of the early repercussions of the contract system within the enterprise in the late 1980s inevitably leads to the conclusion that contracts did not achieve their intended regulatory goal during this phase. But a more detailed look at the changing economic and social environment of the reformed labour society in the early 1990s leads necessarily to an acknowledgement of the far-reaching effects of marketisation and contractualisation of labour relations on Chinese society. Contractualisation was the first step in defining a market framework for labour relations. Regardless of the resistance by units or workers, a re-definition of this environment (which involved more working opportunities and the availability of different sources of income in the urban market) was about to change both the enterprise's role as a social organiser and the worker's strategy towards employment.

Scepticism about the effectiveness of this set of reforms centred around contract regulations also emerged among Chinese commentators. The major reasons for opposition were rooted in the nature of the work-unit system:

> ... the labour contract system is not the best among the labour and employment systems that man has devised. Its positive advantages are often offset by its disadvantages. For enterprises in the East, in particular, it is certainly not the best option. Like a streak of bright colour on a quietly elegant painting, it jars with the harmony unique to the enterprise management system [based] so strong on personal feelings that has developed in the East (China is no exception). To make the labour contract system the predominant labour and employment system in Chinese enterprises will spell no end of trouble for the future.[45]

This uncommonly outspoken article goes on to list the major disadvantages for the unit of using the labour contract system on a large scale: pressure to cope with the short-term interests of the workers, thereby neglecting the long-term interests of the unit; the development of a psychology of 'what is outside the labour contract is none of my business' and the weakening of workers' feelings for the company; an increase in worker-management disputes; uncertainty about the duration of work relations; economicism in labour relations, etc. All of these disadvantages involve differences in the 'Eastern'[46] conception of the work-unit and labour relations as compared to the marketised relationship of Western enterprises. As largely demonstrated by more recent literature on working conditions inside 'Eastern' enterprises within China,[47] the so-called 'Eastern' management of labour relations has proven even more exploitative than others and it certainly is not more effective in complying with demands for a greater say by the workers in the production process.

According to this view, however, the central issue is the reform of enterprises rather than reform of the labour system. 'Given genuine enterprises,' that is, enterprises with entrepreneurs, 'workers will show new initiative even without any change in the existing labour and employment system.'[48]

Despite changes in the labour system, during this phase the unit still remained the central focus. Its autonomy from the state, acquired through administrative reform as well as through reform of property rights and distribution of the surplus, faced the challenges of becoming an independent economic unit, and it had to cope with the conflicting interests deeply embedded in its structure and a rapidly changing society.

6

BEYOND SOCIALIST LABOUR

The Labour Market Debate in the 1990s

6.1 Labour Market: An Open Issue

In the 1990s, moving beyond many of the remaining ideological and theoretical barriers, the discussion of the labour issue became more pragmatic, on the one hand (due to the increasing need to integrate the discussion of unit-level labour organisation and income distribution with that of macroeconomic and social instabilities related to development, modernisation, and mobility), and increasingly focused on the nature rather than the legitimacy of marketised labour, on the other, as a result of the far-reaching changes in the economic premises of socialism. The recognition of the commodity nature of labour and the increasing role of the market relationship both inside and outside the work-unit were accompanied by the emergence of different and conflicting opinions on the role of labour markets: some, very radical, opinions argued the superiority of markets and their ability to regulate and determine the accommodation of macroeconomic relations, and some opinions, more moderate, were more concerned with the deregulation process in a search for an intermediate solution in the process of abandoning public welfare and social security.

Both inclinations were accompanied by a further deepening of the social and cultural processes which originated in intellectual circles during earlier stages of the reform period (the opening up of the scientific community to the outside world, the re-emergence of the social sciences, the end of the rigid ideological legacies, etc.), as well as by a consequent greater understanding, deepening, and increasing visibility of factors of social and economic instability, related to administrative and organisational reform of labour allocation and wealth distribution.

In the field of policy debate, the focus on the labour market and the enlargement of the concept of labour reform towards a comprehensive 'labour and personnel' reform, involving cadres and white collar workers to demolish the 'iron' labour security, contributed to the emergence of new actors in the labour debate, such as professional associations and trade unions, the latter largely interested in the protection or redefinition of their long-held prerogatives within the new environment.

As of the Fourteenth Party Congress in 1992, the expression 'socialist market economy' (*shehui zhuyi shichang jingji*) or simply 'market socialism' was officially accepted. In the same year, a new trade union law (*gonghui fa*) was approved,[1] along with some other regulations affecting the protection of employees' rights, such as the 'Law on the Protection of Women's Rights.'[2] These legislative measures were a necessary prelude to the new labour law discussed from the beginning of the labour reform process.[3]

Although it was not yet clear how this new theoretical shift would influence the labour economy, one major change immediately became evident. If the planned commodity economy was intended to favour the commoditisation of products but not of production factors, 'socialist market economy' recognises the need to put all production factors on the market, albeit a state-supervised one. This basic assumption laid the groundwork for resolving the dispute over whether or not labour is a commodity, but it also completely changed the perspectives and viewpoints of the labour debate.

It was argued that in order to evolve from a 'planned economy containing market mechanisms' to a 'socialist market economy,' production factors, such as land, financial resources, labour, information, and technology had to be marketised.[4] The market set up during the initial phase of the transformation of the Chinese planned economy was only a 'half-way market that cannot get anywhere,' one which used market mechanisms only to adjust demand but not to adjust supply, a sort of one-sided market.

This view, which in particular emerged among the economists of the CASS Institute of Economics, shed a different light on the way in which the issue of labour was to be addressed. Since labour is only one of a number of production factors and since the market is, at the same time, a set of unifying mechanisms for the allocation of production factors, the next logical step was de-regulation, debureaucratisation, and the abolition of central or planned allocation, as well as of the 'three-in-one' policy allowing for the integration of collective, self-employment, and central planning.

In addition to economic research, however, the investigations of the social scientists into the effects of labour reform (and its related phenomena) had a different focus outlining many of the issues which might be a source of instability in China's development. Studies of social stratification, income differentials, labour migration, and social crises relevant to economic stability, etc., contributed to mitigating scientific optimism over China's economic future within the framework of a deregulated market environment.[5] Micro-level sociologists studied such phenomena as poverty in marginal communities and migration, exposing the re-emergence of some socio-economic characteristics typical of Chinese development, thereby making the idea of a pure (and blind) market more problematic: for example, the emergence of an efficient family economy despite the context of 'rationalisation' and modernisation, and the downsizing of industrial activities due to the emergence of 'rural industries' (*xiangzhen qiye*). These contradictions were accentuated by the size of the problems facing China, by the lack of infrastructure, and by the crisis in rural production, which were understood as major risks, not only in themselves but also in their possible consequences for the stability of the economy.

6.2 The Mechanism of Labour Allocation

The magic word needed to move out of the theoretical impasse created by the emphasis on markets was 'mechanism' (*jizhi*). In most academic presentations of the market economy, the rationale and scientific foundation for socialist planning was replaced by equally scientific market mechanisms – the role of which was in part to resolve the remaining irrational economic behaviour under market socialism – in a 'logic and vocabulary informed by neo-classical economic theory.'[6]

In the official language, political awareness and good behaviour were replaced by the promotion of individualism and independence, in an environment where 'merit, which was once bestowed symbolically for employees' political consciousness, will be earned in the marketplace in the form of money.'[7]

In the second half of the 1980s the extenuating labour/commodity issue had dominated the labour debate, favouring the emergence of two positions: one arguing in favour of the existence of labour markets under socialism, and the other against it.

The need to establish (and therefore accept) labour markets was seen as a consequence of the existence of a (planned) commodity economy, which required the emergence of production factor markets, including a labour market:

> Socialized commodity production demands not only that there be unified social measurement standards for the flow of key elements of material production ... but also that there be social criteria of measurement and exchange processes for the flow of labour as a key element in production. Opening a labour market is therefore an essential condition for socialist commodity production itself.[8]

This simple and in fact realistic position (acknowledging a situation which was already in place in the real economy), which was to become dominant in the early 1990s, contrasted sharply with the confusing and complicated justifications offered by its challengers, who played with words to deny the labour market while admitting its existence under 'different forms.' The term *laowu shichang* (labour service market) was preferred to *laodongli shichang* (labour force market) when referring to labour exchange, as it implied a difference and separation between labour and the means of production.

> Under conditions of market socialism, labour service constitutes a special commodity; its value is invisible. The socially needed amount of labour expended in the labour process constitutes the value of labour service. Workers cannot sell labour on the market, but can sell or provide labour services.[9]

In a discussion of labour markets in China, Feng Lanrui attempted to explain this subtle and sophisticated distinction to me by means of one apparently simple example:

> Imagine you need to have a dress made and you bring
> cloth and other materials to a seamstress. In that case you
> are the owner of the production materials and the seam-
> stress only contributes her labour as a service. This is an
> example of labour service. In the labour service market,
> you can only sell services, not labour.[10]

Unfortunately, the difference is still not clear to me! In fact, it
seems that only self-employed workers can sell their own labour,
not employed workers whose labour (and the possibility of producing) depends on production materials, such as those in industrial enterprises.

Furthermore, labour power (*laodongli*) is distinguished from
labour (*laodong*), a distinction which tends to keep industrial
labour separate from other 'services' but also establishes an arbitrary distinction between production factors and labour.

As already mentioned, the basic contradiction in the commoditisation of labour was largely resolved at the end of the eighties,
clearing the path for the publication of important and influential
theoretical works discussing the previously forbidden term 'labour
force market' (*laodongli shichang*).

Nonetheless, usage of this new and powerful term could not
avoid the emergence of at least one clear distinction between the
two major approaches: on the one hand, the importance of market
forces in the regulation of labour relations was stressed, while the
demand for social equality was progressively neglected or postponed and the importance of policy (state) regulation downsized.
On the other, political and social scientists tended to focus on the
importance of constraints (*xianzhi*) and of natural or objective
limits to the full deployment of market laws in the field of labour
exchange.

More simply, the debate was between a free market and a regulated market, between state intervention and 'freedom of choice'
(*xuanze ziyou*). At the beginning of the 1990s, the defenders of the
superiority of market forces could rely on a decade of experience
demonstrating the efficacy of market allocations of labour to
improve performance and productivity in industrial enterprises as
well as widespread optimism about the regulatory ability of markets in other economic fields. In contrast, the advocates of a
restriction of the boundaries of labour markets stressed the
increasing differential in income distribution, both geographically
and socially, as well as the risks of deregulation; they agreed to

eliminate the hypocrisy of the earlier jargon – 'labour service' markets and people 'waiting for employment' – and to adopt the categories of the labour market and the commoditisation of labour relations, but they could not accept the market as the only principle for the regulation of labour flow and industrial relations. Their image of a labour market was still more related to an extension of the contract system, and was based on the right to a 'bi-directional choice' (*shuangxiang xuanze*).

In assessing the limits of the new dispute, I will use two definitions that came to represent the two positions. They are taken from the two major works on the issue of labour markets published during the early 1990s in China. One is Dai Yuanchen's *The Formation of Labour Markets and Wage Reform in China*, published in 1994; the other, *On China's Labour Market*, edited by Feng Lanrui, with Gu Liuzhen, Zhang Weiyu and Hou Yufu, was published in 1992. Dai is a senior researcher at the CASS Institute of Economics, while Mme Feng is a former deputy director of the Institute for Marxism, Leninism, and Mao Zedong Thought, also at CASS. Both scholars, during interviews, claimed paternity for the term 'labour market' in China.

In her introduction, Feng writes:

> We believe that labour markets are the result of a developed commodity economy, and their emergence and growth require the existence of some necessary conditions. As far as the workers are concerned, they must enjoy individual freedom and legally protected independence; they must become the owners of their own workforce and the subject of individual interests. ...
>
> Based on historical evolution, analysis of reality, and theoretical research, we propose a model for the Chinese labour market: a *national*, *unitary*, and *controlled* labour market. This is only a roughly sketched project. The market we have in mind is a real, not nominal, market; it is a market subject to macro control and not totally free; it is national and unitary, not regional and scattered. The major difference between our national, unitary and controlled market and a 'labour services market' is that ours is the sum of 'trade' relations (*maimai guanxi*). It is subject to the regulations of market mechanisms and the macro control of the government. Public control is indirectly realised through economic, legal, and administrative

means. It is an arena for economic relations and not only for the selling and purchasing of the labour force.[11]

This definition is innovative from several points of view. Labour is a commodity and workers are the owners of their workforce. The 'selling and purchasing' of labour are accepted as the foundation of the labour market, while individual rights are safeguarded by the individual possession of rights and 'individual freedom.' Nevertheless, market forces must be moderated by state intervention, employment policies, and 'administrative measures.'

What Feng, as a political scientist, is postulating here is probably not only a project for the future development of labour markets, but also the rectification of the widely accepted analytical categories; in a few sentences, she goes beyond some of the major theoretical debates of previous years (labour/commodity, individual ownership of labour, legalisation and individualisation of labour relations). However, now that the 'labour market' as a concept has been introduced by means of this paradigmatic definition, the debate is open as to what these new 'words' will mean in the discourse on labour economy.

Furthermore, a 'national and unitary' market is necessarily the result of nonmarket forces, namely public intervention, which must be able to cope with the increasing regionalisation of the Chinese economy and the emergence of scattered markets. The national market is one in which interregional and intersectoral labour mobility and migration must be controlled by administrative means and not merely by the pull and push of market factors.

Dai Yuanchen's interpretation of the labour market implies a different view of China's development path:

> After the emergence of the concept of a 'planned market economy,' different opinions were raised, and among them were some intent on limiting very strictly the role of market laws. It was argued that only labour products belong to the 'commodity' category and not production factors, such as land, financial capital, and labour. Therefore, if the market is limited to commodities, and it is not extended to production factors, its boundaries are those of a 'planned economy with some market mechanisms.' ...
>
> [This is] very similar to what the Polish economist Oskar Lange[12] called a 'simulated market' [*mosi shichang*]

in the 1930s. But China has already passed the stage of a simulated market; it has built a real market and demonstrated the effectiveness of market functions.[13]

In order to justify the demand for a 'real' market with the least possible control by the state, Dai begins with a re-evaluation of the 'individual freedom' (*geren ziyou*) of workers. This, according to his interpretation, is the very foundation of the theories of Marx and Engels.[14] Allowing the state to control allocation would mean treating the worker 'as if he were a screw that, once tightened to a surface, will never be removed.'[15]

> ... the government should no longer intervene by means of unified allocation (*tongbao tongpei*) and distribution through administrative orders as it did under the traditional system. Rather, enterprises and labourers, that is, the demand and supply sides of the labour market, should be allowed to exercise their free choice in accordance with the principle of voluntary participation, so that the market mechanism can play its role in the deployment of labour resources.[16]

The direct consequence of this definition of a labour market and of state intervention is that 'according to *correct* [sic] economics, salaries are the average price deriving from the encounter of demand and supply of labour power.'[17] The development of a labour market in China and the deployment of this new role of salaries as the price of labour's trading relations still suffer from administrative constraints. Two of them are major concerns in the study by Dai and his group:

> [...] the first is the free mobility of labour, as the permanence of a life-tenure system of 'one time allocation' is non-market behaviour; the second is the reform of the system for salary determination, as state intervention in this field also is nonmarket behaviour.

As in many other fields of discussion during the recent years of Chinese reform, the debate on labour centered on policy options in which the major point was what role the state should play and the amount of freedom it should allow for market 'mechanisms.' This debate is much more familiar to Western observers than the earlier debate. Despite some attempt to keep track of Marxist ideologies (sometimes in very strange forms, such as taking Marx and Engels as defenders of the market and of the free deployment of market forces), the major point is now the growth of the market and the policy options it implies.

This cannot but influence the prospects for a social re-engineering of Chinese society:

> The monetarization of economic interests is a basic guarantee for the rationalization of behavior. More specifically, this means that we must establish a rational interest structure whereby labourers can partake in market exchange through their possession of labour, that is, partake in this interest structure so that the overall objectives of the society at large can find full embodiment in the behavior of individual staff and workers.[18]

The faith expressed here in the ability of individual economic interests to become determinants of 'rational' behaviour in the market was not shared by all. Those who generally did not agree tended to point out the many constraints to a harmonious relationship between individual interests and the needs of the social and economic system.

Commenting upon the above passage, Howard and Howard see in the dialectic of Dai Yuanchen and Du Haiyan the influence and 'epistemological violence of reductionist economics.' The 'neo-conservative' discourse arguing for the self-regulatory power of the market in the field of labour and the importance of consumption in tackling employment problems under market conditions are seen by these commentators as a reverse plot to eliminate definitively the remnants of the labour security system.

Thus the Howards state:

> The discourse of Western neo-conservative economics is being used here in such a way as to suggest that there is only one way to conceptualize economic relations and practices in a market economy. It is being used to delegitimate and drive to extinction *alternative* conceptual frameworks. The technical discourse and the mechanistic framework exclude the vocabulary of political economy. Discussion of power, authority, rule, legitimacy, consent, rights and responsibilities in the workplace is gradually

being displaced by the scientific jargon of a managerialist discourse. What this discourse reflects is the increasing dominance of economic reason not only in Chinese social sciences but in everyday life. It reflects the gradual displacement of an ethical world view based on solidarity, community, cooperation and a cooperative commonwealth.[19]

The Howards do not specify that what we are comparing here are two alternative discourses rather than two real worlds – one based on the community ethic, the other on aggressive economics. Their considerations allow us nonetheless to understand to what extent the labour debate in China has changed the theory of labour relations, and how far we now are from the ideological assumptions of the late 1970s. The path followed by the labour debate began with Marx and is finishing, more or less willingly, in the open arms of Milton Friedman's neo-liberalism.

In fact, the influence of American neo-liberalism has become more and more relevant as an increasing number of Chinese researchers have obtained postgraduate degrees from U.S. academic institutions and scholarly exchanges between Chinese and U.S. universities have intensified. In 1988, quite significantly, Milton Friedman took part in a conference in Shanghai on China's economic reform,[20] together with other American scholars.

Despite the existence of direct influences[21] – too clear and too relevant to be ignored – they are probaly insufficient to conclude that the American conservative market fetishism has become the most important determinant of the Chinese economic debate and the major inspiration for labour policies. In fact, in Chinese liberalist discourse, the emergence of the market as a key element and faith in its ability to solve problems is sometimes also the result of wholly internal and empirical considerations, such as disillusionment with the effectiveness of full employment policies:

> Labour is a micro-factor for production and management, but is also a fundamental factor of macroeconomic development; this factor has to be distributed among different enterprises and different productions. The problem is: what type of distribution grants the optimum allocation as well as the most efficient use of this production factor? [My research] demonstrated that the best method is the market. ...

The model for market organisation of the labour economy comprises: (1) individual ownership of labour by
workers, and the right of the employing units to hire and
fire workers. ... (2) the price of the labour factor basically
determined by the market and jointly decided by the
worker and the enterprise. ... (3) as for employment
opportunities and open job competition, employees
should be subject to examinations, comparisons, and trial
periods by the hiring unit which should be able to choose
a worker that is appropriate in terms of skills and knowledge, for the kind of job and remuneration level openly
offered. In society there should always be an adequate
reserve labour force to exercise constant competitive pressure on actually employed workers.[22]

This position reflects the dualistic approach towards labour as an
economic factor as well as the re-emergence of macroeconomic
considerations in the field of labour economics. Employment, as
we saw earlier, was a major concern for policymakers during all
stages of the labour reform, and *positive* considerations on the role
of unemployment had already emerged in the late 1980s.[23] The
issue of a 'reserve army' (*houbei jun*) of workers is generally
understood as an inevitable consequence of labour reform, and
'zero-rate unemployment' (*ling shiye lü*) is no longer an issue in
setting the objectives of policy activity.

Full-employment policies definitely do not fit the objective
of zero-rate unemployment, and in reality zero-rate unemployment does not exist and is not achievable. That is
because: (1) an adequate creeping unemployment rate can
create a reserve army of workers to help the structural regulation of the economy and the new relationship between
labour and capital; (2) in order to favour the inclination of
workers to change jobs frequently, in the labour market
there must also be some voluntary unemployment; (3) the
cycle of reproduction of fixed assets can make the overall
cycle of employment fluctuate.[24]

Acceptance of the positive role of a limited rate of unemployment
is common to all analysts. What is not accepted by advocates of a
controlled labour market is that the existence of a reserve army
should be used positively as a tool to exercise pressure on workers'

attitudes toward labour, as this is the mechanism through which 'on-the-job labour exploitation' (*zai zhiye de boxue*) takes place under capitalism. Unemployment (*shiye*) is therefore accepted exclusively as a temporary result of the *natural* development of production, and the contradiction among population, productive forces, and productive capital. The ultimate (and utterly utopian, as rates of up to 20 percent of actual urban unemployment are common in industrial cities) objective of labour policies remains full employment![25]

The mechanical nature of 'closed' and limited labour market relations is a major concern of supporters of extensive state intervention in the macro labour economy:

> There can be many characters, playing different economic roles in the labour market. But the actors in a labour market are in reality only two: the supplier of labour – the worker – and the demander of labour – the enterprise (or any other hiring body). There cannot be a third party. Intermediary or public officials are not actors in the labour market. The government itself is not a direct actor in the market. The role of government, representing the public interest in the market, is that of control, guidance, and adjustment of the market, and not that of a participant in the deployment of labour trading relationships.[26]

The role of the state as a *super partes* referee in the match between seller and buyer should therefore be one affecting the macroeconomy, the overall adjustment of the labour factor in the economy.

The simplified labour market scheme emerging from this description is based on simple, two-sided relationships, rather than on the complex set of interrelations that generally characterises market dynamics. In fact, it still requires that market activities be limited to some of the complex economic links that constitute a developing commodity economy.

In contrast to this simplification, a more 'liberal' view of the labour market tends to consider such factors as diversification of income sources and multiple jobs on the supply side, progressively harder budget constraints, as well as technological, financial, and productive boundaries on the demand side, making the state's ability to control the levels of the demand-supply balance and of income distribution progressively less effective.

This more economic-driven view tends to stress the importance of the mutual influence of consumer prices and wages. It tends also to suggest the elimination of what remains of the 'non-market behaviours' of most state enterprises, where salary policy is still not market-driven and remains strongly influenced by irrational decisions at the enterprise level:

> The widening of the income gap between workers is due to the lack of development of market mechanisms. It is influenced by non-market factors and it is neither reasonable or just.[27]

Unlike this author, I conclude that full deployment of market forces will lead to an increase rather than a decrease in income differentials.

However, faith in market forces and in their self-regulatory capability reveals an enlargement of the analytical field that is no longer limited to worker-enterprise contracting. The 'double-track' system (*shuanggui zhi*) of labour allocation involving the co-existence of market and state allocation of the labour force and income is giving way to a multiplication of income sources and salary systems, slowly amplifying the importance of factors other than the actors' behaviour.

This new attitude and the larger role enjoyed by neo-classical economic theory have led to a re-shaping of the labour discourse in the 1990s, in which it is now argued, with all foreseeable consequences for policy and propaganda, that competition and individual attitudes toward the market can lead to both general development and the growth of individual well-being.

6.3 The Reshaping of Labour Relations

The acceptance of the labour market had wide-ranging implications for the acknowledgment of new labour relations and the further enlargement of the debate. The resolution of the dispute on the commoditisation of labour was to push the discussion towards a more realistic and practical understanding of the labour economy. The progressive redefinition of the nature and roles of labour market actors shifted the focus of the discussion from labour as a comprehensive and abstract concept, to the behaviour of labourers and the interests of work-units.

Labour relations (*laodong guanxi*) have been radically transformed by the reforms of the last two decades, not only because central allocation and the labour distribution mechanism have been extensively replaced by the action of market or market-like forces – much earlier and for far more people than the actual theoretical debate openly recognizes – but also because they reflect the evolution of relations between workers and enterprise management which were once 'largely cooperative in nature' but are now based 'primarily on an exchange of economic interests.'[28] On the other hand, a major change is still underway in the fields of administrative interpretation of labour relations and legal reform. These two are strictly interrelated as they both involve the approval of a new labour law (*laodong fa* – 1994), with the complex process of its formulation and implementation, and the major re-organisation of the All-China Federation of Trade Unions (ACFTU) resulting from the new trade union law (*gonghui fa* – 1992).

As mentioned above, the most popular interpretations of the labour market tend to simplify and purify it by reducing the number of actors involved in the formation of labour demand and supply and consequently also to exclude outside intervention by non-market bodies, while sometimes admitting and allowing for regulatory intervention by the state. This necessarily implies that trade unions, up to this point a Leninist bridge between the party and the masses, will have to decide on their field of action, their objectives, nature, and structure according to the demands of marketised labour relations if they want to have a future role in the new labour economy. At the same time, the party is faced with the controversial decision of how much longer it will unconditionally support the working class that it created from scratch in the 1950s.

The new labour law (notwithstanding its importance as a further step in the legalisation of labour relations) was partly an attempt to rationalise the new dimension of industrial relations and partly an effort to complete the redesign of the new role of trade unions that faced a double crisis of identity: the first stemming from their inability to represent working class interests in a completely competitive environment and in a much more privatised economic environment, and in the face of a new class of managers rather than the state; the other resulting from the relatively low status of workers' organisations inside the party hierarchy, due to their lack of an autonomous revolutionary background and to the ten years that they were closed out from the political arena during the Cultural Revolution. The emergence of a labour market and the changed nature of relations inside industrial enterprises have endangered the very existence of a mass organisation that, despite corporatively representing the working masses, was never really able to express and represent the conflicts embodied in the old and new contradictions in the labour system.

The reform of the trade unions targeted 'effectiveness' in the same pragmatic way as the economic reform in many other fields in China. The question is: what is the substance of the issue of effectiveness?

If we acknowledge that the new structure and organisation of the Chinese economy is now more appropriately described by categories typical of a market economy, we see that the parameters of the effectiveness of trade unions are objectively different today from what they were in 1978 when the All-China Federation of Trade Unions was re-established after the Cultural Revolution.[29] Greater effectiveness was then indicated by the ability to mediate between the pressures of management/state and those of the workers in all major economic issues and to back the party as the organiser of political activities inside the unit. In both cases the role of trade union was mainly limited to the micro-society of work-units, and was aimed at a prevention and reduction in conflicts.

What does effectiveness mean at this new stage and what does it imply at a functional level? Probably exactly the opposite of what it meant in the past: the ability to represent and support the interests of just one party – the workers – to address criticism in the name of and on behalf of the working class and individual workers, to take care of the growing number and variety of processes occurring *outside the unit* and intervening in the process of the formation of a labour market, to limit the pervasiveness of public intervention while maintaining the advantages of public assistance as much as possible, to force and favour conflicts in order to obtain advantages for the 'represented.'

This is at least the kind of effectiveness that seems to be expected by the workers and which is also emerging in the new pragmatic attitude of trade union leaders.

The twelfth Congress of the ACFTU held in 1993, for example, expressed concern about these new forms of effectiveness by exposing the new areas of workers' discontent and economic weakness, largely identified in the mostly un-unionised and highly exploitative labour management systems introduced by market behaviour and many foreign enterprises and by the new sweatshops of the private economy.[30] Despite regulations, trade unions are not prepared to enter the arena of open conflicts such as those of private and for-eign-funded enterprises, and they often try without success to involve the private sector in the same institutional relationship that they have with human resource management in SOEs.

The 1992 Trade Union Law still describes ACFTU as a mass organisation, which, 'while defending the common interests of the whole people, defends at the same time the legal rights of the workers.'[31] Its main political objective thus remains the public interest, not that of a class or a social group; hence it is not allowed to act as a mere syndicalist body. At the same time, while it is not free from control by the state, it lacks even a minimum of support from the workers, who do not see the ACFTU as representative of their interests as a class, whether on the shop floor level or in the general economy.

The law defines the right of trade unions to intervene, as sole representatives of the workers, to adjust the relationship between workers and work-units in the process of the legalisation of labour relations, in the definition of individual and collective labour con-tracts[32] (art. 18), and in the resolution of labour disputes (*laodong zhengyi tiaojie* – art. 20). The signing of a collective contract is to be previously discussed (no mention of approval appears in the text of the law) by the unit's workers' congresses (*zhigong daibiao dahui*). Strengthening the impression that the legal reform of labour was strictly tied to that of the trade unions, the unions were also entitled to exclusive power to underwrite contracts by the 1994 labour law.[33] The presence of a trade union representative on the 'committee for adjustment of labour disputes' (*laodong zhengyi tiaojie weiyuanhui*) inside the enterprise and on the 'arbi-tration commission for labour disputes' at the municipal (*shi*) or district (*xian*) level was granted by the 1993 Regulations on the Resolution of Labour Disputes in Enterprises.'[34]

The role of trade unions is therefore affirmed inside the slightly conflictual administrative framework of labour relations, but it is still a sort of peace-keeper. The new laws simply redefined the role and functions of the old organisation but did not radically change the nature of trade unionism in China.

Those who drafted these regulations seemingly understood effectiveness in the traditional way in their attempts to introduce the presence and activity of trade unions into the multifaceted economy, with no actual change in their nature. Significantly, as just one example of the organisational reform of trade unions, the new law lists among the possible sources of revenue an item mysteriously called 'other income' (*qita shouru*), totally unlimited by any further definition, which de facto allows unions to enter the market economy independently and behave like an enterprise both within and outside the boundaries of its institutional activity.

Yet the 1992 law did not introduce any major changes in the comprehensive structure of trade unions in China. It deals with the role and function of only one well-identified trade union federation (the ACFTU) and it is not a law on trade unionism. The regulations deal with functions, not rights; when rights (*quanli*) are mentioned they are attached to the organisation and limited by that framework. The law grants trade unions the possibility to act and exercise rights *on behalf* and *in representation* of the workers. Significantly, Section Three of the law, listing the functions of the organisation, is entitled 'Rights and Duties of the Trade Union,' thereby limiting by law the flexibility of its role.

No change in nature is conceded. Trade unions are still mass organisations 'realizing the unity of class and mass nature,' subject to the leadership of the Chinese Communist Party. The representation of workers' interests is still achieved through administrative channels and not by consensus. The contradiction between the need for autonomy and the limits of the reform is well described by the statement 'Trade unions are the mass organisation of the working class in which staff and management willingly engage.'[35]

Nonetheless, the new trade union law, which replaced that of 1950 and injected new optimism into disheartened trade union officials within and outside work-units, has improved the understanding of the crisis among the trade unions leaders. The limited scope achieved by the law was probably also due to the slowdown in the debate on labour reform following the 1989 student and worker movements. The ACFTU Congress of October 1988 had indicated that reform of trade union practices was necessary and that radical reform of the structure and functions of the federation could no longer be postponed.[36] The congress elected Zhu Houze as its first secretary-general since the Cultural Revolution (up to that time it had had only a president, Ni Zhifu), but he only held this position until August when, following the crackdown on the student movement (June 1989), he was accused of approving an official donation of 100,000 yuan to the Beijing Red Cross to be used for support and assistance to the student movement.[37] Although much research has targeted episodes of the formation of unofficial trade unions during the period of popular unrest,[38] it is not yet possible to ascertain to what extent these episodes influenced the debate inside the ACFTU on its forthcoming reform. In any case, the crackdown brought to an end a process of reform that seemed to have gone well beyond the level later set by the 1992 trade union law.

The workers' movement of 1989 was probably the result of 'independent spontaneous protest from below' and 'ACFTU institutional agitation from above,'[39] and demonstrated, on the one hand, the interest of the ACFTU in lobbying for a redefinition or a rewriting of its corporate prerogatives in the new framework of a reformed China; on the other, the distance between workers' interests and their capacity for representation in the trade unions. Interviews with trade union leaders demonstrate that the existence and uncontrollability of independent trade unions were not only a challenge to the party-state but also were generally perceived as a danger to the corporatist primacy of ACFTU worker representation, mainly in nontraditional fields of intervention of official organizations (private enterprises, for example, where trade unions are almost nonexistent).

Some fundamental points of the reform policy were addressed particularly by the debate in and on trade unions. The first was the change in industrial labour relations and their transformation from bipartite (state-worker) to tripartite (state-management-worker) in the state-owned enterprises forming the core of China's industrial production. The implications were that the unions would have to become representatives of economic interests in face of the other two parts and obtain legitimation from workers and acknowledgement from management and the state. In fact, the passage from representing shared, collective, and top-down defined political interests to defending structured, divided, and bottom-up individual and group interests meant a radical transformation in the role of trade unions and a further crisis of legitimacy.

A second point was the emergence of new fields of intervention for trade unions, such as privately-owned enterprises, Sino-foreign joint ventures and wholly foreign owned enterprises, that had sprung up without the burden of bipartite labour relations and with the advantage of a low-cost workforce and were therefore not ready to forego their competitive advantages. Unions were thus unable to exercise any kind of restraint on the exploitation of the workforce, as they lacked both shop floor organisation and political support from either the workers or the state.

A third issue was the legal reform of labour relations, which was a necessary prerequisite for unions to 'shake off their image of hidebound agencies which have faithfully done the government's bidding ever since 1949.'[40] This process began in 1990 with the ratification by the National People's Congress of the International Labour Organisation Convention on Tripartite Consultation[41] and was 'completed' by the 1992 trade union law and the 1994 labour law.

An enlightening text on the situation of grassroots labour relations and the role of unions was published in 1993,[42] and was mainly concerned with the meaning and implications for the work and evolution of trade unions of the redefinition of the behavioural patterns and composition of the Chinese working class after the reform and in the context of the 'bitter taste of early capitalism.' The picture emerging from this research is one of a double strategy on the part of unions, searching at the institutional level for recognition from the party-state to participate in the allocation of new corporatist privileges in the representation of workers' interests, while facing at the practical level the need to understand what consequences the workers were facing once their labour force was thrown into the market:

> Chinese workers are beginning to savour an economic system strikingly similar to that of early capitalism in the West. To Chinese workers who grew up with the concept and experience of security and social equity, it tastes bitter right down to the core. ...
> Market forces have educated Chinese workers to become shrewd and calculating.[43]

Therefore, the corporate practice of trade unions addresses both theoretical and practical efforts to mitigate the effects of such changes, to sweeten this taste. In the field of policy recommendation, trade unions have become the strongest institutional advocate of a controlled labour market as well as of a slowdown in the process of abandoning the public system of social security.

During this period in which the labour market became the pivotal point in the labour debate, macro control by the state and 'guided employment' (*zhidao zhiye*) were advocated in trade union journals as a means of keeping the effects of labour market deregulation under control and to increase the quality of the use of the labour factor, reduce workers' unused time, and minimize the effects on employment of the growth of the population.[44]

The content of the entire debate can be summarised under the label of 'labour relations' as comprising three major issues: actors, reform of property rights, and legal development. Labour relations, as a new concept in Chinese labour theory begin, in fact, to be described as 'relations between the owner of the labour force and its user.'[45] These are mediated by the market and consist of both social and economic relationships. In particular, the definition of individual labour rights and strategies for their protection are a major concern of the unions. In the official view of the party, China is steadily advancing towards a rule-based society, in which the civil and social rights of individuals are progressively recognized by law.

The role of trade unions is a sum of rights and functions: 'representation, protection, participation, and control' are generally listed as their major functions under the new system.

> The right of representation means that the trade unions have the power to represent the workers' interests; protection includes helping and guiding the workers when signing an individual or collective labour contract (*jiti hetong*), contributing ideas for the handling of workers by the enterprise, participating in the resolution of labour disputes, as well as granting legal support and services to the workers, participating in the resolution of strikes and slowdowns; participation means taking part in the democratic management of enterprises and the management of general affairs in the enterprise; control means verifying the application of contracts and the democratic management in order to safeguard workers' rights.[46]

Although this functional description depicts the activity and role of trade unions as more conflictual *vis-à-vis* the enterprise, there is still no clear distinction between the two parties, due mainly to the fact that trade unions are not yet allowed to acknowledge the existence of a structural contradiction between the class of wage workers and that of the new bosses in the management. This also derives from the incomplete reform of property rights, as well as from the corporatist behaviour of unions which continue to claim the right to take part in enterprise management and the decision-making process, despite the marketisation of labour relations.

To safeguard the corporatist power of the unions, the new laws have introduced a new version of the labour contract, that is, the collective contract (*gongbao hetong* or *jiti hetong*), which has been correctly interpreted by the unions as a way to obtain collective representation (and consequently power) in front of management as the sole administrative body allowed to act on behalf of the workers and their interests. The collective contract in its original form was to be signed by the workers' congresses and enterprise management,[47] but in fact the law only names the unions as the representative,[48] requiring them to present the draft of the contract to the workers' congress for discussion.[49]

What is most striking in the definition given by the trade unions of the collective contract is its description as a comprehensive tool with which to organise labour relations *inside* the factory. Its nature as a contract, that is, as a deal stipulated between the parties under the pressure of market forces, is just a secondary factor, and *gongbao hetong* is seen as a tool for bargaining industrial relations within the archetypical SOEs:

> There are four major elements to the collective contract: the first consists of the objectives, including productivity, efficiency, technological improvement, cultural construction, labour administration, and improvement of workers' lives; the second regards the responsibilities: those of the manager, the party organisation, the trade union, and the workers; the third concerns distribution: wages, bonuses, welfare, etc.; the fourth is contract management and includes control, settlement of disputes, general appraisement, etc.[50]

The collective contract is depicted as a sort of 'social deal' (or a 'framework agreement'[51]) between the parties inside the factory. It is not an instrument with which the work-unit establishes a relationship with the market. It regulates the working conditions and roles of each party inside the unit, and seemingly constitutes a basis for the hiring of new workers. What is strange is that generally no attention is paid to the action of market forces (prices, salaries, the reserve army of workers outside the enterprises, or labour costs in the market). The unit is still understood as an independent and self-reliant economic entity.

6.4 Conclusion

This account of how China approached the issue of the labour market reveals that the theoretical conflict between two developmental strategies reached its climax under the compelling need to find practical solutions to new and impelling social and economic problems. After the elimination of the heavy burden of ideological legacies, labour reached the central stage of discussion as a social question and an economic factor. The contention did not focus on the meaning, nature and relationship of labour anymore, rather the debate concentrated more clearly on the changing characteristics of the labour society. The complexity of labour relations emerged from observation of the changes taking place both inside and outside industrial enterprises. While in the late 1970s and early 1980s the labour discourse was still centred on the political nature of policy decisions, the superiority of their aims with respect to other societies, and the socialist nature of the labour relationship, in the 1990s the demise of a socialist discourse on labour became clear. 'The theoretical conviction that in socialism there is no unemployment,' a Chinese author noted recently, 'was a theoretical obstacle to the acceptance of unemployment. Unemployment is spreading to the entire world, and, accept it or not, it is coming to you and to me as well!'[52]

This pragmatic disillusion, as we saw, was reinforced not only by a dramatic turnaround in the sources of inspiration of economic literature, but also by the conviction of the inevitability of the trend towards globalisation among policymakers and in the leadership. The deepening of the process of restructuring of the industrial system required that the issue of labour be dealt with in a more radical way, with carrot and stick, to contrast, at least on paper, the progressive deterioration of labour relations that had become inevitable. The deregulation accepted by policies and the emergence of a 'weak' labour discourse were challenged only marginally, in a prevailing atmosphere that accepted the new situation with no major contention, while institutional actors such as the trade unions were unable to think, express and represent an alternative way of development, and remained at the margins of the debate, willing to find a role for themselves in the puzzle of reforming bureaucratic relationships, rather than in expressing the interests of their members.

The 'demise' of socialist labour discourse, however, not only meant the abandonment of a labour theory and the embracement of liberalism, but was also accompanied by (and largely the result of) an increase in the organisational complexity of China's labour society, as I shall try to address in the epilogue of this history.

7

EPILOGUE: LABOUR
MARKET AND THE STATE

Informalisation or Institutionalisation?

Who is driving the process? I have spent many pages describing the conflicting relationship between theory and policy, during a period when the myth of socialist labour gradually faded away, but now we are faced with the question of what is determining the shape of today's marketised labour relations. Is it the market that, with its deregulatory power despite the efforts of central and local bureaucrats, is dominant, or is the state, with its agencies and its indirect intervention, still in control? The reader may not be satisfied with a Solomonic answer, but I do believe the two elements conspired together to create the institutionalised labour market that China experienced in the 1990s. This epilogue is my only way to conclude my assessment of the demise of socialist labour in the last globally significant socialist country surviving at the end of twentieth century. By the time this book goes to press, China will already be much farther on its path although the final direction is still uncertain.

7.1 Informalisation and the Labour Market

The major question in this epilogue concerns the emergence of a multifaceted labour market strategy in the development of the labour economy in China in the 1990s, while, concurrently, deregulation and informalisation increased social complexity and made institutions less relevant components of the social engineering process. Although major theoretical recognition has recently legit-imised the concept and mechanisms of the labour market as well as granting them a pivotal role in the reform of the economic system, it is hardly conceivable that the long history of public inter-vention in the field of labour management reached its end in the 1990s. Nonetheless, many policy options taken, as well as some consequent and uncontrolled outcomes of the economic strategy pursued in recent years, have radically modified the environment for labour competition. The search for competitivity in enterprises gradually made the burden of overstaffing in industrial SOEs unsustainable, and gradually turned the economic inefficiency of enterprises into a social problem, due to the growing incidence of lay-off policies; the growth of the individual and private sectors contributed to enlarging the choices in the labour market, and to accelerating the crisis of the 'life-tenure dream'; the chaotic growth of urban economies, the potential for higher revenue and the con-solidation of familial strategies increased the readiness of labour suppliers to undertake labour mobility; informalisation grew in tandem with the process of reproletarianisation as a consequence of a still high rate of bureaucratic intervention in the economic system and the growth of a hidden (or second) economy.

Different from other experiences in emerging economies, and from what theory tells us,[1] in China's dual-labour market there is no clear-cut distinction between its formal and informal sides. Elements generally associated with informalisation (deteriorating working conditions, instability, high turnover, insecurity in the work place, and interest networking) were also visible in the first market, while, at the same time, informality was in some cases associated with opportunities for greater income generation in those activities not controlled by the state (services, craftsmanship, and petty commerce, in particular).

The role of the informal sector, in particular in the Chinese urban economy, has become increasingly important since the mid-1980s, although it grew considerably in the 1990s due to the reduced ability of administrative means to control some of the processes traditionally relegated to centrally-planned human economic management, such as labour allocation, population redistribution, intersectoral equilibrium setting, urban economic planning and bureaucratic re-distribution of wealth.

The decline in the institutions overseeing this process did not, however, signify a collapse; the informalisation in the labour arena had to cope with the evolution of an incomplete and still highly

148

institutionalised transitional bureaucracy that was able to deal with the 'regulatory mobility' of the markets. The actions of both the market and institutions (or institutional market players) prevented the deployment of all the positive regulatory effects of the labour market, while, at the same time, reducing the margin of protection generally granted by socialist institutions to the working class. The effects were evident both in the formal and informal sectors of the labour market, for both traditional actors in the urban economy (the established worker elite) and the newcomers/outsiders who flooded the urban markets in the late 1980s and early 1990s. State policies to control mobility gradually lost steam and had less of an influence on the strategic individual decisions of potential migrants. Zhao Shukai, for example, reveals that in 1994 over 79 percent of migrant workers already at destination were unaware of the documents necessary for their out-migration and employment.[2]

According to one research study conducted by the Ministry of Labour and the Institute of Economics of CASS,[3] despite the changes in the hiring mechanisms, the ways to enter registered enterprises (SOEs, COEs and POEs) were little changed throughout the 1980s and the early 1990s. Almost 70 percent of new recruits (between 1980 and 1989) entered units after 'graduate assignment' (*biye fenpei*), 'examination' (*zhaogong kaoshi*), or 'transfer from another unit' (*wai danwei tiaoru*). The increase in the latter category from 12.5 percent in the 1960s to 27.5 percent in the 1980s (together with a decrease in *dingti* – substitution – practices from 12.9 percent to 4.7 percent)[4] indicate greater mobility of the official workforce, but on the whole the data reveal a certain stability in workforce composition that has not yet been radically changed by the contract system. A few considerations are necessary, however, in order to understand how deeply the allocation process and the participation of workers in the new competition have been influenced by the recent political and economic reforms.

First, the number of contract workers in enterprises (an indicator of declining immobility, if not of increasing mobility) was still low at the time this CASS research was completed in 1992; a relevant increase was recorded since 1995 when the total reached 39 percent of the state industrial workforce (almost double the percentage in the previous year).[5] The survey also shows that the percentage of those hired by examination (that is, through a selection process at the enterprise level and not by assignment) reached 48.4 percent if only contract workers are considered.[6] We can therefore predict that the proportion of formal workers facing market mechanisms will grow steadily, in tandem with the growth in the number of workers hired under the contract system, although preferential channels will still be used for cadres and highly skilled personnel in the formal sector.

Second, we have to consider the rapid increase in non-*danwei* employment, namely the individual and informal sectors, which are involving more and more people who have little or no access to the state sector or to official paths of employment.

In 1994, there were about 12.25 million urban employees in the registered individual sector (25.5 million – more than double as many – in the flourishing rural individual enterprises), as compared to over 112 million employed in the state-owned sector.[7] But the size and dynamism of non-*danwei* employment is much greater than the statistics show.

Therefore, although the channels for recruitment remained largely unmodified as far as urban industrial units were concerned, the number of urban people legally or illegally employed outside the *danwei* system became increasingly significant in the analysis of real labour markets flows.

This out-of-system labour market sector is made up of those employed through informal channels in tertiary and small handicraft industries, as well as those illegally employed without welfare and insurance protection in enterprises (mainly in the construction industry) that subcontract major works from state-owned or large collective units. Their exact number is difficult to compute, nonetheless the observation of widespread labour practices suggests a dramatic increase in informal labour in recent years.

The informality of labour practices emerges, for example, in the registered individual enterprises (*getihu*). In spite of their name, they frequently enlarge their scope and dimensions by employing other members of the household. According to one survey in Shanghai, the average number of workers per *getihu* is over five, but only the individual entrepreneur is on the books in the fiscal departments.[8] This practice is a part of the intense accumulation strategy of the Chinese family economy, which is essential for establishing and developing productive and commercial activity. The extraordinary propensity for savings in the Chinese household is emblematic of one of the most powerful engines for the take-off of the Chinese economy.[9]

Family members generally contribute unskilled labour, while the *getihus* can always fish in the large labour pond for skilled or technical SOE employees interested in extra salaries. Many workers in SOEs (and especially those labelled as 'redundant' and not engaged in production) are ready to start their own business or to sell their labour to existing private enterprises, thereby helping to solve the basic deficit in know-how generally found in small businesses.

Some large SOEs hire a large number of temporary workers while a corresponding number of their employees are made redundant and taken out of production; the rationale for this is found in the lower costs of temporary labourers and in the larger availability of labour supply for second jobs.

The so-called 'second job' (*dier zhiye*) seekers are stimulated to enter the informal labour market by a greater availability of spare-time as a result of their hidden unemployment, by the diminishing purchasing power of monetary wages as well as by the possibility of higher remuneration in the private sector, without losing the welfare, services, and status they enjoy in the state unit.[10]

Research conducted by the Ministry of Labour in 1991 in eighteen localities found that around 10 percent of the labour force is engaged in second jobs, with relevant differences from place to place. Much higher figures were found for example in Guangzhou and Wenzhou, where the presence of private business was more significant, but other metropolitan areas such as Beijing (10 percent), Shanghai (15 percent) and Tianjin (8–10 percent) were also experiencing the same phenomenon.[11] In Guangzhou a later survey revealed that workers with second job increased from 15 percent in 1984 to as much as 50 percent in 1995.[12]

Second jobs, especially for technicians, have been recognized by law since 1986,[13] as a means of solving the chronic labour supply shortage in this specific area of the labour market, and probably as a way of rewarding those with better skills. Skilled workers enjoyed greater chances to enter the second job market during the entire period of labour reform: by 1987, about 13 percent of the technical and skilled personnel in SOEs nationwide had reportedly taken second jobs.[14]

An official 1988 document pointed out that some problems had emerged with the 'extra-time collaborators' (*yeyu jianzhi*), and mandated that workers engaging in a second activity outside the unit could only use 'non-working time' (and not working hours as was apparently the case), provided that they successfully accomplished the duties of their main job inside their own unit.[15] Second jobs remain an accepted feature of the labour market system and of the relationship between the formal and informal, as well as between the state and private, sectors.

Second jobs usually generated higher incomes than the main urban jobs, while the latter gave the worker access to *danwei* welfare, housing, and labour protection for himself and his family.

Personal income varied considerably from industry to industry, with petty commerce topping the ranks with revenue ranging from one tenth to several tenths higher than salary. A late eighties estimate puts the total annual revenue from second jobs between 6 and 12 billion RMB (the higher estimate being about 6.2 percent of the national annual monetary wage bill in 1989).[16]

The emergence of such an informal labour market is a side-effect of the growth of the individual urban economy, and generally is based on family or friendship, as the advantages of accumulation tend to be maintained within the framework of the household. Family businesses and related informal practices are a good way to resist administrative and bureaucratic pressures, to limit the costs of enlargement and of increasing competition in an overheated and competitive commercial market.

These practices, however, can not be labelled as an informal labour market in a traditional way, as they largely rely on the existence of formal structures that greatly influence their existence and determine their development. This kind of informality would not, in fact, be possible without the indirect support offered to workers by the safety net of the formal employment sector. On the other side, formal enterprises and danwei suffer from the resource-draining effects of on-the-job unemployment, second jobs and brain drain.

On a different level there is, however, a much more traditional form of informality that largely relies on the availability of unskilled and unprotected labour flowing into the cities from the countryside with no support other than their own working ability and personal connections in the cities.

7.2 The Labour Market and the Floating Population

Another part of the informal or parallel urban market is the migrant economy that generates informal/illegal labour recruitment practices. The size of the so-called 'floating population' (*liudong renkou*) is a major topic of discussion among Western and Chinese specialists. Estimates range from 80 to 100 million people (figures that might tend to be exaggerated), taking into account all persons temporarily or permanently living in a place other than that indicated in their *hukou* documents. Some population surveys,[17] for example, exclude from this category persons only temporarily residing in a different place (less than one year), thereby correctly excluding all business travellers or visitors traditionally considered floaters, but also most seasonal workers coming to the cities from the countryside during certain periods of the year.[18]

Furthermore, as one writer states, 'the floating population, as the term suggests, is elusive and seasonal. Within any year, its size tends to be larger in the winter season when demand for work on the farms is low, and usually reaches its peak in February or March, immediately after the Spring Festival. Also typical at this early stage of mobility transition is a significant amount of seasonal and circular migration.'[19]

In general – and officially – the difference between floaters (*liudong renkou*) and migrants (*qianyi*) is that only the latter (a small number) have obtained a change of *hukou* status. Only with an urban *hukou* do rural floaters become migrants. Floaters are largely the result of rural to urban migration flows and are living evidence of the increasing complexity in both urban and rural societies and of the progressive demise of the *hukou* system's ability to determine rural-urban boundaries.

The presence of a floating population in large Chinese cities has increased in the 1990s. In May 1995, there were 3.29 million floaters in Beijing (of which 2.88 million were not visitors or travellers), while the entire registered (*huji*) population of the capital was 6.2 million.[20] That means that one out of three persons in Beijing was not entitled to a permanent residence certificate in the city and therefore had major difficulties in accessing the formal and state-led labour markets, as well as the welfare facilities still reserved for urban dwellers. Of these about 75 percent had become workers or were engaged in petty commercial activities.[21]

In 1990 the estimated percentage of floaters in rural areas ranged from a minimum of 11.1 percent to a maximum of 27.5 percent.[22] In Guangzhou about one-third of all urban workers were *waidi* (outsiders)[23] and urban authorities admitted that they were an important source of cheap labour for the local economy where the local workforce was insufficient.[24]

A large number of these migrants without status, however, end up doing marginal and dirty jobs as a result of the large demand for temporary employment in industrial enterprises and the service sector. The needs of the construction industry, for example, employing about one fourth of all rural workers in big cities, match the requirements of most rural labourers for low-skill, temporary activities in the cities.

The recruitment and organisational mechanisms of the construction industry is relevant here to understand the extent to which industrial and economic conditions determine the attitude maintained by local authorities in a highly competitive and deregulated labour market. While almost losing entire control of the process, they progressively rely on informal organisations (often extensions of native place networks) that provide a tool to maintain social stability, and to employ cheap labour for economic construction. At the same time, local authorities in the places of origin, willing to export their surplus labour, have established bureaucratic links with their counterparts in the cities (both government agencies and mass organisations) in order to facilitate the export of labour.[25]

As noted by Solinger, the traditional models for interpreting migration flows collapse in China 'under the weight of the state – a state much more involved in regulating its populace's mobility than most other states,' that 'created and exacerbated push factors that drove poorer people out of the less promising rural areas,'[26] while turning a largely deregulated market (for work and capital) into a powerful pull factor.

At the same time, the retreat of the state from its role as organiser of social networks left space for the re-emergence of traditional and despotic patterns in the labour market, mainly along the lines of interpersonal or 'ethnic' networks. The institutional control still at work on the mobility of these newcomers in the cities facilitated the duties of the new bosses, marking a path towards draconian management on one side and ethnic organisation and familial self-exploitation on the other. The first is well exemplified by the extent to which teams or 'gangs' have been able to organise and exploit rural labourers, mainly in the construction industry of large and medium cities; the second is exemplified by the size of the safety nets that 'native place networks' have been able to organise within large cities.

The myth of 'blind flowing' (*mangliu* – a clue to the justification for restrictive policies towards migrants) is dispelled, as Ma and Xiang show,[27] by the different strategies and decisions adopted by migrants in their native places. Connections, skills, and the availability of capital are important variables in the decision to initiate a migration project, in the choice of a destination, in the forms of organisation, as well as in the possibility for success.

According to Zhao Shukai, migrant farmers initiate a labour market of their own, a sort of 'protomarket' (*chuji xingtai shichang*), which is extended, multifaceted, flexible and vital. It is, however, also scattered, has a low degree of organisation and suffers from 'small peasant attitudes', from limited circulation of information and, in general, from a lack of regulation.[28]

In Jiangxi province, in 1992, about 85 percent of outmigrants had chosen self-initiated ways or peasant informal organisations to outmigrate.[29] The levels of informality of this segment of the market remain very high and the attempts by the government to 'regulate' (*guifan*) the relationships established in this parallel market appear largely ineffective. The advantages of a flexible market for the employer derive from its very lack of regulation and from the lack of control over the implementation of labour regulations, assignment, registration, protection etc.

For this reason, some policy analysts are now suggesting that 'blind movement' is to a certain extent a risk that cannot be avoided, and they greatly emphasise the need for a regulatory action that focuses on the spreading of information in the market and among market players, rather than a fully-fledged regulation of the flow. Ineffective attempts to fully regulate the blind flow would only be 'the refraction of a traditional mentality of economic planning on today's employment question.'[30]

7.3 Working for a Boss: The Case of the Construction Industry

The construction teams (*baogong dui*) working as contractors or subcontractors in the booming construction industry of the large cities employ mainly rural workers (*nongmin gong*) who have temporarily or permanently left their rural jobs. There were about 550,000 construction workers in Beijing in 1994, 93 percent of whom were 'rural workers' (*nongmin gong*), constituting about 21 percent of all immigrants in the city.[31]

Many of the construction teams are based or originate in the countryside. At the beginning of the 1980s, local 'construction stations' (*jianzhu zhan*) were directly dependent on the rural governments and were contracted for public or 'popular' (*minban*) construction projects. At that time, they were not different from a public agency that could recruit temporary workers. In the following years, when the modernisation of China's economy demanded increasing numbers of construction workers and the need for agricultural labour fell drastically, the 'stations' underwent a massive process of privatisation. In order to maximize profits and work opportunities, they split into several 'teams,' working in a larger number of smaller projects. Many of the more experienced workers set up their own construction teams, under the name of their original construction stations, and they compensated the original stations with an annual 'management fee' (*guanli fei*).

In the mid-1980s, with the booming demand for construction work in the cities, growing competition among urban construction enterprises, and difficulties in recruiting labourers from among the urban elite, a number of rural teams were authorized (*jinshi xuke*) to work in the cities.[32] Later, the urban authorities in Beijing established a system of authorisation for construction teams from outside, issued in connection with the local authorities in their places of origin. This gave the team leaders the official recognition they needed to enter the protected urban market and to act as an employer both in the localities and in the urban markets. They often operate in the same market as the illegal teams with which they compete, thus making work conditions even more difficult.[33]

The construction fever in Chinese cities did not abate in the 1990s, and *baogong dui* were a major outlet for workforce suppliers from the countryside. The high competition among the workforce, the large amount of full or partial subcontracting, and the lack of protection for these workers have contributed to making construction work very difficult, unprotected, and poorly remunerated. For a total daily wage of 7 to 10 yuan[34] (about 80 percent of the floating population earns less than 300 yuan a month[35]), the rural workers spend 14 to 16 hours at the construction site, and are therefore largely dependent on the team boss for such facilities as accommodations, transportation, and food.[36]

Almost militarily organised, with poor living and working conditions, in which roles are hierarchically defined and team bosses (*baogong tou*) exert almost tyrannical power over the workers, the construction teams, and especially those who work without authorisation, are the least integrated migrants groups in the urban society and economy. Often collectively recruited from the same village, they generally do not speak nor do they learn either the national language or the Beijing dialect. Unlike the *lao shifu* (old masters), who tend to remain for longer periods and enjoy higher rankings in the hierarchy, the unskilled workers have a very high rate of turnover.[37]

Urban authorities also tend to consider construction teams as a way to maintain control over migrants,[38] while workers, by means of a 'privileged' relationship between their bosses and the police authorities, often manage to escape the required registration.

Recruitment generally takes place in the countryside, where the team boss has better control over the workers and can rely on the binding role of family and kinship.[39] Most of the construction workers recruited in the countryside to work in the city, generally youth (aged 18 to 30), do not intend to permanently migrate or to remain in the city and therefore they do not easily integrate into urban society. Only occasionally and under pressure do the bosses hire workers directly in the cities.

The team bosses are also referred to as 'white-collar rural workers' (*bailing nongmin gong*). They are a sort of intermediate entrepreneur, spending considerable amounts of money (mainly in bribes and gifts) to secure subcontracts from enterprises and, with some capital at their disposal, to cover the costs of recruitment and to set up a building site. They generally have good connections with urban key bureaucrats while maintaining strong influence also in their places of origin, from where they recruit labourers.[40] Since payment is usually due only upon the completion of work, it is very important for bosses to have a reliable team of loyal workers, who are able to work hard, and who are flexible in terms of wages:[41] 49.3 percent of the floating population works for 30 days a month, while 56.4 percent works longer than the maximum 8 hours daily stated in the labour law.[42] This of course has consequences both for the quality of construction work and for safety conditions. A quality check of 341 projects in Wuhan revealed that less than 23 percent of those carried out by rural teams met specifications.[43] Official statistics report that 1601 people died from over 6500 officially registered serious work-related injuries in the construction sector in China only during 1994. Considered the high rate of informality in the sector, the real number must be much higher.

Informality and labour injuries seem to be directly proportional also in other industries. A general survey in Zhangjiakou (Hebei) revealed that, between 1988 and 1993, 74.1 percent of the labour injuries involved rural workers.[44] Mining, another sector with high incidence of floating rural workers, tops this macabre ranking with 11.529 deaths in 1994 (4590 of which in rural collective enterprises).[45]

The *baogong dui* rarely has full control over a project since it is mainly a subcontractor. For example, of the 65,000 construction workers from Jiangsu working in Beijing, only about 5,000 are engaged in 'whole contracted projects,' while all others are working on subcontracted sites.[46]

The practice of subcontracting (*zhuanbao or fenbao*) is a common feature in the urban construction industry and both state-owned and collective construction companies have different options for engaging in subcontracting: (a) to hand over the work to a rural enterprise after deducting a fixed amount called a 'management fee' (*guanli fei*), generally around 20 percent of the total amount; (b) to assign the work to a member of their own unit who recruits workers from the market; (c) to sell the contract to one or more individual *baogong tou* to execute the work with their own teams.[47]

Subcontracting and dividing work among different executors also increases the number of people intending to profit from a certain job, thus reducing the profit margins as well as the salaries of the workers. The contractor (*chengbao*) often becomes a contractee (*fabao*) and the revenue of the final contractor is inversely proportional to the number of subcontractors involved in the process.

In June 1994 the Beijing government amended the 1988 'Provisional Regulation on the Administration of Construction Enterprises from Outside Working in Beijing.' The new regulation forced non-Beijing based enterprises to register with the municipal Construction Office in order to be entitled to 'legal rights,' and it prohibited local Beijing enterprises 'from employing workers from other localities.' If an enterprise is found to be sub-contracting to an unregistered team, it can be fined up to 10,000 yuan.[48] This regulation will probably increase the number of registered enterprises as well as the tax revenues, but it is not likely to improve the quality of life and labour relations in the construction teams.

The construction industry is only the most obvious example of how a parallel labour market partially out of the control of the urban authorities was developing as an integrated part of urban development. The influx into Beijing of almost three million people from other provinces, for example, responded to the needs of an increasingly rich urban residential and commercial economy. If we exclude those who went to Beijing as members of construction teams (about one-half million) and the small percentage (12–13 percent) who regularly reported to the municipal authority to apply for jobs, the rest found jobs either through personal ties or in the informal market.

In Beijing, several places have become famous as living 'labour markets:' the walkway in front of Dongdan Hospital, for example, is one of the most crowded. In this '*baomu* (nannies) market,' men and women, mainly from the rural province of Anhui, offer temporary or long-term services to Beijing residents, especially after the emergence of families where both wife and husband are employed and the breakdown of unit-level service networks and childcare during the reform period have increased demand for such services.

But many other marginal jobs, such as bike repairs or carpentry, as well as all kinds of heavy labour, are also offered on the street, mainly by immigrants who have neither the skills nor the connections to obtain better jobs in the city.

7.4 Ethnic Economies: The Case of Ethnic Villages in Beijing

Another example of the way in which informality in economic activities is shaping the labour market independently from official labour institutions is the ethnic enclaves. Unlike the individual strategies of rural construction workers, ethnic economies generally reflect the emergence of longer-term organisational strategies.

Ethnic enclaves are the result of long-term and far-reaching chains of migration that produce a concentration of economic activities in a geographically identifiable and socially organised area, making defence from urban pressures and the organisation of informal production generally easier.

In this case, the effects of administrative pressures are balanced by the entrepreneurial activity and the relatively high level of organisation of the communities. The level of participation in the municipal commercial and economic network is much higher than that of other migrants, although life inside these ethnically organized communities is extremely inward-looking.

The major and most famous example is 'Zhejiang Village' (*Zhejiang cun*), that has recently attracted research interest both in China and abroad.[49]

'Zhejiang Village' is the name given to a large community of migrants from the Wenzhou area (mainly Yongjia and Yueqing counties) who settled in Fengtai district, the southeastern suburbs of Beijing, east of Dahongmen Road. In 1994 Yueqing accounted for over 75 percent of the 50,000 Zhejiang migrants engaged in clothing production who were living in this area, testifying to the solidity of native place ties. Unlike other areas where migrants mixed with local dwellers, in Dahongmen the Wenzhouese rapidly outnumbered locals, who often found it more convenient to rent out their houses and move to other areas.[50]

Although the initial settlement began in the early 1980s, the conditions for the formation of a large-scale, concentrated, integrated (production and trade), and specialised 'ethnic' economy developed when administrative controls on migration were relaxed in 1985–86. At that time, a large flow of migrants reached the capital, while the reform of the city's commercial system offered the Wenzhou community more space for both them and their products.[51]

The arrival of the first Wenzhou tailors in the early 1980s was viewed favourably by the Beijing authorities, in particular because of the chronic shortage of consumer goods in the city at that time. The growth of the community, its concentration in some areas, and the subsequent extension of its commercial activity to markets in south Beijing favoured the development of a network of producers, which has rapidly become an important economic factor in the city. The hundreds of workshops in the previously quasi-agricultural district of Fengtai were mainly involved in leather and clothes production. Their products (and principally the leading article, leather jackets – *pi jiake*) were sold in the stalls of most large clothing markets in the Chinese capital, especially in the area south of Qianmen, but *Wenzhou hua* (the local dialect) could be heard spoken in other markets as well, a sign of a rooted and growing presence of the economic interests of Zhejiang Village inside the city.[52] Although reliable data[53] in this field are not available, it is widely recognised that the Zhejiang people have gained control of a large part of the distribution (and production) of shoes, leather products, and clothes, mainly in the lowest quality niche of the market.

As sometimes argued,[54] the concept of 'ethnicity' in the migrant communities is related more to their place of origin, language and kinship ties, than to other ethnic differences, such as religious and cultural practices, customs, or facial characteristics (over 95 percent of the migrants are *Han*). The ethnic link, coupled with a family interest in the enterprise, allows for the actors in the economy (both shop owners and workers) to accept longer working hours, poorer living conditions, and lower remuneration. It also leads to accumulation and solidarity among the workers/family members. Ethnic links also have an effect on the dynamics of the labour market: recruitment for Zhejiang Village's Beijing workshops is often carried out in the more distant but more reliable Wenzhou market.[55]

The workshops were originally set up on a family basis and only occasionally involved outsiders who were recruited through friendship or kinship networks. Yet the recent growth and stability of Zhejiang Village is becoming a source of employment for other migrants. Of the over 90,000 people living in the Dahongmen area in 1994, at least 40 percent were immigrants from other provinces working in Wenzhou-invested workshops.[56]

The capital needed to set up a new business in Beijing is generally raised in Wenzhou prior to migration. This is typical of the Wenzhou people's business-oriented migration. Money can be borrowed from usurers (*gaolidai*), from the so-called *taihui*, a sort of mutual help organisation, or directly from family members. Investment in technology, which has become increasingly necessary, due to growing competition, can increase the dependency of the workshops and the families on capital providers, with labour often the only guarantee that debts will be repaid. The multiple sewing machines typically in the middle of the living and working space in the villagers' houses, although second-hand, can cost up to 130,000 yuan.[57] 'Deviant practices' in the capital market in Wenzhou have contributed to making 'underground' private financial institutions the most important sources of capital for the boom of the individual economy in Wenzhou in the 1980s (almost 95 percent of the total capital needed by the private sector).[58]

Remittances from migrants, at least in the case of this enclave, also seem to demonstrate that migration strategies have much to do with the growth of the economy of native places. Yongjia county, for example, in the first years of reform (1978–85) exported only 15 percent of its labour force. But in 1985 48.9 percent of the total rural income came from remittances.

The area where the Zhejiang migrants settled had the advantage of both low-cost housing and low administrative pressures, and at the time of the greatest influx was still in the belt between city and countryside, that is, where most residents were not required to have 'fully' urban registration. On the other hand, the area was poorly equipped and lacked infrastructure, especially in view of the high concentration of productive population that was to arrive later with its burden of waste materials. Growing demographic pressure boosted speculation and soon created a disproportion between low salaries (200–300 yuan per month) and the cost of housing (up to 1000 yuan per room/month); thus, living space was generally shared by up to eight to ten persons and was used for both living and production.

Kinship-based recruitment does not shield workers from draconian exploitation. Typically, new recruits work for no compensation other than room and board. The major advantage is the protection they enjoy in the administratively and culturally hostile urban environment.

This kind of community which profits from marginal sectors and particular features of urban organisation, such as low administrative and housing pressures, has recently been called, quite appealingly, 'interstice community' (*jiafeng juju*)[59] in Chinese specialised literature.

Their status as migrants has greatly limited their access to urban services (medical care, schooling, housing). As already mentioned, this situation is the result of the contradictory effects and incomplete reform of the household registration system, which keeps the social status of migrants separate from that of urban residents, and stimulates the emergence of substitutive social tools, mainly based on the self-organisation of a mutual help network. Inside the village, clinics supplying simple medical care have been set up as have private kindergartens.[60] Once children reach school age, families are faced with the choice of either paying several thousand yuan per year to send them to public schools or sending them back to Wenzhou until their primary education is completed.[61]

The village also seems to be an almost independent unit inside Beijing municipality. Conversations with officials show that the Beijing municipal government regards Zhejiang Village as a 'district' (*shiqu*), and is not about to intervene in its affairs as long as its economic relevance does not endanger public security. There are periodical clean-up campaigns, but the workshops that are closed down generally re-open a few weeks or months later.[62]

The growth of the village also marked a change in the dimension of its trade and in its ability to improve the visibility of its 'trademark.' While Dahongmen earlier had been known as a market for cheap garments and clothes, the opening – between 1992 and 1998 – of several buildings (funded by both local authorities and private Wenzhouese[63]) turned it into a flourishing commercial area in the south of the capital and into a symbol of the very success of the community in its efforts to attain status.

Some recent agreements and regulations between Beijing and the Wenzhou municipal government[64] regarding the size and protection of productive and commercial activities of Zhejiang Village, suggest that a new policy is emerging with respect to this district of the city. They also demonstrate that the community has enough political power to negotiate rights and duties with the authorities.

What does the experience of Zhejiang Village tell us about labour markets in urban China? The development of the village's external politics is an example of how shadow economies live an independent economic life only as long as they need to remain protected against an external environment that exercises a pressure on them. As soon as the economic and political environment becomes more acceptable, a cooperation between the two sectors appears as a viable way to keep social evolution under control. As was the case for the construction industry, municipal authorities have no better way to keep the situation under control other than relying on informal organisations. In this particular labour market the 'free' interaction between labour demand and supply is moderated by the action of closed native place networks, who are given almost unlimited freedom as long as their businesses do not ignite social instability or unrest. As for migrant workers, they accept harsher working conditions as a way to participate in a process of potential status enhancement that would not be guaranteed by the administrative labour market.

There are at least three other major communities of migrants in Beijing, namely Henan, Xinjiang, and Anhui villages.[65] The one that is most strikingly different from Zhejiang Village is Henan Village, in the Liulitun area east of the Sanlitun diplomatic compounds. Henan people concentrated in this area (about 30,000 in 1995, but my impression during my most recent field visits in the summers of 1996 and 1997 suggest dramatic growth) are mainly employed in the construction industry, but many of them live as scavengers along the roadsides. Their village, unlike the productive and *relatively* well-organised and orderly Zhejiang Village, appears as a huge garbage dump dominated by a 'gang' economy, increasingly resembling that of Latin American urban slums.[66]

Henan village in Liulitun developed – along a typical interstitial path – in an area that had been prepared for the construction of the eastern part of the fourth ring road in Beijing. The postponement of the project left free space to be used for collecting waste materials, until the 1999 fiftieth anniversary of the PRC when the urban authorities completed the construction work and eliminated, as much as possible, the migrants settlements; the migrants then moved to nearby places, or to other areas in the city, thus partly diluting their geographic concentration.[67]

A similar occurrence took place in the so-called Anhui Village (*Anhui cun*) in the northwestern area known as Wudaokou. This was a much smaller community of about 2,000 people, two-thirds of whom worked as scavengers, such that the village was nicknamed the 'garbage village' (*peilan cun*) by the migrants themselves.[68]

The comparison with slums is intended to bring to mind a vital form of migrant organisation rather than a frightful, totally negative or degenerated model. The gangs in Anhui Village, for example, are complementarily organised by job into groups: families may be separated, while male and female workers generally share living quarters with other people of the same sex and the same working times. There is no hierarchical organisation outside of that of the families, and individual workers claim to be 'on their own' (*ziji ren*). Apart from scavenging, some villagers engage in petty commercial activities, mainly selling fruit, vegetables, or seafood in the local markets or on the roadsides. Indeed, garbage collection is generally reserved for middle-aged or elderly people (40 to 70 years of age), while youths prefer to look for less dirty and relatively more remunerative jobs, for example in construction. Scavenging is done both during the day and at night (to take advantage of the reduced control), and the collected materials are sold individually or piled on collective grounds.[69] Certain groups of migrants have the power to set the price and to purchase the materials from the scavengers, and they generally resell them to enterprises that recycle them for production. Such materials as paper or metal are extremely scarce in China and thus can earn profits. The middlepersons in this trade generally benefit the most from these activities. We can infer that these migrants lack the connections or opportunities to secure better jobs and are thus relegated to such marginal sectors.

In general, one major difference is immediately evident when comparing Wenzhou migrants (and economic migrants in general) with other migrants: the Zhejiang settlement seems to be a complete economic system in which production, distribution, and services interact, something resembling an ethnic enclave. That is why it produces opportunities for upward social mobility almost independently of the surrounding economic system (though growing commercial links are gradually increasing its dependency on external economic factors).

Other migrant groups lack both entrepreneurial spirit (and opportunity) and economic autonomy, and generally present themselves in the local labour markets as individual labourers, mainly in construction teams. When a community does exist, it generally plays the role of mediating between individual migrants and local labour demand; should it succeed in organising autonomous sources of revenue, this is usually in the marginal and residual sectors of the local economy, such as scavenging.

Informal labour markets therefore open a totally new vista for analysis of labour policies during the reform period. For the first time, market forces reveal their disruptive though powerful side. While control of the labour allocation system is still constrained by state intervention, an increasing number of workers are finding other ways to enter the secondary labour markets, where supply and demand meet, apparently, more freely, and where there are few or no policy restrictions or control.

7.5 The 'Mechanism' of Formal Labour Markets

As we saw in the previous chapter, 'market' is the keyword for both policy reform and socioeconomic changes in the field of labour. In the 1990s, mechanisms of a labour market were officially implemented among the enterprises in the formal sectors, and labour was recognised as one component in the larger category of production factors.

As the experience of the informal sector shows, official recognition is no longer a *conditio sine qua non* for the emergence of market behaviour; nonetheless, another labour market, subject to a regulatory bureaucracy, has developed under the influence of administrative channels parallel to a highly deregulated market. But the ability of the system to control allocation has been greatly reduced in the market environment, especially in the cities.

The number of new workers and staff hired in urban centres through the official allocation system decreased steadily from 5.02 million in 1985 to 2.84 million in 1994,[70] although both the population and labour opportunities have continued to grow in the urban centres. Only the number of *zhuanda biye* (graduates from high schools and universities) entering urban units recorded consistent growth, almost reaching the 2 million figure in 1994 (0.885 million in 1985), testifying to the importance of allocation for cadres and highly skilled labour personnel.

In the 1990s there was an increase in the importance of official employment agencies as go-betweens in the supply-demand game. The role of talent exchange centres, for example, as regulators of the mobility of highly skilled personnel in the labour market took off when they were no longer simply involved in inter-unit 'transfer' of personnel and became instead real intermediaries, offering services to workers and enterprises. Their importance grew together with their number: there were more than 8,000 such centres and employment agencies in the entire country by 1991, eight years after the first talent exchange centre was established in Shenyang. A general exchange centre under the Ministry of Personnel was created in 1984. For quite some years, and in some cases until today, these centres were accessible only to local *hukou* holders, and were entitled to hold the workers' 'personal files' (*dang'an*) during the time of transition from one unit to the other.[71]

A new role was stressed in the management instructions to local talent exchange centres published by different local governments in about 1992. According to the 'Provisional Method for Tianjin Municipality's Talent Markets,'[72] as well as the numerous similar local regulations that followed in other places,[73] the institutional duties of these public agencies include consultancy, registration, and intermediation, both for enterprises and for individual labourers.

As the leaflet advertising one such talent exchange centre in Beijing states, its main professional tasks include:

(1) To start a Beijing talent market, to establish a talent information system, to gather supply and demand information on talent, to direct all kinds of talent to obtain employment, to recommend talent for jobs, to provide services covering the entire process, and to advertise for talent;

(2) ... To collect, run, and distribute insurance funds on behalf of the Beijing municipal government;

(3) To manage the personal files of floating personnel, to expedite the procedures of going abroad for private reasons, to provide managerial services for personnel matters for all kinds of non-profit institutions and enterprises;

(4) To coordinate and arbitrate the dispute of talents concerning the floating of talents ... ;

(5) To develop international talent exchanges, cooperation, and academic communications ... ;

(6) To carry out training work, including professional skill training or re-skilling before employment;

(7) To test the quality of work and the ability of talent employed by domestic or foreign customers;
(8) To set up scientific and technical entities ... to increase labour opportunities for youths waiting for employment.[74]

Those interested in such services included retired or laid-off technical, skilled personnel and managers; self-funded (*zifei*) students who have graduated from universities, high schools, or vocational schools and are not included in the allocation system; registered managers and technical workers from outside the city; and already employed workers (*zaizhi gongren*) with university degrees or high school diplomas.

Talent exchange centres (*rencai jiaoliu zhongxin*, or otherwise called *rencai tiaojie zhongxin*) provide advice and consultancy to enterprises in the process of contacting, selecting, and stipulating contracts with workers by collecting information both on enterprises and on suppliers of labour.

The deputy director of one such station in Beijing (inside the People's Cultural Park, *Renmin wenhua gong*) once showed me a set of computers containing labour market information at the disposal of both enterprises and applicants.[75] At this talent exchange centre – the largest of the seventeen in the municipality (at both the district and county level) – a special 'talent fair' (*rencai jishi*) was held every Wednesday. The number of people in search of new jobs taking part in the weekly event averaged 1,500 to 2,000. About 90 percent of them had high school certificates or university degrees, while 80 percent were under the age of 30; the majority were male. All applicants paid a small fee to enter the fair.[76] Although the rate of immediate success of the interviews was relatively low (about 8 percent), the fair provided a good opportunity for introductions to the enterprises. Periodically (once in the spring and once in the autumn), the centre also organised larger fairs, in parks or at the International Exhibition Centre. Such initiatives are also undertaken by other organisations, such as the trade unions or the women's federation, in an attempt to diversify their services to members and to control the drop in membership in recent years.

Also symbolically, these large skilled labour 'markets' are the best expression of a willingness to have labour supply and demand meet directly, albeit under the administrative control of the state. Only about 30 percent of the enterprises taking part in these initiatives in Beijing are SOEs; the rest are collective, rural, or private enterprises. SOEs probably still use the official channels for recruitment more than these quasi market agencies; then again, they are no longer the most important employers nor the most attractive: looking only at the figures for annual new urban recruitment, in fact, SOE employment decreased from 67.6 percent in 1986 to 41.1 percent in 1994.[77]

Enterprises generally refer to these agencies when they need skilled labour, but unskilled labour can also be recruited through public agencies under the Ministry of Labour, which constitute a part of the so-called 'labour system' (*laodong xitong*).

About 13,000 such offices operated in China in 1994, constituting about 86 percent of the *zhiye jieshao jigou* (employment bureaus). The rest (about 2,100 stations) are organised by trade unions, the women's federation and other mass organizations, associations, street committees, or individuals. Of the workers employed through the public system, almost all are rural workers (67 percent) or youth in search of first employment (27 percent), and most obtain jobs as common workers.[79] In Tianjin, 31.2 percent of the 684,300 people who entered the formal labour market in 1994 found a job. This percentage was almost unchanged from the previous year, but the total number of people involved with employment agencies was more than double (it was 296,000 in 1993).[80]

In official evaluations,[81] the labour system has become more flexible and suited to diverse situations and different labour markets, allowing for the coexistence of private (or popular, *minban*) and public agencies. Five major models, taking the names of different urban centres, have been singled out in the official analysis:

(a) the Changchun (or 'comprehensive' – *yitiao long*) model, a system in which employment agencies (*zhiye jieshao suo*) cover all phases of intermediation, evaluation, training, and other administrative practices necessary to both the worker and the enterprise; this method has become a model in more recent policy documents;[82]

(b) the Yichang model, in which high levels of informatisation help the standardisation of procedures and criteria, and increase the productivity of coordination;[83] this model also allows for cross-district recruitment;

(c) the Nanchang model, a 'pure' (*tun*) model, in which agencies act only as go-betweens, avoiding all administrative intervention in any phase of the recruitment process;

(d) the Wenzhou model, which arose in an area where the large development of private and individual business boosted the creation of private employment agencies under different forms; in order to standardize and monitor the work of such agencies, the labour bureau made available a building, from which these private agencies now act under public supervision; therefore the role of the public system is apparently only one of coordination and supervision while practices are deregulated and in the hands of private agencies. In Wenzhou (where there were almost 40,000 private wage-labourers already in 1985) the tolerance towards privately hired workers was much greater than that in the rest of China since the beginning of the reform period, and the role of public agencies grew in tandem with that of a spontaneous labour power market and private 'labour introduction centres' (*laodong jieshao suo*).[84]

(e) the traditional model, characteristic of the less developed and border areas, privileges administrative means and excludes all other organisations.

Access to urban labour markets appears to be divided along several lines: an administrative divide, as workers have different access to allocation according to their administrative status; a quality divide, as allocations of unskilled and skilled labour go through different channels and involve different levels of bureaucratic pressure; a geographic divide, as the occupational situation of different cities requires an adaptation of recruitment mechanisms (both formal and informal); and a formal/informal divide, as the two worlds have little or no contact in the field of labour recruitment, although informal practices have emerged in the recruitment of the formal labour force.

Official labour bureaucracy maintains a certain control in areas where there is a more limited demand for labour and where informal practices are therefore less developed. Thus, more the private sector is developed, the less effective seems the intervention of public agencies in both recruitment and regulation of the labour market. Although informalisation, once again, is not only a characteristic of private and 'grey' enterprises, but of the state sector as well.

7.6 Mobility and Immobility in the Labour Market

By concentrating on the urban side of the issue, as I have done in this book, I have tended to give only marginal consideration to more complex phenomena occurring elsewhere (namely in the rural areas) while maintaining a theoretical division between city and countryside which, despite continuing administrative constraints, no longer corresponds to the reality of a scattered and complex situation. The bureaucratic boundaries, as pointed out several times during this study, were progressively modified and deregulated during the 1980s and early 1990s, with a totally different level of effectiveness than at the beginning of the reform era.

In this final section, I will draw on the results of a labour market survey run by CASS in 1992 to assess the depth and thoroughness of labour market transformations.[85]

The fascinating thing that strikes observers viewing the entire labour reform process from an historical perspective is the extreme flexibility in both policies and ideological background, which in the long term (though in a step-by-step approach) have accompanied the dramatic overall transformation of practices. The changes have affected the role of state intervention and of economic factors in the labour process, such that the present system is far more complex than can be described by the artificial categories of 'formal' and 'informal' used here.

Thus, the ground has been laid for the coexistence of contending situations in China's labour economy in the 1990s:

(a) the 'dark side' of the labour market described earlier, which more than official statements reveals the extent of the transformation and the prospects for future labour relations in post-socialist China; while

(b) public intervention is still highly effective in the field of employment and in the definition of labour relations in the formal sector, where the introduction of profit-driven management mixes with administrative constraints.

Administrative actors and constraints, therefore, still play a concurrent regulatory role in marketised relationships in defining labour mobility patterns as well as in shaping labour demand in the formal sector. Public institutions, however, have long lost their prerogatives as implementation agencies for central policies in a scattered environment that has witnessed the rise of local players (enterprise management, local governments, and lower echelons of the bureaucratic system).

Recruitment

The immobility of the Chinese traditional labour market has been noted repeatedly in this study as one of the features preventing China from having a real market-driven labour-force flow. In recent years there has been a marked relative increase in mobility, due partly to the informalisation processes described above, and partly to the reform of the unit system. In particular, the simplification of administrative practices for the recruitment of non-*hukou* migrants under the contract labour and temporary systems have greatly increased rates of turnover inside units, as well as the ability of workers to move from one unit to another, from one industry to another, or from one 'ownership level' to another.

In the 'Labour Market Survey,' of the 3322 interviewees who had a migration experience (about one-third of the entire sample), more than half (56.9 percent) had moved after the beginning of the reform period (1980–1991).[86]

The kind of mobility in the formal sector emerging from this survey is less the result of upward social mobility trends than of horizontal mobility. A look at the working situation of migrants at the time of 'migration' for the same period shows that over 71 percent already worked in state-owned enterprises. Tables 1 and 2 show that the ability of SOEs to maintain workers is slowly being eroded by the growth and increasing attraction of collective and private enterprises, even though the state sector still remains the most attractive. Also, the rush towards SOEs from collective and private enterprises was, already in 1992, coming to an end. Indeed, the trend is towards a progressive though not dramatic 'privatisation' of the formal workforce, down on the scale of property (that is, from the highest level of socialist state ownership towards collective or private ownership, generally considered to be the 'less socialist' among ownership forms).

The kind of movement registered by this survey is still strongly related to administrative actions. During the 1980s and early 1990s, 34.8 percent of these migrants moved for labour adjustment reasons, 27.3 percent were 'assigned' (after graduation or training) to units not in their place of origin, about 16 percent migrated for family reasons (to accompany a spouse or to get married in a different place), 8 percent were demobilized from previous (mainly military)[87] assignments, and 5 percent moved as a result of 'substitution' practices (which almost disappeared after 1990). This means that over 70 percent of the staff and workers interviewed entered the unit where they presently work as a consequence of administrative measures, and due to market practices, and that inter-unit mobility is still largely subject to administrative decisions or controls.

Table 7.1: 'Inter-ownership' Mobility (1979–1984)

To	State-Owned Enterprises	Collective Enterprises	'Sanzi' Enterprises	Other Ownership
From				
State Owned Enterprises	57.3%	24.4%	13.5%	0.9%
Collective Enterprises	25.9%	54.3%	18.5%	1.2%
'Sanzi' Enterprises	–	–	–	–
Other ownership	56.5%	23.9%	19.6%	–

Source: CASS Labour Market Survey

Table 7.2: 'Inter-ownership' Mobility (1985–1991)

To	State-Owned Enterprises	Collective Enterprises	'Sanzi' Enterprises	Other Ownership
From				
State Owned Enterprises	42.8%	29.3%	26.3%	1.7%
Collective Enterprises	20.8%	42.4%	36.0%	0.8%
'Sanzi' Enterprises	6.7%	0	93.3%	0
Other ownership	41.8%	24.6%	28..4%	5.2%

Source: CASS Labour Market Survey

The practice of assignment (*fenpei*) to a post remains extremely important for staff and workers who have graduated from universities (61.3 percent) or technical high schools (30 percent). Workers with less training generally have to take examinations to get jobs; indeed, almost half of the contract workers are hired by examination (*zhaogong kaoshi*).

Technical personnel (Table 7.3) are assigned (48.7 percent) or transferred from other units (24.6 percent) confirming suspicions about a more institutionalised path of recruitment for this group, while workers who take a formal examination already constitute about one-third (32.9 percent) of the total. Breaking down the data along the lines of the relationship to the enterprise (Table 7.4) we note that less steady relationships correspond to more informal recruitment.

As many as 45.4 percent of temporary workers, for example, enter the enterprise through personal relationships, while state cadres are almost entirely hired or transferred through formal channels. As predicted, the overall number of contract workers is increasing,[88] and this will probably also further reduce the proportion of contract workers formally assigned to enterprises.

Table 7.3: Hiring Methods by Working Position

	Workers	Technical personnel	Managers	Auxiliary personnel
Assignment after graduation	15.9%	48.7%	22.8%	17.2%
Demobilized soldiers	5.2%	2.6%	6.4%	15.4%
Examination and selection	32.9%	12.7%	22.9%	12.6%
Promotion	2.5%	3.3%	5.0%	5.7%
Substitution (*dingti fumu*)	9.0%	2.5%	5.0%	3.9%
Personal relationships	7.5%	1.3%	2.8%	5.4%
Recommendation from an employment agency	1.7%	1.0%	1.5%	1.1%
Transfers from other units	18.1%	24.6%	27.5%	26.3%
Transfers from subsidiary units	1.3%	0.5%	1.0%	0.8%
Other	6.0%	3.0%	5.0%	4.5%

Source: CASS Labour Market Survey

Table 7.4: Hiring Methods by Working Status

	State cadres	Permanent workers	Contract workers	Temporary workers	Other
Assignment after graduation	44.6%	15.6%	15.7%	3.6%	12.5%
Military demobilization	8.2%	7.7%	2.3%	1.3%	5.5%
Examination and selection	7.3%	25.2%	48.4%	29.5%	31.6%
Promotion	6.0%	3.7%	1.5%	1.0%	5.5%
Substitution (*dingti fumu*)	1.8%	9.8%	4.5%		5.8%
Personal relationships	1.0%	2.5%	7.4%	45.4%	4.6%
Recommendation from an employment agency	0.8%	1.1%	2.5%	4.3%	3.0%
Transfers from other units	26.9%	27.7%	12.7%	2.3%	17.6%
Transfers from subsidiary units	0.6%	1.3%	1.1%	1.0%	0.6%
Other	2.9%	5.4%	4.1%	11.6%	13.4%

Source: CASS Labour Market Survey

From these initial data we can see that the influence of market practices – though growing – was still unable, in the early 1990s, to reshape hiring procedures in the formal labour market and to reduce the influence of both *guanxi* and central planning, the two contradictory forces coexisting under the traditional system and hindering the process of market rationalisation of labour mobility and labour flow, that were the main target of the labour reform in the 1980s and 1990s. Contracts have played, and will continue to play, an important role in marketising labour relations, but until now they have been regarded mainly as a means of internal regulation of labour relations rather than as a mutually satisfactory agreement between demand and supply.

The growth of mobility in the 'formal' market has not followed the same patterns as the more general social mobility. Mobility is only partially a result of the 'bi-directional choice' (see Chapter 4) advocated by the Chinese theorists and is more clearly a result of the greater flexibility of administrative practices and the greater autonomy enjoyed by enterprise management. Also contributing to the increased mobility have been relevant changes in workers' attitudes towards their jobs and the emerging role of employment agencies that act as almost fully marketised go-betweens. This marketisation has resulted not only in intra-sector mobility and competition and improved prospects for worker elites (both skilled and trained staff) who can take advantage of growing demand for technicians, but also in a restriction of opportunities for social mobility among disadvantaged groups on the supply side.

As the two sectors of the market roughly corresponded to the still active administrative divisions of city and countryside, and despite the demise of the unit-based welfare, the urban groups increased their advantage through better access to training and education; education and training being the main divide between those who can benefit from market rules and those who are forced into even greater dependency on the enterprise or on the requirements of the labour market. Not surprisingly, the sample shows that the highest level of education is not among cadres or managers (for whom party membership remains an important prerequisite), but among technical workers, about 60 percent of whom have graduated from college or university, where only 7.8 percent of nonskilled workers received college educations.[89]

Employment pressures and redundant workers

The existence of a labour market, with its increasingly demanding competition and a 'reserve army' outside the enterprise, together with the high discretionary power assigned to factory managers after the implementation of the economic responsibility system, are the major factors influencing the deterioration of labour relations inside the enterprise. The 'ideology' of reform has invariably argued that an increase in the income gap among different sectors of society is justified, but this has proved to be a major turning point for the work-unit system: as the Chinese industrial economy is still very much labour-driven, workers face great pressures from managers eager to accomplish ambitious production targets.

One study of state-owned textile factories (where, despite mechanisation, the labour factor remains extremely important and pressure from outside – mainly from rural unemployed females – is particularly high), reveals that the new situation has radically changed labour relations inside the plants along two lines:[90] (a) managers have developed a cynical (though 'scientific') attitude towards production organisation, aimed at obtaining higher rates of productivity by increasing working hours, applying punitive measures in the calculation of production bonuses, and using Taylorist methods of rationalisation of working cycles, thereby destroying the image of Chinese state factories where 'workers work at a leisurely pace and enjoy all manner of perks;'[91] (b) the methods of 'socialist' production have been amply modified to fit the new productivist ideology; for example, participation in 'labour emulation,' that is, the periodic campaigns to increase individual productivity on the shop floor, were declared to be 'voluntary' by the 1995 Labour Law. Voluntary 'labour emulation,' however, involves more workers today than it did earlier as individual productivity and work attitudes and behaviour, although no longer related to 'political performance' (*zhengzhi biaoxian*), are the parameters for calculating the largest part of monetary wages (the floating basic wage, bonuses, incentives, and subsidies).

In some of the mills investigated, the four-shift labour organisation that had been introduced in the mid-1980s has reverted back to a three-shift system. Overtime labour and work during holidays[92] are generally paid at normal rates, while sick leave is up to the manager, and sometimes involves cuts in wages. To obtain family leave (mainly requested by women), workers are sometimes required to pay a temporary substitute from their own pockets in order to avoid large salary cuts (the practice is called 'shift purchasing' – *maiban*).[93]

The authors of this research contend that, contrary to what is generally argued about the inability of the labour reform to radically modify labour relations in Chinese industry, the case of the textile industry shows a radical change in labour practices, in particular as far as worker-management relationships and production levels are concerned. I would argue that this is largely due to the increasing pressure exerted by open market forces on the contractual position of workers *vis-à-vis* management as well as by the remaining administrative constraints on the position of the enterprises in front of the state.

Paradoxically, the increase in workload has accompanied 'on-the-job unemployment' (*zaizhi shiye*) and redundant workers in SOEs.

According to a survey by the Commission for the Reform of the Economic System (*Jingji tizhi gaige weiyuanhui*, or *Tigaiwei*) carried out in Tianjin in 1995, the number of redundant workers in the 3,362 SOEs in Tianjin in 1994 reached 124,651 (with an average of more than 37 per enterprise).[94]

According to general policy, redundant workers should be shifted to other units or to *ad hoc* affiliate enterprises under the control of the mother firm, but this is possible for only some. In the Tianjin chemical sector, only 36.2 percent (9,687 workers) of the personnel classified as 'redundant' (*fuyu*) were relocated during 1994. The rest mainly were kept in the factory on 'production vacation' (*shengchan xing fangjia* – 51 percent), long-term sick leave (*changqi bingxiu* – 24.2 percent) or 'internal unemployment' (*changnei daiye* – 11.8 percent).[95] Apparently these workers are almost completely outside of the production process and it is difficult to relocate them (due to age or low skills). They remain under the protection of the enterprise, whose burden of social costs has become increasingly heavy after the independence of enterprise accounting was introduced and the costs of welfare shifted from state books to the enterprise. The same research in Tianjin revealed, for example, that in one large glass factory 9,100 workers were actively producing, while 5,300 were receiving pensions from the enterprise, amounting to one pensioner for every 1.7 active workers. Nationwide, the retired to active workers ratio dropped from 1:30 in 1978 to 1:5 in 1994.[96]

Urban unemployment also greatly increased as a consequence of the greater enterprise autonomy and the further drive towards privatisation and efficiency. In most cases, the bureaucratic re-employment system failed to offer a real solution to the problem. Nationwide, only 26 percent of *xiagang* workers had been re-employed by 1996, while an even smaller 13 percent had been able to receive a training from the system.[97] Higher unemployment rates (estimates foresee 13 to 16 percent in the cities by the year 2000) also created tensions especially among the generation that had experienced the forced movements of 'down to the countryside up to the mountains' (*xiaxiang shangshan*) before and during the Cultural Revolution, who felt that they were once again been betrayed by the government, and they were bearing 'the burden of both revolution and reform.'[98] Over 50 percent of the *xiagang* workers in 1996 was under the age of 45, roughly the same generation that made over 70 percent of the unemployed in 1980–81, during the previous – post-Cultural Revolution – unemployment tide.[99]

Wages and benefits

As the nominal wage (or 'position' wage) is only half or less of the entire salary, a worker's monthly revenue generally depends on the bonuses he/she receives as floating integration from the enterprise. Bonuses are calculated by points (on a one hundred or one thousand point scale), in a way that does not differ too greatly from the previous workpoint system. Thus, workers are dependent on a wide variety of parameters, some productive and some behavioural (but no longer 'political').[100] The Taylorist attitude of the new scientific management of SOEs is leading to exaggerated control over all moves made by workers who are subject to an endless row of checks. More than as an incentive to increase production, this attitude by the management is generally perceived as a continuous threat to the workers' wage-level protection. The monthly wage therefore remains largely undefined and the real wage more often is lower rather than higher than expected: a sort of 'reverse' use of the floating wages (punishing instead of compensating) as bonuses are a major component of the salary that can be cut at will or as punishment for deviant behaviour.

The CASS 'Labour Market Survey' attempts to compute the incidence of the floating part of the salary on the workers' monetary income. Although this calculation does not take into account the nonmonetary components of the salary, the composition of the monetary part quite clearly shows how wages can be used as a means to control productivity as well as a tool of social control inside the enterprise.

Monetary wages in the investigated industrial enterprises were below 1,500 RMB per year for about 32 percent of staff and workers, while the average value was 1,946.5 RMB per year. 1,500 RMB a year was not reached by the 25 percent of state cadres, 30.7 percent of permanent workers, 44.5 percent of contract workers, and 57.6 percent of temporary workers.[101] There is an important average difference between party members (2,818 RMB and only 7.6 percent under 1,500 RMB) and nonparty members (2,197 RMB and 24 percent under 1,500 RMB), but this is mainly due to the concentration of party members in the highest ranks of the enterprise system and to their low number in absolute terms (8.1 percent of the entire sample).

Temporary workers constitute the sector of the internal labour market subject to the highest wage pressures. The uncertainty of income is confirmed by an extremely low position wage (44 percent of the total wage) and a relatively high percentage of such components as piece-rate work (8.9 percent). Contrary to what was expected at the beginning of the reform period, the wages of both permanent and contract workers have an almost negligible piece-rate component. Piece-rate wages have proven to be more efficient for extremely low-tech sectors, that is, those that employ temporary workers, as piece-rates are unlikely to match the needs of management to control and increase the productivity of workers in longer term and more specialised production processes.

The situation was exacerbated by the financial difficulties of enterprises: in 1997 more than 10 million employees saw their salaries either reduced or they did not receive any salary at all (*jianfa, dingfa*), constituting a total debt towards workers of 19.7 billion yuan (US$ 2.4 billion). In the provinces of Heilongjiang and Sichuan – where there is a high concentration of SOEs – 1.58 million and 1.18 million industrial workers respectively received no salary at all.[102]

Table 7.5: Composition of Wages by Position

	Average Wage	Basic Wage %	Floating Wage %	Piece rate wage %	Bonuses %	Labour Insurance- Subsidies %	Price Sub- sidies %	In Kind %
State Cadres	2577.9	57.2	7.0	1.2	15.9	3.3	14.0	1.5
Permanent Workers	2307.2	54.8	7.1	2.3	14.1	3.3	17.0	1.5
Contract Workers	2052.5	49.1	7.1	3.1	16.6	4.6	17.1	2.4
Temporary Workers	1899.8	44.1	9.5	8.9	14.3	5.6	11.8	5.9
Other	2180.1	57.0	5.9	2.0	13.9	2.9	17.0	1.3

Source: CASS Labour Market Survey

The relatively high level of price subsidies and of subsidies in kind (the latter are especially high for temporary workers) reveal that enterprises have hardly relinquished their role of 'distributor' of goods and services to workers, even after the decline of the 'comprehensive' role of the *danwei*. Even more interesting is that there is no significant difference in this category between SOEs (where 15.9 percent of the salary is distributed as price subsidies), COEs (17.6 percent) and *sanzi* enterprises (14.1 percent). Although SOE data may be influenced by the larger presence of cadres, the over-all numbers show a tendency on the part of all enterprise to inte-grate salary with supplements in kind and services.

In SOEs – at least until the recent reform in 1998 – the one major traditional allowance was housing. The average urban household[103] spent 28.79 yuan (per capita) for housing rent in 1994, that is, about 0.8 percent of per capita income, slightly more than 1 percent of total annual living expenditures, and one-four-teenth of the annual expenditures on clothing.[104] Considering that in developed market economies the ratio between income and housing costs ranges from 2:1 to 6:1, we can easily infer that hous-ing remained, in the early 1990s, the major welfare item distrib-uted by Chinese enterprises and the state, and thus not surprisingly an area that has been the target for major reform initiatives.

The quality, or even the availability, of housing, as well as other nonmonetary factors constituting the worker's income and affect-ing the household's well-being, were long a result of state planning decisions. Significant portions of the state budget were expressly allocated for social welfare and housing construction, while the 'ranking' (based on ownership, size, and industrial sector) of the enterprise was a determining factor in deciding the allocation of public housing space. This gave a major advantage to SOEs and, among them, to large and strategic enterprises. Collectives were assigned almost no housing funds.[105]

We would therefore expect that, after the start of the reform, not every enterprise was able to guarantee housing to their staff and workers; indeed, housing has remained a major demand from workers, in particular from short-term workers who do not bene-fit from urban welfare and did not 'inherit' a house from the old system. But, quite surprisingly, the 'Labour Market Survey' revealed no relevant difference between SOEs, COEs and POEs, with regard to the percentage of workers living in 'public houses' (*gongfang*): 83 percent, 78 percent and 81 percent respectively.[106] Only 15 percent of the urban workers investigated (nevertheless a meaningful slice) already lived in private homes.[107]

The reform of housing in urban centres has introduced the pos-sibility for workers to purchase houses and for enterprises or the state to sell them, thereby boosting the real estate market. However, this process has not until recently substantially reduced the role of work-units in housing assignment, either as owners of the buildings or as the distributing body. In 1990, 59 percent of urban housing was still owned by work-units,[108] with significant differences from place to place. In Shanghai, for example, the percentage of work-unit-owned housing space was only 12 percent in 1990, but about 86 percent of the new investment for public housing construction in the same year had actually been raised by enterprises, a sharp increase from 55 percent in 1980.[109] While an increase in the speculative use of funds for construction projects should be taken into account, this still could be indicative of a tendency by enterprises to continue to maintain their original 'comprehensive' approach towards workers, even in the new, almost 'privatised' system of wealth distribution.

From the perspective of the commoditisation of the housing market, work-units will be able to cash in from their control over such a scarce commodity as housing (4.0 square meters per capita in 1980, 7.5 square meters in 1993),[110] in a market with increasing demand.

As the data on the influence of housing on the household budget show, the major aim of the housing reform (to increase rent and convince workers to purchase housing) has not been achieved and has allegedly been abandoned by many work-units. The increase in private real-estate investment in these years has mainly been due to the greater availability of capital and the profitability of housing investments rather than to increased housing costs or the reduced availability of rented housing on the 'public' or private markets.

Private housing, however, accounting for 71 percent of the total in 1950, had declined to 24 percent by 1976 and decreased further, despite the reform drive, until 1990 when it reached a low of 21 percent. The reform of housing allocations that began in 1993 – again in an experimental way – and culminated in 1998 with the end of assignments did not entirely eliminate *danwei* control over housing and its distribution. In many cases, the sale of houses followed the same criteria as assignments, by privileging one's own workers and insiders over outsiders (sometimes with housing facilities sold considerably below their market values) and the work-unit did not become a market oriented real-estate agency as might have been expected.

As observed by commentators, after the reform 'the distribution of commodified housing is similar to the old system, except that housing is no longer free,'[111] while the reform increased, rather than reducing, the role of work-units in housing. Housing is still considered a reward or way of preventing key staff from leaving the unit (in many cases such decisions as wedding arrangements are largely influenced by the time and conditions of a housing assignment – *fen fangzi*). The market is, in fact, still very much influenced by the intervention of the work-unit, in the form of housing distribution (as production bonuses or incentives), 'soft loans' (or loans whose repayment scheme is extremely long), and discounts,[112] making the alienation of public housing a part of the redistributive process rather than the result of market behaviour.

Work-units, therefore, remain in control of many of the distributive processes (in the form of both monetary remuneration and nonmonetary or welfare benefits), reaffirming their role in marketised labour relations.

The kind of labour market emerging in the urban formal sector is thus also one in which workers maintain a certain degree of dependency on the work-unit while they are increasingly exposed to outside pressures – a labour market in which the socialist work unit is trying to redefine its role as 'marketised,' 'cost-reducing,' or 'independent', but is, in the end, still all-encompassing. This situation does not contradict the general aim of the reform of China's industrial system. The marketisation of labour relations in SOEs may resemble models supplied by Korean or Japanese corporations.[113] Their integrated economic strategies allow the large SOE with low profits to enjoy the advantage of market mechanisms and to keep consumer spending under control, without releasing high rates of independence to the workforce.

7.7 A Highly Institutionalised Labour Market

In China, the 'labour market' is basically seen as a mechanism able to solve employment problems related to the restructuring of the economic system and the development of a market economy affecting labour relations. Therefore, the concept of a labour market that has emerged during this transitional stage is a highly institutionalised engine, confronted on one side by the challenge of informalisation, and on the other by the difficulties of managing formal unemployment and the so-called 'rational flow' of the labour force dismissed from the SOEs.

The control and development of such a labour market will face some major difficulties in the future:

A. *A narrowing of 'relocation' opportunities, growing in tandem with the saturation of the ability of SOEs to absorb new labourers.*
Because of the redundant labour force inside the units, SOEs are

not eager to hire new personnel. Therefore, demand remains largely insufficient for the growing supply, and the role played by nonstate-owned enterprises (although increasing) is still too small to insure the absorption of large numbers of urban and rural dwellers, thus forming a urban reserve army. In Tianjin, for example, of the 87,000 workers relocated during 1995, only 15 percent accepted jobs in the nonstate sector, while the number of unemployed grew by another 32,500 persons, thereby reaching an official unemployment rate of 2.6 percent.[114] But even official data tend to paint a much worse picture: according to the 1996 1% population survey[115] – excluding *xiagang* – the number of urban unemployed had already reached 9.98 million, that is, 7.5 percent of the active population (against an official 2.9 percent for the same year). Including only the part of *xiagang* workers (that is, the workers who have been made redundant but who still receive subsidies from the enterprise) who receive less than 100 RMB of subsidies per month from the employer (72.5 percent), the unemployment rate is 9.2 percent.

B. *Constraints on the free choice of workers.*
Despite the growth of managerial autonomy in SOEs, both hiring and dismissal of employees are subject to policy limitations. Although dismissals have grown at an increasing rate in some urban centres (the case of Mudanjiang is noteworthy, where 60 to 80 percent of SOE workers has been forced to *xiagang*), the Chinese authorities have complained that, while the demand for labour in the nonstate sector is still the highest, redundant workers in SOEs are reluctant to accept posts in the private or collective sectors due to the bad reputation these enterprises have as below-standard employers with little or no respect for labour regulations.[116] 46 percent of the redundant workers who have not been relocated never applied for new jobs and relied only on the bureaucratic re-employment system, while 11 percent did not accept positions they were offered in the labour market.[117]

On the other side, driven by economic interests, the demands of enterprises privilege the advantaged segments of the market (gender, age and specialisation are among the most important criteria for selection), thereby excluding most of the workers made redundant by readjustments, who make up the largest proportion of urban workers seeking employment or relocation. About 62 percent of redundant *xiagang* workers have primary school education while only 3.77 percent have university degrees.[118]

C. *The inadequacy of labour management tools at the enterprise level.*

From the point of view of a competitive market for labour resources, the reform of the labour system is still incomplete. Nevertheless, there continues to be a clear contradiction between the differing status of workers inside the enterprises (permanent, contract, and temporary workers), which are mainly the result of their different administrative positions (urban dwellers, rural migrants, or floaters) at the time of employment. The contract system, which was expected to be a way to foster a stratified labour market, is still far less effective than expected. Again in Tianjin, in 1995 only 50 percent of the enterprises implemented a 'full contractualisation' policy (*quanyuan laodong hetong zh*i).[119] According to the Guthrie's findings, the full implementation of contracts is faster and more comprehensive in enterprises in poor financial and economic shape, while well-performing enterprises generally tend to maintain a portion of the old workers under the iron rice bowl system.[120] An analysis inside the enterprises, much deeper than what I have presented here and focused on the implementation of labour policies, would be necessary to explain more clearly to what extent labour policy at the work-unit level is a result of central stimulation, or rather of the economic constraints faced in the local, national, and international markets.

D. *The incomplete reform of employment agencies.*

Employment agencies have been growing in importance in China's institutionalised labour market, even though they are not yet able to exercise control over labour market dynamics which should be their main task as government agencies. Apart from in some urban cases, in fact, the agencies still lack the infrastructure and ability to spread the information needed to develop contacts between demand and supply. Furthermore, they are not able to create viable training or retraining opportunities for young workers and for those dismissed or made redundant by production readjustments, and they are often constrained by their role as 'hubs' for unemployed waiting for rare second opportunities.

The agencies develop their activities according to the shape of demand. In one municipal *laowu shichang* (labour market) I visited in Tianjin in 1995, where the focus should have been on the allocation of low-skilled workers, I found that due to pressure from enterprises (mainly looking for skilled workers), special meetings were organised for skilled workers and enterprises.

Agencies operate differently in different areas of the country: the lower the influence of the labour market the higher the importance of the state-led recruitment system, and vice versa. In areas where private business dominates there is much more unofficial recruitment, and kinship networks and private employment agents play a dominant role, while inland areas with scarce employment opportunities still rely on the regulatory power of state agencies.

E. *The role of work-units as organisers of distribution.*
This has not changed much since the start of the reform. The formal market is strongly influenced by the distributive role played by work-units: while a cynical and productivist attitude has emerged in labour relations, work-units, despite the increased independence of economic management, continue to play a major role in the redistributive system. Worker dependency is probably even more extensive since the reform, as the enterprise is now a direct actor and no longer the long arm of state welfare.

Thus the labour market that has emerged in the early 1990s is replete with contradictions that will not be solved in the short or even the medium term. The ability to control the flow of labour was greatly reduced in the twenty years of reform as a consequence of the decentralisation of the economy and the emergence of new social and economic phenomena such as large scale informalisation, previously less relevant or even absent.

In trying to establish a labour market using the tools of a command economy, the Chinese leadership radically divided the urban labour economy into two disparate sectors, over only one of which it has partial control. Macro labour allocation policies and the actions of state-led labour market institutions are aimed at assuring that the central government does not lose the limited control it has over that sector, but it is forced to deal with the contradictions between a highly bureaucratic system of allocation and a dynamic market economy in which the rules of the market and their consequences are becoming increasingly clear to both managers and workers.

The emergence of widespread market behaviour among actors (enterprises, workers, and the state) will probably not be the final act of China's enigmatic transition towards a commodity economy. The behaviour of enterprises and workers might well be led by apparently non-market considerations, in particular as a response to the infrastructural inadequacies of public structures to replace the previously state-led distributive system.

7.8 Conclusion

The aim of this work has been to place the entire process of labour reform in an historical perspective and to describe, in parallel, the goals, actions, and the eventual achievements of the policymakers, while highlighting the institutional as well as economic roots of China's labour market in the making.

To achieve this goal, this book focused mainly on the evolution of labour discourse, in some cases as a reflection of broader processes going on in society at large, in other cases as an internal constituent of the decision-making process. In an historical perspective – a longer term picture of the evolution of a society and of its leading organisational discourse – the outcome, partly unexpected initially, was the emergence of major paradoxes in the relationship between the initial goals and final outcomes, as well as major clashes in the ongoing and contradictory relationship between theory and practice.

Continuities in the political leadership, the behaviour of the elite, and policymaking, have only been marginally challenged by the emergence of these paradoxes. However, the deepening of the reform has contributed to transforming labour-related social problems into major factors of instability, and therefore from a future-oriented perspective, into a social threat and a challenge to the elite.

In 1977–78, China was emerging from an intense and violent period of political struggle, and was confronted with a labour economy that had dramatically impoverished the working class whose role, as 'vanguard of the people,' was itself in danger. Politics had gone too far in manipulating individual destinies and the dominance of administrative constraints over individual and social mobility had clearly put China on a dual track development path sharply dividing city and countryside.

Even the most audacious among the reformist thinkers who took part in the 1977–78 conferences on the reassessment of 'distribution according to labour' as a guiding principle for the redistribution of wealth, probably did not expect the final outcome of both theory and practice to result in the final dismantling of the public labour-based welfare system outlined in the most recent policy steps; nor was it likely that they expected that the making of a legal environment in the field of labour would grow in tandem with the deregulation and informalisation of the labour economy. Even less was it likely that they envisaged that the foundation and referent ideology for 'theoretical work' on labour would change so sharply, in a smooth and silent escape from the narrow boundaries of socialist thinking towards the proud embrace of a policy-driven form of capitalism that has recently become the new scientific foundation for the socialist economy.

This book also places the theoretical debates in the context of policymaking and sheds historical light on the contradictions which emerged within a process of reform generally seen to be straight and univocal. To challenge this view, it should be noted, the clarity of one political objective (stability) and one economic goal (efficiency) are balanced by the experimental nature of virtually all policy steps undertaken in these twenty years. The focus on experiments during the entire process of labour reform continues to this day and is still confronting challenging and worrying difficulties – raised by the rebuilding of the welfare system on the ashes of the *danwei* system (the privatisation of health care and pensions in particular) and the reallocation of millions of *xiagang* workers, victims of the necessary reform of the state ownership system.

To mark even more sharply the distance between the present situation and the labour economy in 1977–78 (a mere 20 years ago!), Chinese newspapers, in the period of the Fifteenth Congress and the 'fourth generation' of leaders, are filled with stories of the success of experiments to retrain unskilled personnel, and with personal stories of workers forcefully – but successfully – 'diving into the sea' of petty private business (*xia hai*) after being laid-off from factories where they had worked for decades. The government recognises the need to create 160 to 180 million new jobs during the Ninth Five Year Plan (1996–2000),[121] a number that includes both the 'geographic' movement of the labour force away from the countryside and the 'administrative' movement of redundant workers (for whom mobility means unemployment) from inside to outside the subsidised state labour system.

The dimension of unemployment in China sets a new agenda for labour reformers. While the theoretical clashes of the late 1970s were mainly the result of artificial attempts to combine socialist ideology and market forces, the new theoretical positions are largely liberated from this constraint and thus regard labour as a factor of production. This new interpretation of the political meaning of the word 'labour' has been accompanied by an unexpected 'minimal' interpretation of the socialist ideal (a leading economist recently declared socialism to be nothing but 'social justice plus a market economy').[122]

At the end of the second decade of the reform, labour policies in China are completing a privatisation process characterised by political and economic *decentralisation* on one side, as a direct result of political options, and by increased *mobility* and *informalisation* of economic and labour relations on the other – two features (resulting from the so-called process of the 'liberation of productive forces') that appear difficult to control.

Labour underwent some major contradictory readjustments as it was progressively privatised, initially as a result of spontaneous involvement by farmers in private business and then as a consequence of the restructuring process and labour 'diet' of state owned enterprises. Although a conscious privatisation (that is, the osmosis of industrial state labour into a private industrial sector and an urban tertiary sector) of labour relations was not a theoretical goal of the debate until recently, its emergence has been cashed in on by economic reformers as a positive result for the aim of raising productivity both inside industrial units and in the overall economic system, as it was related to the growth of the non-industrial and urban service economy that remains a major prerequisite for China's marketisation.

The privatisation of the economy, although advancing at unprecedented speed for a socialist country, could not avoid the problem of redundant personnel in SOEs. Once the political and theoretical disputes on DATL were settled, the focus slowly shifted from wealth distribution (in the years of economic recovery in the late 1970s) to the relationship between efficiency and employment, thereby creating theoretical categories that will eventually lead to the final abolition of the *danwei* system. These all-encompassing structures that were once the major social, economic and political reference for the largest majority of urban workers and employees during the 'classical' period of Chinese socialism lost their appeal step by step as the dependency of workers began to decline and the urban market began to offer diversified and better opportunities to cope with basic needs and economic desires.

Industrial work-units, once the only source of wealth redistribution, became self-accounting economic entities that behave in a profit-driven manner. They have lost their political and social roles and accordingly their very essence as an organising unit of socialist society.

In the light of recent steps in industrial policy (such as the establishment of so called 'pillar-industries' and the rush to merge industrial enterprises into huge conglomerates), the *danwei* system may not be simply dismantled but more concretely transformed into a feature of *chaebol*-like state conglomerate. This would mean that, while eliminating the idea of a work-unit based economic and political society, China is ready to reshape and modernise the concept for the organisation of large, high-tech, and less labour-intensive industrial SOEs. This would coherently respond to the socialist claim that the urban industrial economy is a strategic national resource and must be maintained under the direct control of the state, while, at the same time, it is given a sufficient level of strategic and operational autonomy to deal with both internal labour relations and with an increasingly hostile national and international market. The claim recently aired by the Chinese media,[123] that China lacks any multinational enterprises able to compete with international competitors and to maintain a dominant position in the domestic market seems to envisage a 'large enterprise' strategy for the next decade. This is a field where the *danwei* dream might be revisited. Economies based on large state-protected conglomerates of the Korean type have proved very effective in fast developing countries, where the state is still able (albeit in spite of regional contradictions, and decentralisation, and its weaknesses during the recent Asian financial crisis) to maintain control over major macro-economic indicators.

From the point of view of labour relations such 'new' work-units might reignite in a different form the paternalist socialist *danwei* discourse, although the process of informalisation and privatisation of the labour economy, as well as the global economic conditions within the country, envisage a much larger differentiation of activities and employment opportunities in China in the next decades than those in Korea in the 1970s.

An unprecedented number of unemployed have been released in the urban centres, reinforcing the reserve army of unskilled labour already present in great numbers in the once-closed Chinese cities. A report from the World Bank[124] identifies rates of unemployment as high as 20 percent in some cities in 1995, while official rates are still under 3 percent due to underestimation and non-consideration of those workers still formally belonging to a work-unit even though they have no jobs and do not receive salaries. The fast and disorderly growth of tertiary activities is still largely insufficient to cope with the masses of workers expelled from enterprises, and the excess of unskilled workers generally has been accompanied by a shortage of skilled personnel. Back-up strategies, such as the bureaucratic re-employment network, have not been efficient;

retraining is not as valuable a tool as the authorities had hoped as most *xiagang* workers are uneducated, while there is a labour shortage only for a highly specialized segment.

This situation, together with the flow of farmers from the countryside and the so-called floating population, fostered an informalisation of the labour economy. Informalisation can be considered to be among the unexpected results of the economic reform, which, paradoxically, emerged when Chinese official policy and theory aimed at creating a legal environment for labour relations, thus replacing political correctness with basic individual rights. This eventually resulted in the enforcement of the labour law in 1995.

The entire process that led to the political and legal achievements of labour reform was one of experimentation, such that my initial time-frame would have probably been useless had *events* (rather than major discontinuities) been taken into consideration.

One of the processes largely untouched upon here – and that I hope will enter the agenda of future research – is that of the relationship between enterprise decision making and central policies. The reform can be described as an elastic process of experimentation > success > policy formulation > implementation, where the central policies (on which I focus in this study) were only the final outcome of local experiences and pioneering initiatives, and were themselves experimental and underwent major readjustment over time.

The 'history' (historians will excuse the improper use of the term) of labour reform depicts a process that has generally been understood as gradual (probably because it did not originate with any radical political or elite changes) but, due to the enormous contradictions with which it had to deal, had a tremendous impact on both social life and political ideology. The 'experimental development' of labour policy produced a scattered and contradictory environment in the labour arena that resulted in deregulation and localisation of labour organisation as well as different levels of depth and coherence in the implementation of central policy. Furthermore, labour reform implied a diversification of players and an adaptation of their behaviour to the unexpressed forces of market rules. Despite a late (early 1990s) ideological *recognition* of the regulatory mechanism of market forces in the labour arena, internal competition, the search for further efficiency, and the booming private and semi-private economies in both city and countryside had sown the seeds of market rules much earlier and much deeper than the cryptic and contradictory descriptions of theoreticians during the 1980s might have predicted.

This reality-driven recognition of a deregulated labour market (taking clearer shape in urban centres but involving most of the rural population as well) and the influence of market forces on the increasing labour mobility do not mean, however, that China has consciously taken the road towards 'sole-market' management of the labour force. China's policymakers are conscious of the fundamental lack of social institutions able to manage the dismissal of the 15 percent of SOE workers who are now redundant. Recent efforts to establish a pension system (based on social pooling plus individual contributions) and an unemployment fund still suffer from both administrative (eligibility is still mainly limited to urban registered workers) and financial limitations emerging from decades-long soft-budget constraints and the hoarding of redundant personnel.

My conclusion is that the economic and political environment in China today is one in which the labour market has been assimilated, both at a theoretical level and in the daily life experience.

This assimilation has been the result of both the internationalisation of the economy which requires higher rates of efficiency for survival, and the decentralisation of political and economic control, accompanied, as I have tried to show, by privatisation and informalisation.

Although highly deregulated at the lower levels, what we now (at the risk of oversimplification) call the Chinese labour market is still dominated by a high level of institutionalisation, mainly in the urban areas, primarily concerned with the reform and reorganisation of SOE employment.

A labour market is up and running, while the most problematic issues continue to exist under a highly institutionalised administrative umbrella. Keynesian and neo-liberal views contend in the theoretical field, while policymakers are confronted with the need to balance demand (too low in both industrial and service sectors compared to the rate of development of the economy) and supply (abundant in unskilled but lacking highly needed skilled labour).

NOTES

CHAPTER 1

1 Michael Korzec, *Labour and the Failure of Reform in China*. New York: St. Martin's Press, 1992.

2 François Gipouloux, *Les cent fleurs à l'usine: agitation ouvrière et crise du model sovietique en Chine 1956–1957*. Paris: L'ècole des Haute Etudes, 1986; Jackie Sheehan, *Chinese Workers: A New History*. London: Routledge, 1998; Elizabeth Perry, *Shanghai on Strike: The Politics of Chinese Labor*. Stanford: Stanford University Press, 1993.

3 Andrew G. Walder, *Communist Neo-Traditionalism: Work and Authority in Chinese Industry*. Berkeley: University of California Press, 1986. Though Walder's book is devoted almost entirely to the Maoist period, the final chapters forecast a future of continuity in the practice of work authority in a different environment characterised by increased paternalism at the enterprise level, and by a focus on productivity rather than on politics in the field of policy. A perspective on the reform period is offered in Ching Kwan Lee, 'From Organized Dependence to Disorganized Despotism', *The China Quarterly*, no. 157 (March 1999).

4 Jutta Hebel, 'Der Betrieb als Kleine Gesellschaft: die Bedeutung des chinesischen Betriebstyps für den Prozess der Reform des Arbeitssystems,' *Soziale Welt*, no. 2 (1990); idem, 'Institutional Change in a in an Enterprise-based society and its Impact on Labour: the Case of the People's Republic of China,' in Gerry Rodgers, Klara Foti, Laurids Lauridsen (eds.), *The Institutional Approach to Labour and Development*. London: Frank Cass, 1996; Jutta Hebel and Günther Schucher, *Die Reform der drei Eisernen, Strukturwandel im chinesischen Arbeitssystem*. Berichte des Bundesinstitut für Ostwissenschaftliche und Internationale Studien, no. 44 (1992); Yves

Chevrier, 'Micropolitics and the Factory Director Responsibility system,' in Deborah Davis and Ezra Vogel (eds.), *Chinese Society on the Eve of Tiananmen*. Cambridge: Harvard University Press, 1990; Walder, *Communist Neo-Traditionalism*; Lü Xiaobo and Elizabeth J. Perry, (eds.), *Danwei. The Changing Chinese Workplace in Historical and Comparative Perspective*. Armonk, N.Y.: M.E. Sharpe, 1997; Li Hanlin and Wang Qi, *Research in the Chinese Work-Unit Society*. Frankfurt: Peter Lang, 1996.

5 Dorothy Solinger, *Contesting Citizenship in Urban China: Peasant Migrants, the State and the Logic of the Market*. Berkeley: University of California Press, 1999; Laurence J.C. Ma and Biao Xiang, 'Native Place, Migration, and the Emergence of Peasant Enclaves in Beijing,' *The China Quarterly*, no. 155 (September 1998); Frank Pieke and Hein Mallee (eds.), *Internal and International Migration: Chinese Perspectives*. London: Curzon Press, 1999; Børge Bakken (ed.), *Migration in China*. Copenhagen: Nordic Institute of Asian Studies, 1998; Thomas Scharping (ed.), *Floating Population and Migration in China: The Impact of Economic Reform*. Hamburg: Institut für Asienkunde, 1997.

6 Peter Lee, 'Enterprise Autonomy Policy in Post-Mao China: a case study of Policy Making,' *The China Quarterly* no. 105, (March 1986).

7 Barry Naughton, *Growing Out of the Plan: Chinese Economic Reform 1978–1993*. Cambridge: Cambridge University Press, 1995, p. 7.

8 Jean C. Oi, *Rural China Takes off: Institutional Foundations of Economic Reform*. Berkeley: University of California Press, 1999, p. 138. Oi's use of 'local state corporatism,' while validating the idea of a corporatist attitude in China's state-society relations, focuses on a structure coordinated by local authorities, rather than the central state, that leads to the emergence of 'corporatist rather than a free market system, at least at the local levels,' pp. 2–13.

9 Yia-Ling Liu, 'Reform from Below: The Private Economy and Local Politics in the Rural Industrialization of Wenzhou,' *The China Quarterly*, no. 130 (June 1992).

10 Walder, *Communist Neo-Traditionalism*.

11 Ching Kwan Lee, *From Organized Dependence to Disorganized Despotism*. Idem, *Gender and the South China Miracle: Two Worlds of Factory Women*. Berkeley: University of California Press, 1998

12 Fei-Ling Wang, *From Family to Market: Labor Allocation in Contemporary China*. Lanham, MD: Rowman and Littlefeld, 1998, pp. 7–10.

13 I adopt here Kornai's definition, which refers to Maoist China as a 'classic' form of socialism.

14 Korzec, *Labour and the Failure of Reform*.

15 Elizabeth J. Perry, 'Shanghai's strike wave of 1957', *The China Quarterly*, no. 137 (March 1994).

16 Akio Takahara, *The Politics of Wage Policy in Post-Revolutionary China*. London: Macmillan, 1992.

17 A significant example of this position is the commentary by Prof. Pu Shan on a paper Milton Friedman discussed at a 1988 conference in Shanghai. The opposition between 'free' and 'socialist' markets is

clearly outlined here: Wang Xi and Tu En [James Dorn] (eds.), *Zhongguo jingji gaige: wenti yu qianjin* (Economic Reform in China: Problems and Prospects). Shanghai: Fudan daxue chubanshe, 1994.

18 Wang Chengying, *Zhongguo zai jiuye* (China's Re-employment). Chengdu: Sichuan daxue chubanshe, 1998.

19 Susan Shirk discovered, for example, that all new recruits in 1979 were children of retired employees in some enterprises. 'Recent Chinese Labour Policies and the Transformation of Industrial Organization in China,' *The China Quarterly*, no. 88 (December 1981). See also Korzec, *Labour and the Failure of Reform*.

20 David Granick, 'Multiple Labour Markets in the Industrial State Enterprise Sector,' *The China Quarterly*, no. 126 (June 1991).

21 On *dingti*, see Korzec, *Labour and the Failure of Reform*, and Deborah Davis, 'Urban Job Mobility,' in Davis and Vogel (eds.), *Chinese Society on the Eve of Tiananmen*, pp. 85–108.

22 Janos Kornai, *Economics of Shortage*. Amsterdam: North Holland, 1980. The book was translated into Chinese in 1986 and was very influential in shaping subsequent debates: *Duanque jingji xue*. Beijing: Jingji kexue chubanshe, 1986.

23 Flemming Christiansen, 'The Legacy of the Mock Dual Economy: Chinese Labour in Transition,' *Economy and Society*, vol. 22, no. 4 (November 1993).

24 Charles Tilly, *From Mobilization to Revolution*. Reading, MA: Addison-Wesley, 1978.

25 Andrew G. Walder, 'The Remaking of the Chinese Working Class, 1949–1981,' *Modern China*, vol 10, no.1 (1984).

26 The rustication policies of the late 1950s were probably resulted from the 1949 baby boom, as the urbanised farmers had already been sent back to their places of origin. Ibid.

27 Ibid.

28 Sally Sargeson, *Reworking China's Proletariat*. London: Macmillan Press, 1999, p. 30.

29 Gipouloux, *Les cent fleurs à l'usine*.

30 Perry, 'Shanghai on Strike.'

31 Elizabeth Perry, 'From Native place to Workplace: Labor Origin and Outcomes of China's *Danwei* System,' in Lü and Perry (eds.), *Danwei*, p. 43.

32 Sheehan, *Chinese Workers: a New History*.

33 Ching Kwan Lee, 'The Labour Politics of Market Socialism', *Modern China*, vol. 24, no. 1 (January 1998).

34 On the issue of resistance, see the recent Elizabeth J. Perry and Mark Selden (eds.), *Chinese Society: Change, Conflict, and Resistance*. London: Routledge, 2000, especially Ching Kwan Lee's 'Pathways of Labour Insurgency.'

35 Solinger, *Contesting Citizenship in Urban China*, pp. 1–8. The assumption is based on T.H. Marshall's work on citizenship.

36 Flemming Christiansen, 'Social Division and Peasant Mobility in Mainland China: The Implications of the *Hu-k'ou* System,' *Issues and Studies*, vol. 26, no. 4 (April 1990); Tiejun Cheng and Mark Selden, 'The Origins and Social Consequences of China's Hukou System,' *The*

China Quarterly, no. 139 (September 1994); idem, 'The Construction of Spatial Hierarchies: China's *Hukou* and *Danwei* systems,' in Timothy C. Cheek and Tony Saich (eds.), *New Perspectives on State Socialism in China*. Armonk: M.E. Sharpe, 1997, pp. 23–50.

37 On the crisis and the attempt to reform the *hukou* system, see Hein Mallee, 'China's Household Registration System under Reform,' *Development and Change*, no. 26 (1995).

38 An indication of *hukou* type is still very important in application forms, even in the most advanced labour market fairs, which are periodically held in major urban centers to meet the demand for skilled labour. In many urban labour agencies only local *hukou* holders have access to the services.

39 Sargeson, *Reworking China's Proletariat*, p. 104.

40 Dorothy J. Solinger, "Temporary Residence Certificate' Regulations in Wuhan, May 1983,' *The China Quarterly*, no. 101 (1985). The role of redistribution was increasingly played by the enterprises during the 1980s.

41 See, for example, John P. Burns, 'Rural Guangdong's 'Second Economy', 1962–1974,' *The China Quarterly*, no. 88 (December 1981) and Anita Chan and Jonathan Unger, 'Grey and Black: The Hidden Economy of Rural China,' *Pacific Affairs*, no. 3 (Fall 1982).

42 See Liu, *Reform from Below*.

43 Naughton, *Growing Out of the Plan*, p. 13.

44 David Stark, 'Bending the Bars of the Iron Cage: Bureaucratisation and Informalisation in Capitalism and Socialism,' in Chris Smith and Paul Thompson (eds.), *Labour in Transition: The Labour Process in Eastern Europe and China*. London: Routledge, 1992. The term informalisation is used here to describe a process opposed to bureaucratisation.

45 Solinger, *Contesting Citizenship*, pp. 142–143.

46 Huang Weiding, *Zhongguo de yinxing jingji* (China's Shadow Economy). Beijing: Zhongguo shangye chubanshe, 1992.

47 Frank Pyke, Giacomo Becattini, and Werner Sengenberger, *Industrial Districts and Inter-firm Co-operation in Italy*. Geneva: International Institute for Labour Studies, 1990.

48 For a long time the expression 'waiting for employment' (*daiye*) was the only accepted term for 'unemployed' (*shiye*); the latter has only recently become part of the official language, together with more crude expressions such as *xiagang*, the term used to refer to SOE workers who have been dismissed from their jobs.

49 Ma and Xiang, 'Native Place, Migration and the Emergence of Peasant Enclaves in Beijing.'

50 Akio Takahara, for example, in his analysis of wage policy in socialist China, identifies some regular annual cycles made up of two politically-led seasonal antithetical political campaigns, with the final aim of influencing policy decision. Takahara, *The Politics of Wage Policy*.

51 For a useful definition of market socialism, see Janos Kornai, *The Socialist System: The Political Economy of Communism*. London: Oxford University Press, 1992.

52 Actually, of the four members of the gang, the one who deserves the greatest attention when discussing the labour issue is Zhang Chunqiao because of his vigorous and repeated attacks on the principle of 'distribution according to labour.'

53 In March 1978, during a campaign to link wages to enterprise performance, Deng circulated comments in support of DATL, criticising the long-term practice of 'distribution according to politics' (*an zheng fenpei*).

54 It was not uncommon that the Marxist origins of the theory were stressed also by using the German rather than the Chinese expression. See the discussion of the terms of the debate on this specific issue in Feng Lanrui, *Anlao fenpei, gongzi, jiuye* (Distribution According to Labour, Wages, and Employment). Beijing: Jingji kexue chubanshe, 1988.)

55 Ibid.

56 I use this term conscious of the negative meaning generally associated with it. In this usage it refers to the restoration of a *status quo ante*, prelude for the reform drive. I am sure that, in historical terms, the use of 'restoration' in this case is at least as controversial as the term 'revolution' associated with the 1966–1976 decade. My major concern is to address the issue of a possible comparison between the 1950s and the early reform policies.

57 For a discussion of Stalinist discourse in 1950s China see Deborah A. Kaple, *Dream of a Red Factory: The Legacy of High Stalinism in China*. London: Oxford University Press, 1994.

58 A higher worker mobility rate, as in the Soviet Union, is generally considered a sign of more rational labour allocation.

59 Korzec, *Labour and the Failure of Reform*, pp. 44–50.

60 Walder, *Communist Neo-Traditionalism*.

61 Luo Shouchu, 'Laodong li liudong he laodong zhidu gaige chuyi (Initial Analysis of Labour Mobility and the Reform of the Labour system,' *Zhongguo shehui kexue*, no. 5 (1986).

62 New recruits originally meant greater allocation of state funds to the enterprise.

63 At this time, in the discussion of the question of labour mobility in the changing economic environment and the attempt to provide a theoretical answer to the question of the original nature of labour relations in a 'socialist market economy,' a well supported opinion argued, that the division of labour actually exists also in a socialist market economy; the double status of workers (as owners of the means of production and suppliers of labour) is in fact a functional separation giving origin to an 'exchange' in terms of labour contribution, which is similar to the commodity-labour exchange described by Marx for capitalist market relations. The real difference in the socialist market is the 'bi-directional choice' (*shuangxiang xuanze*), the theoretical assumption that labour is not paid at its market value (the reproduction value), but at a price to be calculated according to wage plus the part of redistributed social wealth which the worker produces and of which he/she benefits. Luo Shouchu, 'Laodong li liudong he laodong zhidu gaige chuyi.'

64 The debate was particularly intense in 1986 and 1987 and hundreds of pages were devoted to this topic in the major political and economic journals. For an interesting example of the various positions see, *Zhongguo shehui kexue*, no. 1 (1987), in which four different articles are collected under the title 'Shehui zhuyi tiaojian xia laodong li shi bu shi shangpin' (Is the Labour Force a Commodity under Conditions of Socialism?).

65 As will become clear from analysis of the debate, this was not a *real need*, but more a dialectic necessity to allow the debate to proceed. Actually, a *de facto* labour market was already developing, but the official definition was still that of a *laowu shichang* (a labour functions market) and not, as later recognised, *laodong li* (labour force) or *laodong* (labour) market.

66 Despite many statements on the commodity nature of labour, at the conference on the labour market held in Beijing by the Institute of Economics of the Chinese Academy of Social Sciences (CASS) in 1995, this heated issue came up and was vigorously discussed.

67 The first official text dealing with the issue of labour in terms of a labour market is Feng Lanrui's *Lun Zhongguo laodong li shichang* (On China's Labour Market). Beijing: Zhongguo chengshi chubanshe, December 1991. The basic theoretical assumption of the book, that I shall discuss in further detail in Chapter 6 is that 'under certain conditions' the relationship between workers and their own labour force can become an 'economic property relationship' (*jingji guanxi de suoyou zhi guanxi*). The book had a very limited circulation but was very influential inside CASS.

68 This policy was decided upon at the 'National Conference to Discuss Party Work on Labour,' held in Beijing in August 1980.

69 Dai Yuanchen, *Zhongguo laodong li shichang peiyu yu gongzi gaige* (The Growth of a Labour Market and the Reform of Salaries in China). Beijing: Zhongguo laodong chubanshe, 1994.

70 See Gordon White, 'Social Security Reform in China: Toward an East Asian Model?, in Roger Goodman, Gordon White and Huck-ju Kwon (eds.), *The East Asian Welfare Model: Welfare Orientalism and the State*. London: Routledge, 1998.

71 Dai, *Zhongguo laodongli shichang peiyu yu gongzi gaige*, pp. 172–73.

72 Wang Yiying, et al., *Zhongguo laodong fa shiwu* (The Chinese Labour Law in Practice). Beijing: Jinri zhongguo chubanshe, 1994, pp. 64–65, helps provide an understanding of the basic difference between the two categories.

73 *Zhonghua renmin gongheguo laodong fa, Zhonghua renmin gongheguo gonghui fa* (The Labour Law and the Trade Unions Law of the People's Republic of China). Beijing: Zhongguo fazhi chubanshe, December 1994, pp. 4–8.

CHAPTER 2

1 Michael Burawoy, *The Politics of Production*. London: Verso, 1985, p. 156–57.

2 Miklos Haraszti, *Worker in a Worker's State*. London: Penguin Books, 1977.

3 The Red Star Tractor Factory, where the Hungarian sociologist worked in 1971–72.

4 Michael Burawoy, 'Piece Rates, Hungarian Style,' *Socialist Review* (January 1985).

5 Harry Bravermann, *Labor and Monopoly Capital*. New York: Monthly Review Press, 1974.

6 I include in this group also Janos Kornai's *Economics of Shortage*.

7 This was the case despite the fact that Kornai had lectured in China.

8 Su Shaozhi and Feng Lanrui, 'Bo Yao Wenyuan anlao fenpei chansheng zichan jieji de miulun' (Get Rid of Yao Wenyuan's Absurd Theory that 'Distribution According to Labour' Gives Birth to a Bourgeois Class), *Renmin ribao*, 9 August 1977.

9 Also among the *Critique*'s argument in the Chinese edition of *Marx and Engels Selected Works*, *Makesi Engesi xuanji*. Beijing: Renmin chubanshe, 1972, vol. 3, pp. 10–13.

10 The 'Gang of Four' was the nickname for the radical leftist clique that was accused of putchism and of constituting a shadow dictatorhip in the last years of the Cultural Revolution and at the end of Mao's life. During a public trial that marked the symbolic end of the Cultural Revolution in winter 1980, they were found guilty of unjustly persecuting over 700,000 persons.

11 As Deborah Kaple points out, the numerous translations of Soviet industrial manuals was not paralleled by a corresponding number of visits to Soviet plants. The application of the Soviet industrial model during the First Five Year Plan was mainly based on a theoretical explanation of the extensively translated soviet manuals. Deborah Kaple, *Dream of a Red Factory*.

12 Li Honglin, 'An lao fenpei shi shehui zhuyi yuanze haishi ziben zhuyi yuanze?' (Is DATL a Socialist or a Capitalist Principle?), *Renmin ribao*, 27 September 1977.

13 Yu Guangyuan, born in Shanghai in 1915 was vice president of the Science and Technology Commission and vice president of CASS. Yu Guangyuan, *Zhongguo shehui zhuyi chuji jieduan de jingji* (The Economy at the Initial Phase of Socialism in China). Guangzhou: Guangdong jingji chubanshe, 1998, esp. pp. 362–429.

14 Though he is well known for his work as a political scientist, Su has been trained as an economist.

15 When CASS was founded in November 1977, Hu was appointed president, and Yu Guangyuan and Deng Liqun were vice presidents.

16 Takahara, *The Politics of Wage Policy*, p. 67.

17 Renmin ribao teyue pinglun yuan (People's Daily Special Commentator) 'Guanche zhixing anlao fenpei de shehui zhuyi yuanze,' (Carry on the Socialist Principle of Distribution According to Labour), *Renmin ribao*, 5 May 1978 was then republished with slight revisions in Feng Lanrui, et al., *Lun anlao fenpei* (On Distribution According to Labour). Beijing: Beijing renmin chubanshe, 1978.

18 Karl Marx, 'Critique of the Gotha Program', in *Makesi Engesi xuanji*, vol. 3, pp. 10–11.

19 'The role of Proletariat in the Russian Revolution,' in *Lienin xuanji*. Beijing: Renmin chubanshe, 1972, vol. 3, p. 62.

20 *Mao Zedong xuanji* (Selected Works of Mao Zedong). Beijing: Renmin chubanshe, 1951, vol. 1, p. 93.
21 Renmin ribao teyue pinglun yuan, 'Guanche zhixing anlao fenpei de shehui zhuyi yuanze.'
22 Sheehan, *Chinese Workers*, p. 197.
23 Takahara, *The Politics of Wage Policy*.
24 The most appealing was that of Yu Guangyuan in his opening address at the 1978 conference: 'Yu Guangyuan tongzhi zai di sici anlao fenpei wenti taolun hui kaimu shi hui shang jiang hua' (Opening Address of Comrade Yu Guangyuan at the Fourth Conference to discuss DATL), 25 October 1978, in *Guanyu anlao fenpei wenti* (On Distribution According to Labour). Beijing: Sanlian shudian, 1979.
25 Karl Marx, *Critique of the Gotha Program*. Moscow: Foreign Languages Press, 1947 [1875], p. 25.
26 The most complete references of the three 1977 conferences are in *Guanyu anlao fenpei wenti jingji xuejie 1977nian sanci huiyi de chubian* (References of the Three 1977 Conferences of Economic Circles on the Issue of Distribution According to Labour). Beijing: Sanlian shudian, 1978.
27 Feng Lanrui, *Anlao fenpei, gongzi, jiuye*, pp. 108–9.
28 In German in the Chinese text.
29 Feng Lanrui, *Anlao fenpei, gongzi, jiuye*, p. 108.
30 Li Honglin, 'An lao fenpei shi shehui zhuyi yuanze haishi ziben zhuyi yuanze?'
31 Renmin ribao teyue pinglun yuan, 'Guanche zhixing anlao fenpei de shehui zhuyi yuanze.'
32 Wen Min, 'Yinian lai guanyu anlao fenpei wenti de taolun qingkuang' (The Debate on DATL during the Last Year), *Jingji yanjiu*, no. 1 (1978).
33 Wu Xinmu, 'Laodong baochou xingshi shang you dai shentao de jige wenti' (Some Problems Related to the Method of Labour Rewards that Need to be Accurately Discussed), in *Guanyu anlao fenpei wenti* (On Distribution According to Labour), Beijing, Renmin chubanshe, 1979 p. 326 (hereafter *DATL-78*).
34 See Hu Sheng, *A Concise History of the Communist Party of China*. Beijing: Foreign Languages Press, 1994, pp. 730–38.
35 Hu Qiaomu, 'Anzhao jingji guilü banshi, jiakuai shixian sige xiandaihua' (Deal with Things According to Economic Laws. Accelerate the Implementation of the Four Modernisations), *Renmin Ribao*, 6 October 1978. See *Hu Qiaomu wenji* (Hu Qiaomu's Collected Works). Beijing: Renmin chubanshe, 1993, vol. 2, pp. 401–432. Hu's speech was written in the previous July.
36 Takahara, *The Politics of Wage Policy*, p. 75.
37 'Guowuyuan guanyu tiaozheng bufen zhigong gongzi de tongzhi' (State Council Communiqué on the Readjustment of Some Workers' Wages), 10 August 1977, in *Jingji tizhi gaige wenjian huibian* (Collection of Relevant Documents on Reform of the Economic System) (hereafter *Tigai huibian*). Beijing: Zhongguo caizheng chubanshe, 1984, p. 1009.
38 'Yu Guangyuan tongzhi zai di sici anlao fenpei wenti taolun hui kaimu shi hui shang jiang hua.'

39 Bi Shuiying, 'Shehui zhuyi shi laodongzhe geren liyi weiyi lingu de baozheng' (Socialism is the Guarantee for the Stability of Workers' Individual Rights), in *DATL-78*, p. 195.

40 Wang Meihan, 'Guanyu shehui zhuyi zhidu xia de jingji liyi wenti' (The Problem of Individual Economic Rights under Socialism), in *DATL-78*, pp. 224–225.

41 Liu Guangdi, 'Bixu renzhen de yanjiu anlao fenpei guilü de zuoyong, qieshi de anzhao an lao fenpei guilü banshi' (It is Necessary to Investigate the Function of DATL and to Apply the Principle to the Practical Issues), in *DATL-78*, p. 56.

42 Zhao Lükuan and Feng Lanrui, 'Guanyu jijian gongzi he jiangjin de jige wenti' (Some Problems concerning Piece-rate Wages and Bonuses), in *DATL-78*, p. 299.

43 While the management responsibility system was not implemented until 1981, the initial steps for a re-evaluation of cadres and managers were already evident during 1978.

44 Wang Haibo, Wu Jinglian and Zhou Shulian, 'Shenru guanche anlao fenpei yuanze de ruogan wenti' (Some Problems in the Implementation of DATL), in *DATL-78*, p.122.

45 Yi Shijie and Zheng Biqing, 'Anlao fenpei guilü de zhuyao tedian he yaoqiu' (Main Features and Needs for the Principle of DATL), in *DATL-78*, p. 29.

46 'Firmly Uphold Whatever Policy Decision Chariman Mao Made, Firmly Follow Whatever Instructions Chairman Mao Issued.' Promotion of the 'two whatevers' was later considered to be as one of Hua's major political mistakes.

47 Yu Guangyuan, 'Tantan guanyu anlao fenpei zhong de yixie lilun wenti' (On Some Theoretical Issues Concerning DATL), in *Guanyu anlao fenpei wenti* (On Problems of Distribution According to Labour) (hereafter *DATL-83*). Beijing: Renmin chubanshe, 1984.

48 See Lee Lai To, *Trade Unions in China: 1949 to Present*. Singapore: Singapore University Press, 1986; Ng Sek-Hong and Malcolm Warner, *China's Trade Unions and Management*. London: Macmillan Press, 1998; Chiang Chenchang, 'The Role of Trade Unions in Mainland China,' *Issues and Studies*, vol. 26, no.2 (February 1990), pp. 75–98.

49 Zhou Yuanliang, 'Woguo naoli laodongzhe de gongzi wenti' (The Problem of Wages for Intellectual Workers), in *DATL-83*, p. 367.

50 Zheng Li, 'Zhongguo laodong xuehui shoujie nianhui taolun qingkuang jianjie' (The Yearly Meeting of the Labour Research Association Discusses the Present Situation), *Jingji Yanjiu*, no. 5 (1982).

51 Ibid., p. 69.

52 Ibid., p. 68. Zheng describes four positions, but the fourth (that property-rights and use-rights of labour force are separate) did not have a large part in the debate.

53 For a review of the three positions and supporting attitude documentation for the third, see, for example: Zhang Xin, 'Laodong li suoyouzhi yu gongzi guanli tizhi gaige' (The Ownership of Labour and the Reform of Wage Management), in *DATL-83*, p. 244.

54 Zheng Li, 'Zhongguo laodong xuehui shoujie nianhui taolun qingkuang jianjie,' p. 71.
55 Zhang Xin, 'Laodong li suoyouzhi yu gongzi guanli tizhi gaige,' p. 247.
56 'Eating from the same big pot' is an expression referring to the high level of dependence of workers on State allocation of resources, mainly through the *danwei* system.
57 Takahara, *The Politics of Wage Policy*, p. 131.
58 Qian Shiming, 'Lun fudong gongzi zhi' (On the System of Floating Wages), in *DATL-83*, p. 260. The issue of 'floating wages' (that is, an integrated wage made up of a fixed salary plus different forms of incentives) was in fact discussed with the help of empirical data sets showing the results of practical experiments inside the enterprises. See, as an example, Cheng Biding, Xin Qiushui, 'Cong Hefei zixingche chang shixing fudong gongzi de shijian kan gongye qiye gongzi zhidu gaige de fangxiang' (The Perspective for Industrial Wage Reform as seen from the Experiments on Floating Wages Carried out at the Hefei Bicycle Factory), in *DATL-83*, pp. 312–329.
59 See Korzec, *Labour and the Failure of Reform*.

CHAPTER 3

1 *Zhongguo laodong tongji nianjian 1995* (China Labour Statistical Yearbook, 1995) (hereafter cited as CLSYB-95). Beijing: Zhongguo tongji chubanshe, 1996.
2 Barry Naughton, '*Danwei*: the Economic Foundation of a Unique Institution,' in Lü and Perry (eds.), *Danwei*, p. 174.
3 Ibid., p. 180. Naughton calculates 18.6 square meters of housing per worker in large SOEs against 10.4 square meters in light industry, while the rate of primary education among workers was 16.2 percent and 4.4 percent respectively in 1985.
4 *Guowuyuan guanyu tiaozheng bufen zhigong gongzi de tongzhi,* pp. 1009–10.
5 Article 2.3 of the circular declares in fact that 'An adjustment of less than 5 yuan can be upgraded to 5 yuan while an adjustment of more than 7 yuan has to be limited to 7 yuan,' Ibid., p. 1009. See also Takahara, *The Politics of Wage Policy*, p. 68.
6 *Guowuyuan guanyu tiaozheng bufen zhigong gongzi de tongzhi*, art. 2.1.
7 Takahara, *The Politics of Wage Policy*, p. 66.
8 Chen Ruoxi, *Democracy Wall and the Unofficial Journals*. Berkeley: Center for Chinese Studies, University of California, 1982. See also Sheehan, *Chinese Workers*, pp. 157–94.
9 'Guowuyuan guanyu shixing jiangli he jijian gongzi zhidu de tongzhi' (State Council Circular on Implementing Bonuses and Piece-rate Wage System), 7 May 1978, in *Tigai Huibian*, p. 1011.
10 It is interesting to note that the limit in relative terms is not at all low, if we consider that the officially computed general percentage of bonuses and piece rate wages never reached 20 percent in the sixteen years from 1978 to 1994 (17.9 percent in 1994). *CLSYB-95*.

11 In October 1998, at a time when differences were much more relevant and the competition much stiffer, bonuses and piece-rate wages accounted for just less than one quarter of monetary salaries on average (22 percent), and (at least officially), with relatively low imbalances between the different types of registered enetrprises. *CLSYB 1999*.

12 The total amount of SOE wages in 1979 was 52.95 billion yuan and bonuses were 4.18 billion. *CLSYB 1995*, pp. 34–35.

13 *Guowuyuan guanyu zhizhi langfei jiangjin he jintie jinji tongzhi* (Urgent State Council Circular on Controlling Waste in Bonuses and Rewards), 19 February 1979, in *Tigai Huibian*, pp. 1019–20.

14 Ibid. This is generally referred to as a subsidy-in-kind.

15 Writers express different views on the effectiveness of market reforms in the field of labour: Michael Korzec, for example, insists on the 'fail-ure' to reform the labour system in Chinese SOEs, arguing that the major original goals were not achieved due to the resistance from the involved parties. Korzec, *Labour and the Failure of Reform*. Other authors, quite differently point out the noteworthy deregulatory effects of reform on shop floor labour relations and stress the distance between the labour practices of the 1970s and those of the 1990s. See Minghua Zhao and Theo Nichols, 'Management Control of Labour in State-Owned Enterprises: Cases from the Textile Industry,' *The China Journal*, no. 36 (July 1996). On the responses to changing factory regimes see also Walder, *Communist Neo-Traditionalism* and Lee 'From Organized Dependence to Disorganized Despotism.'

16 The abolition or limitation of *fujia gongzi* was explicitly addressed in the 1978 circular.

17 Takahara, *The Politics of Wage Policy*, p. 74.

18 The figure was 98.6 percent in 1952. In 1978 the remainder of the work-force was employed in the 'collective' *(jiti)* sector. Today, most analysts tend to include collective enterprises in the 'nonstate sector,' together with the privately owned, joint ventures, and foreign invested enterprises. In 1994 the proportion of workers employed in the 'non-state sector' reached 26.6 percent. *CLSYB 1995*, p. 17.

19 Feng Lanrui, *Lun Zhongguo laodongli shichang*, p. 30.

20 Despite a net decrease during the tragic years of the Great Leap Forward (1958–1961).

21 The definition of what constitutes the urban population is controver-sial. I refer here only to the official data, generally calculated on the basis of *hukou* (registration) status.

22 At the beginning of the First Five-Year Plan, the proportion of total industrial output produced by light industry was 56.9 percent, but it decreased to 43 percent by the time of the launching of the Great Leap Forward (1958).

23 Feng Lanrui, 'Dangqian woguo chengzhen laodongzhe de jiuye wenti' (The Problem of Urban Employment for the Contemporary Chinese Urban Labourers), in Feng Lanrui, *Laodong baochou yu laodong jiuye* (Wages and Employment). Hong Kong: n.p., 1982.

24 Whyte and Parish quote the same data but from a different source (Zhao Lükuan, 'A Probe into some employment problems,' *Beijing*

Review, no. 43 (27 October 1980), p. 20. Their data is however 1,000 yuan. The source quoted is apparently the same (Zhao was Feng's collaborator) and I would infer that the correct figure is one million (*baiwan yuan*). Martin King Whyte and William L. Parish, *Urban Life in Contemporary China*. Chicago and London: University of Chicago Press, 1984, p. 38.

25 Ibid., p. 55.

26 Pat Howard, 'Rice Bowls and Job Security: The Urban Contract Labour System, *The Australian Journal of Chinese Affairs*, no. 25 (January 1991).

27 Ibid., p. 94.

28 Feng Lanrui, 'Dangqian woguo chengzhen laodongzhe de jiuye wenti,' p. 120.

29 The Chinese expression is '*cong nongcun fanhui chengshi de xiaxiang zhishi qingnian.*' Ibid., p. 122.

30 That means a figure of 16 to 17 million out of an urban population of about 100 million. Whyte and Parish, *Urban Life in Contemporary China*, pp. 39–40.

31 State Statistical Bureau.

32 For the official document on the policy conference see: 'Zhonggong zhongyang guanyu zhuanfa quanguo laodong jiuye huiyi wenjian de tongzhi' (CCP-CC Transmision of the Documents from the All China Conference on Labour and Employment), 17 August 1980, in: *Tigai Huibian*, pp. 616–21.

33 Ibid., pp. 619–20.

34 Feng Lanrui, *Lun Zhongguo laodongli shichang*, pp. 14–16.

35 According to Lee, it was only 'incidental' that the policy papers on this issue were published at the beginning of the Great Leap Forward, as they were part of a policy framework largely abandoned during the years of radicalism. Peter Nan-shong Lee, 'Enterprise Autonomy Policy in Post-Mao China: A Case Study of Policy-making, 1978–1983.' *The China Quarterly*, no. 105 (March 1986).

36 Ibid.

37 Oi, *Rural China Takes Off*, p. 28.

38 Ibid., p. 28.

39 Klara Foti and Flemming Christiansen, 'Transition from the Public to the Private: Different Strategies for the Labour Market in the Transforming Chinese and Hungarian Labour Market,' in Rodgers, Foti, and Lauridsen (eds.), *The Institutional Approach to Labour and Development*.

40 On the practice of *dingti*, that during some periods of China's socialist labour history was also regulated by specific norms, see Korzec, *Labour and the Failure of Reform*.

41 Although more difficult to evaluate, the same mechanism of patronage by large state enterprises may have contributed to the equally extraordinary development of 'rural industry' or 'township enterprises' (*xiangzhen qiye*).

42 *CLSYB-95*, p. 103.

43 'Guowuyuan guanyu keji renyuan heli liudong de ruogan guiding' (State Council Regulations on the Rational Flow of Technical

Personnel), no. 111 (1983), in *Zhongguo rencai liudong zhengce fagui daquan* (Collection of Policies and Regulations on Talent Mobility in China) (hereafter referred to as *Rencai*). Beijing: Jingji guanli chubanshe, 1993, pp. 1–4.

44 Ibid., pp. 2–3.

45 On neighbourhood organisations and their role in Chinese social life see also, Cecilia L.W. Chan, *The Myth of Neighbourhood Mutual Help: The Contemporary Chinese Community-Based Welfare System in Guangzhou*. Hong Kong: Hong Kong University Press, 1993.

46 Whyte and Parish, *Urban Life in Contemporary China*, p. 25.

47 Robert C. Hsu, 'Changing Conceptions of the Socialist Enterprise in China, 1979–1988,' *Modern China*, vol. 15, no. 4 (October 1989); Jutta Hebel, 'Der Betrieb als kleine Gesellschaft: Die Bedeutung des chinesische Betriebstyps fuer den Prozess der Reform des Arbeitssystems,' *Soziale Welt*, no. 2 (1990); Jutta Hebel and Günther Schucher, 'From Unit to Enterprise. The Chinese *Tan'wei* in the Process of Reform,' *Issues and Studies*, vol. 27, no. 4 (April 1991); Andrew G. Walder, 'Factory and Manager in an Era of Reform,' *The China Quarterly*, no. 118 (1989); idem, 'Wage Reform and the Web of Factory Interests,' *The China Quarterly*, no. 109 (1987); Yves Chevrier, 'Micropolitics and the Factory Director Responsibility System,' *in Davis and Vogel (eds.), Chinese Society on the Eve of Tiananmen*; Lü and Perry (eds.) *Danwei*; Li and Wang, *Research on the Chinese Work-Unit Society*.

48 Alessandro Russo, *Ouvrier et* Danwei: *Notes de récherche sur une enquête menée dans deux usines de Guangzhou en Avril-Mai, 1989*, Paris: Cahiers du CIASOC, 1990.

49 Naughton: *Danwei: The Economic Foundations of a Unique Institution*, pp. 172–173.

50 Andrew G. Walder, 'Organized Dependency and Cultures of Authority in Chinese Industry,' *Journal of Asian Studies*, vol. 43 (November 1983), p. 52.

51 Jutta Hebel and Günther Schucher, *Die Reform der drei Eisernen: Strukturwandel im chinesischen Arbeitssystem*.

52 Lee, *From Organized Dependence to Disorganized Despotism*.

53 Nan Lin and Wen Xie, 'Occupational Prestige in Urban China,' *American Journal of Sociology*, vol. 93, no. 4 (1988).

54 Naughton, *Danwei: The Economic Foundations of a Unique Institution*, p. 173.

55 'Guowuyuan pizhuan caizheng bu guanyu guoying qiye shixing qiye jijin de guiding' (State Council Transmits the Ministry of Finance 'Decision on the Establishment of Enterprise Funds in State-run Enterprises'), in *Tigai Huibian*, pp. 784–85.

56 Takahara, *The Politics of Wage Policy*, p. 84. The decision drafted by the Ministry of Finance also specifies different percentages of profit retention for different departments. For example, oil, electricity, and foreign trade departments were allowed only a 5 percent, while the percentage allowed for most of the other departments was 10 percent.

57 'Shangyebu caizhengbu guanyu zai shangyebu xitong shixing lirun liucheng banfa de tongzhi' (Ministry of Trade and Ministry of Finance Circular on Systematically Experimenting the Profit Retention System), 16 March 1979, in *Tigai Huibian*, pp. 791–94.
58 'Guowuyuan pizhuan guojia jingwei, guowuyuan tizhi gaige ban-gongshi, guanyu gongye guanli tizhi gaige zuotanhui huibao tigang de tongzhi' (State Council Circular to Make Public the Report by the State Economic Commission and the Office for Economic Reform of the State Council on the 'Conference on the Reform of Industrial Management'), 1 April 1981, in *Tigai Huibian*, pp. 223–44.
59 'Guowuyuan pizhuan guanyu shixing gongye shengchan jingji zeren-zhi ruogan wenti de zanxing guiding de tongzhi' (State Council Circular on 'Provisional Regulations on Implementing the Economic Responsibiliy System in Industry), 1 November 1981, in *Tigai Huibian*, pp. 276–79.
60 Ibid., p. 276.
61 The best account of the conflicts within units during the re-implementation of bonuses and piece-rate wages is Takahara, *The Politics of Wage Policy*, pp. 143–56.

CHAPTER 4

1 Feng Lanrui, personal written communication, 1 February 1996.
2 'Laodong renshibu guanyu jiji shixing laodong hetong zhi de tongzhi' (Ministry of Labour and Personnel Communiqué on Actively Implementing the Labour Contract System), 22 February 1983, in *Tigai Huibian*, pp. 1079–80.
3 'Laodong renshibu banfa guanyu zhaogong kaohe ze you lüyong de zanxing guiding de tongzhi' (Communiqué on the Ministry of Personnel Methods on 'Temporary Decision on Workers' Selection'), 25 February 1983, in *Tigai Huibian*, pp. 1081–82.
4 As is well known, special economic zones are regions or areas where special regulations on investment, taxation, and labour favour the investment of foreign capitals thus boosting the economy of China's coastal provinces.
5 'Guojia laodong zongju yinfa guanyu zhaogong shixing quanmian kaohe de yijian de tongzhi' (Communiqué of the National Labour Bureau on 'Ideas on Implementing Worker Selection'), 9 March 1979, in *Tigai Huibian*, p. 1021.
6 This statement represents a formal recognition of the right of each worker at his retirement age to decide on the employment of at least one child. For a discussion of this point see Deborah Davis, 'Urban Job Mobility,' in Davis and Vogel (eds.), *Chinese Society on the Eve of Tiananmen*.
7 The term *chuantong zhidu* (traditional system), is commonly used to refer to prereform period.
8 Liu Qintang, 'Laodong zhidu gaige wenti tantao' (On the Problems of Reforming the Labour System), *Jingji wenti tansuo*, no. 8 (1984).
9 Xue Yongying, 'Shengchanli yinsu lun' (A Theory of Production Factors), *Jingji Yanjiu*, no. 8 (1984), p. 66.

10 Jin Bu, 'Laodong li liudong tansuo' (On Labour Mobility), *Jingji wenti tansuo*, n.5 (1984), p. 23.

11 Ibid., p. 24.

12 Ibid., p. 26.

13 Liu Qintang, 'Laodong zhidu gaige wenti tantao,' p. 15.

14 Ibid., p. 15.

15 Ibid., p. 16.

16 Ceng Bizhong, 'Lun laodong fuwu gongsi zai laodong jiuye gongzuo zhong de zuoyong' (On the Role of LSCs in Employment Work), *Jingji wenti tansuo*, no. 7 (1984).

17 The housekeeper market (*baomu shichang*) mainly involves rural women lining up along some streets in Beijing to seek temporary and unregistered jobs with urban families. This has been used as an example of the anarchy of the market.

18 Zhang Yide, 'Kaifang laodong li shichang yu laodong li guanli tizhi gaige' (The Opening Up of a Labour Force Market and the Reform of Labour Force Management), *Jingji wenti tansuo*, no. 1 (1986).

19 For some names of these agencies, see ibid., p. 72.

20 Ibid., p. 73.

21 Jia Guangcai and Zhou Lijin, 'Establishing Labor Markets, Improving Labor Management: Meeting Held in Beijing to Discuss Labour Market Issues, *Jingjixue zhoubao*, 19 January 1986, translated in JPRS-CEA-86–047.

22 Kornai, *Economics of Shortage*. The book appeared in Chinese in 1986. See also Zhang Zhonghua, *Gaobie duanque* (Away From Shortage). Beijing: Zhongguo caizheng jingji chubanshe, 1998.

23 Luo Shouchu, 'Laodong li liudong he laodong zhidu gaige chuyi.'

24 Ibid., p. 61.

25 For an application of the analysis based on the softness of the budget constraint to the issue of labour and wages, see Kornai, *Economics of Shortage*, esp. chap. 16.

26 Luo Shouchu, 'Laodong li liudong he laodong zhidu gaige chuyi.'

27 See for example, Liu Qintang, 'Laodong zhidu gaige wenti tantao.'

28 The following articles are just some examples of the huge debate on this topic, covering a large range of positions: Ceng Nanjie, 'Shehui zhuyi laodong li shangpin xingzhi de biran xing ji qi lilun de shijian yiyi' (The Real Theoretical Meaning of the Commodity Nature of Socialist Labour), *Jingji wenti tansuo*, no. 3 (1987); Chen Xiuhua, 'Laodong li shangpin de jige zhuyao lilun wenti' (Some Major Theoretical Points on the Commodity Nature of Labour), *Jingji wenti tansuo*, no. 5 (1987); Deng Youping, 'Laodong li zhi lun' (On the Labour Force), *Jingji wenti tansuo*, no. 2 (1984), He Ganqiang, 'A Brief Discussion of the Causes and Forms of the Flow of Labor Force,' *Guangming ribao*, 20 September 1986, translated in JPRS-CEA 86–116; Jiang Chenglong, 'Shehui zhuyi jingji zhong cunzai laodong li chengwei shangpin de tiaojian' (In the Socialist Economy Conditions Still Exist for Labour to Become a Commodity), *Zhongguo shehui kexue*, no. 1 (1987); Li Ke, 'Shilun shehui zhuyi tiaojian xia laodong li chengwei shangpin de biran xing' (On the Need to Consider Labour as a Commodity Under Socialism), *Jingji wenti tansuo*, no. 4 (1987);

Ma Conglin, 'Dui laodong li shangpin lun ruogan lundian de zhiyi' (Some Theoretical Points on the Theory of the Commodity Nature of Labour), *Zhongguo shehui kexue*, no.1 (1987); Wang Jue and Xiao Xin, 'More on the Labor Resources Market: A Reply to Comrade Han Zhiguo' *Guangming ribao*, 26 November 1986, translated in JPRS-CEA 87–005; Wei Ming, 'Woguo xian jieduan bixu rang laodong li caiqu shangpin de xingshi heli liudong' (At the Present Stage China Should Allow Labour to Float as a Commodity), *Jingji wenti tansuo*, no. 3 (1987); Wei Xinghua, 'Shehui zhuyi laodong li shangpin lun bu neng chengli' (The Theory of the Commodity Nature of Labour is Groundless), *Zhongguo shehui kexue*, no.1 1987; Wei Xinghua, 'A Brief Comment on the Theory that Socialist Labor is a Commodity,' *Guangming ribao*, 27 September 1986, translated in JPRS-CEA 86–118; Zhou Wenfu, 'Guanyu chuantong de shehui zhuyi laodong li fei shangpin lun de lilun fansi' (Against the Traditional Theory that Socialist Labour is not a Commodity), *Jingji wenti tansuo*, no. 2 (1987).

29 Wang Jue and Xiao Xin, 'More on the Resources Market.'

30 For a very confusing attempt to summarize these options see Gao Wenhan and Gao Mianhou, 'Do Labour Markets Exist Under Socialism? – A Summary of Recent Discussions,' *Jingjixue zhoubao*, 8 March 1987, translated in JPRS-CEA 87–026.

31 He Wei and Han Zhiguo, 'Shilun woguo shehui zhuyi shichang de quan fangwei kaifang' (Discussion of the Opening of a Socialist Market in China), *Zhongguo shehui kexue*, no.2 (1986). Emphasis added.

32 Ma Conglin, 'Dui laodong li shangpin lun ruogan lundian de zhiyi,' p. 35.

33 Wei Xinghua, 'Shehui zhuyi laodong li shangpin lun bu neng chengli.'

34 Wei Xinghua, 'A Brief Comment on the Theory that Socialist Labour is a Commodity.' Emphasis added.

35 Ceng Nanjie, 'Shehui zhuyi laodong li shangpin xingzhi ji qi lilun de shijian yiyi.'

36 Wei Xinghua, 'A Brief Comment on the Theory that Socialist Labour is a Commodity.'

37 As we shall see, the issue was no longer 'officially' problematic after 1992. But at a 1995 conference in Beijing, I witnessed a long and heated discussion on this question.

38 Cao Shengde and Wang Yuejin, 'Shixing laodong hetongzhi haochu hen duo, wenti bu shao' (There are Many Merits and Problems in Implementing the Labour Contract System), *Jingji Guanli*, no. 12 (December 1986).

39 Ibid.

40 Hu Qili, 'Zhengque renshi laodong zhidu de gaige' (Thoroughly Understand the Reform of the Labour System), *Hongqi*, no. 19 (1986), pp. 10–15. Emphasis added.

41 It is interesting to note that once labour became an economic and productive factor, its economic evaluation became based on 'cost.'

42 Luo Shouchu, 'Laodong li liudong he laodong zhidu gaige chuyi,' p. 67.

43 Ibid., p. 68.

CHAPTER 5

1 Hu Sheng, *A concise History of the Communist Party of China*. Beijing: Foreign Languages Press, 1994, p. 768 (emphasis added). Hu Sheng is the director of the Party History Research Center of CCP Central Committee and a former President of CASS.

2 Ibid., p. 768.

3 Foti and Christiansen, 'Transition from the Public to the Private.'

4 'Zhonghua renmin gongheguo zhongwai hezi jingying qiye laodong guanli guiding' (PRC Regulations on Labour Management in Sino-Foreign Enterprises), 26 July 1980, in Li Baiyong and Yuan Shouqi (eds.) *Laodong fa quanshu* (A Comprehensive Book on Labour Law) (hereafter *LDFQS*). Beijing: Yuhang chubanshe, pp. 312–313.

5 'Laodong renshibu guanyu jiji shixing laodong hetong zhi de tongzhi' (Ministry of Labour and Personnel Circular on Actively Experimenting with a Labour Contract System), 22 February 1983, in *Tigai Huibian*, pp. 1079–80.

6 Ibid. p. 1079.

7 'Laodong renshibu fenfa guanyu zhaogong kaohe zeyou lüyong de zanxing guiding de tongzhi' (Ministry of Labour and Personnel Circular on the Provisional Regulations for Recruiting, Testing, and Selection of Workers), 25 February 1983, in *Tigai Huibian*, pp. 1081–82.

8 The circular prohibited the practice of *neizhao* 'unless otherwise explicitly stated in the directives of the Central Commitee or State Council.' Ibid., p. 1081.

9 In 1991 there were 2.16 million contracts and 3.63 million recruits in the state sector. See *CLSYB-95*, pp. 8 and 471. A possible explanation for this trend may be related to the deepening of the reform process in Chinese SOEs after 1992, the reduction in number of new recruits in this sector, and the high number of dismissals from bad performing enterprises, that enlarged the availability and the forced mobility of workers, including also of those with a permanent status.

10 Calculated from *CLSYB-95*, p. 8.

11 'Guoying qiye shixing laodong hetongzhi zanxing guiding' (Provisional Regulations on the Establishment of the Labour Contract System in State-Run Enterprises), 12 July 1986, in *LDFQS*, pp. 223–25.

12 This is not allowed for temporary workers (*lunhuang gong*), whose contract cannot be formally extended (*xuding*).

13 The classification of labour contracts became more accurate and systematic after the 1995 labour law. At that time local governments were invited to produce a standard contract for different types of employment and employing units. See: Zhu Wenzhou and Wang Faxing, *Laodong hetong zhizuo ji wenben shifan* (The System of Labour Contract and Model Forms). Beijing: Falü chubanshe, 1999.

14 'Guoying qiye citui weiji zhigong zanxing guiding' (Provisional Regulations on the Dismissal of Workers Violating Discipline Norms in State Run Enterprises), 12 July 1986, in *LDFQS*, pp. 233–34.

15 For a translation of this document see Xinhua News Agency, 'Provisional Regulations on Government Unemployment Insurance

for State Owned Enterprises,' 12 July 1986, translated in JPRS-CEA 86–109.

16 Ibid., p. 80.

17 Political rights within the enterprise were among the claims of contract workers during unrests in the 1950s.

18 Xiao Yin, 'How to Implement Reforms in the Labour System,' *Jingji daobao*, 1 October 1986, translated in JPRS-CEA 86–124.

19 'Guoying qiye zhaoyong gongren zanxing guiding (Regulations Concerning the Recruitment of Workers in State-Run Enterprises), 12 July 1986, in *LDFQS*, pp. 225–26.

20 Ng and Warner, *China's Trade Unions and Management*, p. 67.

21 Ibid., p. 223.

22 Literally 'diving into the sea,' the expression is used to describe leaving the security of the state sector to enter individual or contract employment in the private sector.

23 Mallee, 'China's Household Registration System under Reform.' Similar cycles of encouragement and discouragement characterized the action of local bureaucracies during the 1990s with respect to the non-*hukou* population. See Solinger, *Contesting Citizenship*.

24 Mallee, 'China's Household Registration System under Reform,' p. 14. For some previous trial reforms of the *hukou* system see also Solinger, 'Temporary residence regulations in Wuhan, May 1983.'

25 Kam Wing Chan, 'Internal Migration in China: A Dualistic Approach,' in Frank Pieke and Hein Mallee (eds.), *Internal and International Migration: Chinese Perspectives*. London, Curzon Press, 1999.

26 Ibid.

27 It is noteworthy that the low number of 'contract system workers' (*hetong zhi* gong) in 1987 may have been due to the change in the official label to 'contract workers' after the implementation of 1986 regulations.

28 Zhu Wenzhou and Wang Faxing, *Laodong hetong zhizuo ji wenben shifan*, p. 259–61. Quite interestingly, this is the only type of contract that still requires that workers show a 'good political record' and that the employer carry out political education.

29 As we saw, contract workers, although less protected in SOEs, were considered 'in the plan' employment.

30 Feng Lanrui, *Lun Zhongguo laodongli shichang*, pp. 36–37. This common notion among Chinese and foreign observers is partly confirmed by official data but may be less true with the passing of time and the further restrictions on employment opportunities in the formal sector.

31 Sargeson, *Reworking China's Proletariat*, p. 35.

32 Ng and Warner, *China's Trade Unions and Management*, p. 67.

33 Sargeson, *Reworking China's Proletariat*, pp. 71–102; Hebel and Schucher, *Die Reform der Drei Eisernen*.

34 Sargeson, *Reworking China's Proletariat*, pp. 78–82.

35 Korzec, *Labour and the Failure of Reform*.

36 Lee, 'Pathways of labour insurgency,' p. 47.

37 Zhongguo Xinwen she, *Serious Misuse of Talented People in Shanghai*, 1 December 1986, translated in JPRS-CEA 86–126.

38 Zhao Lijuan, 'Talent Exchange Centers Enjoy Little Success,' *China Daily*, 25 June 1987.
39 Initially contract employment did not include high school or university students who remained under the state allocation system until 1988.
40 Hebel and Schucher, 'From Unit to Enterprise? The Chinese *Tan-wei* in the Process of Reform,' *Issues and Studies*, no. 27 (1991); See also Korzec, *Labour and the Failure of Reform*.
41 See for example: Howard, *Rice Bowls and Job Security*; Sargeson, *Reworking China's Proletariat*, pp. 125–48; Sheehan, *Chinese Workers*; Lee, *Pathways of Labour Insurgency*.
42 Ibid. pp. 46–47.
43 *CLSYB-95*, p. 41.
44 Andrew Walder and Gong Xiaoxia, 'Workers in the Tian'an Men Protest,' *Australian Journal of Chinese Affairs*, no. 29 (January 1993) and Sheehan, *Chinese Workers*.
45 Xu Haibo, 'Popularization of the Labor Contract System not Advisable,' *Zhongqingnian jingji luntan*, 10 January 1987, translated in JPRS-CEA 87–27.
46 This author seems to be more comfortable with the Japanese and Korean systems as they maintain an identification between workers and the interests of the enterprise. Ibid., p. 68.
47 See in particular Anita Chan, 'Labour Relations in Foreign Funded Ventures, Chinese Trade Unions and the Prospects for Collective Bargaining,' in Greg O'leary (ed.), *Adjusting to Capitalism: China's Workers and the State*. Armonk: M.E. Sharpe, 1998.
48 Xu Haibo, 'Popularization of the Labour Contract System not Advisable.'

CHAPTER 6

1 'Zhonghua renmin gongheguo gonghui fa' (Trade Union Law of the PRC), in *LDFQS*, pp. 455–57. The previous law had been approved in 1950.
2 'Zhonghua renmin gongheguo funü quanyi baozhang fa' (PRC Law on the Protection of Women's Rights), in *LDFQS*, pp. 458–60.
3 The Law was approved by the eighth session of the Standing Committee of the National People's Congress on 5 July 1994, and became effective on 1 January 1995.
4 Dai Yuanchen, *Zhongguo laodong li shichang peiyu yu gongzi gaige* (The Emergence of a Labour Market and Wage Reform in China). Beijing: Zhongguo laodong chubanshe, 1994.
5 For the most recent and relevant studies see, for example, Zhao Shukai, *Zongheng chengxiang: Nongmin liudong de guancha yu yanjiu* (Between City and Countryside: Observation and Research on the Peasant Floating Population). Beijing: Zhongguo nongye chubanshe, 1998; Zhongguo kexueyuan, guoqing fenxi yanjiu xiaozu (Research Group on the National Situation of the Academy of Sciences), *Jiuye yu fazhan* (Employment and Development). Shenyang: Liaoning renmin chubanshe, 1998; Zou Lanchun, *Beijing*

de liudong renkou (Beijing's Floating Population), Beijing: Zhongguo renkou chubanshe, 1996; Yang Shaoming and Zhou Yihu, *Zhongguo danwei zhidu* (China's Work-unit System). Beijing: Zhongguo jingji chubanshe, 1999; Wang Dahai, *Shiye de zhongguo* (China Unemployed). Beijing: Jingji ribao chubanshe, 1999; Yuan Yue, Wang Xin and Zhang Shouli, *Beijing wailai renkou zhong de quanwei* (Leadership among Migrants in Beijing). Beijing: Horizon, unpublished report, 1996; Zhang Jing (ed.), *Guojia yu shehui* (State and Society). Hangzhou: Zhejiang renmin chubanshe, 1998; Gong Wei, *Laodong li waichu jiuye yu nongcun shehui bianqian* (Migrant Labourers and Social Changes in Rural Areas). Beijing: Wenwu chubanshe, 1999.

6 Sargeson, *Reworking China's Proletariat*, p. 22.
7 Ibid., p. 22.
8 Gao and Gao, 'Do Labour Markets exist under socialism?'
9 Ibid., p. 59.
10 Interview with the author, June 1995.
11 Feng Lanrui, et al. (eds), *Lun Zhongguo laodong li shichang*, pp. 2–3.
12 Oskar Ryszard Lange (born in Tomaszov in 1904, died in London in 1965), a Polish economist educated in the United States, held important positions in the post-war Polish government. A Keynesian economist, he was one of the founders of econometrics. He studied the determination of prices in socialst, non-marketized economies, and the problem of the optimum allocation of resources in socialist economies. His major work, *On the Economic Theory of Socialism*, was published in English in 1938 (Minneapolis, Minn: University of Minnesota Press). It is possible that the revival of Lange among Chinese economists in these years was due to Kornai's evaluation of his work as one of the early fathers of 'market socialism.'
13 Dai Yuanchen, *Zhongguo laodongli shichang peiyu yu gongzi gaige*, p. 6.
14 In the paper quoted in the next footnote Dai and Li quite interestingly analyse Engels *Anti Dühring* as if it were an example of high liberalism, founding their idea of free participation to the market economy on the basis of the work of one of the fathers of socialism! Somewhere there must be a misunderstanding!
15 Dai Yuanchen and Li Hanming [Elizabeth Li], 'Zhongguo laodong ziyuan peizhi fangshi de fazhan bianhua' (The Changes and Development of the Modes of Allocation of Labour Factor in China), paper presented at the CASS Beijing Conference on the Labour market, August 1995.
16 Quoted as in Pat and Roger Howard, 'The Campaign to Eliminate Job Security in China,' *Journal of Contemporary Asia*, vol. 25, no. 3 (1995), p. 348. Dai Yuanchen, 'Recognizing Labour Power as a Commodity is a Pre-requisite for Fostering the Labour Market,' *Jingji Yanjiu*, no.3 (March 1993). The same argument is made in Dai's later: *Zhongguo laodong li shichang peiyu yu gongzi gaige*, especially in the opening section *Peiyu laodongli shichang bixu chengren laodong li shi shangpin* (To Open a Labour Market we have to Admit that Labour Force is a Commodity), pp. 3–19.

17 Dai Yuanchen, *Zhongguo laodongli shichang peiyu yu gongzi gaige*, p. 177.

18 Du Haiyan, 'Guoyou qiye de jiuye zhidu gaige de lilun sikao' (Theoretical Thoughts on Reform of the Employment System in State-Owned Enterprises), *Jingji Yanjiu*, no. 1 (January 1993), pp. 26–33. As cited in Howard and Howard, 'The Campaign to Eliminate Job Security,' p. 349.

19 Ibid., p. 350.

20 The conference was held at Fudan University in September 1988 and was sponsored by the CATO Institute and the Fudan University American Research Center. The foreign participants included: Milton Friedman, James Dorn, Don Lavoie, Peter Bernholz, George Selgin, Christine Wallich, John P. Powelson, Gabriel Roth, Thomas R. Dye, John Greenwood, Edward Olsen, David Lampton, Ted Galen Carpenter, Alvin Rabushka, William Niskanen, and George Gilder. The papers and transcripts of the discussion at the conference were not published in China until five years later in 1994, probably due to the restrictions on publications after the 1989 student movement: Wang Xi and Tu En [James Dorn], *Zhongguo jingji gaige: wenti yu qianjing*. The English version was published in 1990 under the auspices of the so-called 'Chicago School' (Chicago: Chicago University Press).

21 One example might be the experience of the Economics Research Center at Beijing University, where a generation of returned Ph.D. holders is taking over most of the training activity in economics. In summer 1995, president Jiang Zemin told a group of Chinese economists based in the United States (off the record) that he had read Friedman's works and he did not see anything wrong with them. A survey of reference lists in recent Chinese publications in the field of economics would probably map the paths through which this influence is taking shape. I refer here to only one collective work that contains many references to foreign economic literature: Beijing Daxue Zhongguo Jingji Yanjiu Zhongxin (Research Center on the Chinese Economy at Beijing University), *Jingji xue yu Zhongguo jingji gaige* (Economics and Economic Reform in China). Shanghai: Shanghai renmin chubanshe, 1995.

22 Zhou Tianyong, *Laodong yu jingji zengzhang* (Labour and Economic Growth). Shanghai: Shanghai renmin chubanshe, 1994.

23 Korzec notes the emergence of such positions prior to 1989. Korzec, *Labour and the Failure of Reform*.

24 Li Jingwen, *Zou xiang ershiyi shiji de Zhongguo jingji* (The Chinese Economy Towards the Twenty First Century). Beijing: Jingji guanli chubanshe, 1995. p. 404.

25 Hou Yufu, 'Kaifang laodong li shichang yudao de jige lilun renshi wenti' (Some Theoretical Problems Encountered in the Process of Opening Up a Labour Market), in Feng Lanrui, et al (eds.), *Lun zhongguo de laodongli shichang*, pp. 185.

26 Feng Lanrui, 'Woguo de laodongli shichang shi tongyi de you kong de laodongli shichang' (China's Labour Market is a Unitary and Controlled Labour Market), in Feng Lanrui, et al (eds.), *Lun zhongguo laodong li shichang*, pp. 196–97.

27 Li Hanming and Dai Yuanchen, 'Shuanggui tizhi gongzi shouru ji qi dui laodong li gongxu de tiaojie' (Wage Income and its Regulatory Function of Labour Demand and Supply Under the Double Track System), paper presented at the CASS Beijing Conference on the Labour market, August 1995.

28 Feng Tongqing, *Zhihua zhishou yu jizeng gonghui zhuxi tantan xin* (Speak without Reservations: Heart to Heart Talks with Grassroots Trade Union Leaders). Beijing: Jingji guanli chubanshe, 1994. The quotation is taken from a translation of the most significant parts of the book, presented in: Feng Tongqing and Zhao Minghua (eds.), 'Workers and Trade Unions under the Market Economy: Perspectives from Grassroots Union Cadres,' *Chinese Sociology and Anthropology* vol. 28, no. 3 (Spring 1996).

29 The ACFTU was banned as a consequence of Liu Shaoqi's purge in 1966. Liu's power base was in the unions and he was accused of pursuing economicism through them.

30 Ng and Warner, *China's Trade Unions and Management*, pp. 102–3.

31 'Zhonghua renmin gongheguo gonghui fa,' art. 6.

32 Collective labour contracts were officially introduced in the 1994 labour law.

33 Significatively, the regulation in the 1994 labour law concerning collective contracts allows workers in enterprises where no established trade union exist to elect (*tuiju*) their representatives to sign the collective contract (we can infer that this concerns enterprises with less then twenty-five employees, the minimum number required to establish a trade union affiliated with the ACFTU).

34 'Zhonghua renmin gongheguo qiye laodong zhengyi chuli tiaoli' (PRC Regulations on the Resolution of Labour Disputes in Enterprises), Zhonghua renmin gongheguo guowuyuan lingdi 117 hao (PRC State Council Order no. 117), 6 July 1993, in *LDFQS*, pp. 762–64. The set of regulations accompanying this order have been collected and published in different forms. Refer for example to: *Laodong zhengyi shenpan shouce* (Judicial Handbook on Labour Disputes). Beijing: Falü chubanshe, 1994, pp. 639–43, or Guo Jun, et al. (eds.), *Laodong fa yu laodong zhengyi shiyong shouce* (Handbook of Labour Law and Labour Disputes). Beijing: Zhongguo jiancha chubanshe, 1994, pp. 582–88.

35 Ibid., art. 2. It is well known that high level levels of unionization in SOEs largely are due to the fact that unions are often the organisers of cultural or recreational activities for their members.

36 Chiang Chen-chang (Jiang Zhenzhang), 'The role of Trade Unions in Mainland China,' *Issues and Studies* vol. 26, no. 2 (February 1990), pp. 75–98.

37 Ibid. See also my 'Operai in un paese di contadini: un caso di conflittualità operaia nella Cina contemporanea,' *Società e Storia*, no. 63 (1994).

38 See, for example, Walder and Gong, 'Workers in the Tiananmen Protest: The Politics of the Beijing Workers Autonomous Federation;' Anita Chan, 'Revolution or Corporatism? Workers and Trade Unions in Post-Mao China,' *Australian Journal of Chinese Affairs*, no. 29 (January 1993); Sheehan, *Chinese workers*.

39 Anita Chan, 'Revolution or Corporatism?'
40 Ibid.
41 This is ILO convention number 144. China signed the convention in 1976. Ng and Warner, *China's Trade Unions and Management*, p. 75.
42 Feng and Zhao (eds.), *Workers and Trade Unions under the Market Economy*.
43 Ibid., p. 59.
44 Shen Qinqin, 'Lun jiuye zhidaodui shengchan li fazhan de zujin zuoyong' (On the Positive Effects of Guided Employment on the Development of Productive Forces), *Gonghui lilun yu shixian*, no. 1 (1995).
45 Guo Jun, et al. (eds.), *Laodong fa yu laodong zhengyi shiyong shouce*, p. 2.
46 Huo Qimai, 'Lun gonghui zai shishi laodong fa zhong de diwei he zuoyong' (The Role and Position of Trade Unions in the Process of Implementing the 'Labour Law'), *Gonghui lilun yu shixian*, no. 1 (1995), pp. 27–29.
47 Feng Tongqing and Zhao Minghua (eds.), 'Workers and Trade Unions under the Market Economy.'
48 Art. 33 of the 1994 labour law. See *LDFQS*, p. 5.
49 Art. 18 of the 1992 trade union law'. See *LDFQS*, p. 455.
50 Bao Jianbing and Zhu Cong, 'Gongbao hetongzhi shi banhao gongyouzhi qiye de youxiao zhidu' (The Collective Contract is the Method to Positively Solve the Issue of SOEs), *Gonghui lilun yu shixian*, no. 1 (1995), p. 30.
51 Ng and Warner, *China's Trade Unions and Management*, p. 91.
52 Wang Dahai, Shiye de zhongguo, p. 3 and p. 1

EPILOGUE

1 Dorothy Solinger discusses M.J. Piore dual market that regards informalisation as a characteristic only of second markets. *Contesting Citizenship*, pp. 203–4.
2 Zhao Shukai, *Zongheng chengxiang*, pp. 33–34.
3 Thanks are due to Professor Dai Yuanchen and Zhu Jianfang for sharing both reports and raw data from the survey 'Zhongguo laodong li shichang peiyu yu gongzi gaige' (The Labour Force Market and Wage Reform in China), presented on the occasion of an international workshop organised by the Institute of Economics of CASS (August 1995) in Beijing. The 1992 survey collected information from 438 enterprises with different ownership structures and in different industries, as well as from 9,432 staff and workers who were interviewed individually. I will hereafter refer to the survey as 'Labour Market Survey'
4 'Labour Market Survey'; see also Zhu Jianfang, Dai Yuanchen and Chen Dongqi, 'Zhongguo laodong li shichang peiyu yu gongzi gaige (tongji baogao)' (Labour Force Market and Wage Reform in China – Statistical Report), unpublished paper presented at the Beijing Labour Market Conference in 1995.
5 Guojia tongji ju (State Statistical Bureau), *Zhongguo tongji nianjian 1995* (China Statistical Yearbook). Beijing: Tongji chubanshe, 1996.

6 'Labour Market Survey.'
7 *CLSYB-95*, p. 7.
8 Huang Weiding, *Zhongguo de yinxing jingji* (China's Shadow Economy). Beijing: Shangye chubanshe, 1996, 2nd edition, pp. 91–92.
9 The data on individual deposits testify to constant growth in recent years, up to 3.33 trillion RMB in 1996. *The Economist Intelligence Unit, Country Report: China and Mongolia*, 2nd quarter 1996, p. 38. In a period of large demand for capital for the restructuring of the state industrial sector (as in the 1990s), and of deep reform of public financial institutions, the role of private savings is central to China's development strategy.
10 Huang Weiding, *Zhongguo de yinxing jingji*, pp. 91–94.
11 Zhongguo laodong bu zhengce fagui si (Department of Policy and Law, Ministry of Labour), *Zhongguo dier zhiye wenti* (China's Second Job Problem). Beijing: Zhongguo laodong chubanshe, 1991, pp. 9–10.
12 Guo Yuanxi, *Zhongguo dier zhiye* (China's Second Jobs). Chengdu: Xinan caijing chubanshe, 1997, p. 10.
13 By the 'Central Commitee Decision on the Reform of Scientific and Technological Sectors' (*Zhonggong zhongyang kexue jishu tizhi gaige de jueding*). See Guojia renshibu liudong diaopei si (State Personnel Department, Mobility Section), *Zhongguo rencai liudong zhengce fagui daquan* (Collection of Policy Documents on Talent Exchange in China). Beijing: Jingji guanli chubanshe, 1993. p. 246 (hereafter *Zhongguo rencai*).
14 Zhongguo laodong bu zhengce fagui si (Department of Policy and Law, Ministry of Labour), *Zhongguo di er zhiye wenti*, p. 10.
15 'Guowuyuan bangong ting zhuanfa guojia kewei guanyu keji renyuan yeyu jianzhi ruogan wenti de yi jian' (Ideas from the State Council Office on Some Problems Concerning Extra-Time Second Employment of Technical Personnel), Guoban fa, 1988, in *Zhongguo rencai*, pp. 246–48.
16 Zhongguo laodong bu zhengce fagui si, *Zhongguo dier zhiye wenti*, p. 11 and *CLSYB-95*, p. 38.
17 Namely, the 1990 census and the 1987 1 percent population survey. Kam Wing-Chan, 'Internal Migration in China: A Dualistic Approach.'
18 For a complete summary of the estimates on the floating population see Solinger, *Contesting Citizenship*, pp. 19–20.
19 Kam Wing-Chan, 'Post-Mao China: A Two-Class Urban Society in the Making,' *International Journal of Urban and Regional Research*, vol. 20, n. 1 (1996), p. 140.
20 Huang Weiding, *Zhongguo de yinxing jingji*, 2nd edition, p. 65. Huang probably is referring to Beijing proper as the estimate of the greater Beijing popoulation exceeds 12 million. A survey by the State Planning Commission in 1994 quotes substantially similar data (3.295 million floaters with a registered population of 10.628 million). Zou Lanchun, *Beijing liudong renkou*.
21 Huang Weiding, *Zhongguo de yinxing jingji*, 2nd edition, p. 65.
22 Ma and Xiang, *Native Place, Migration and the Emergence of Peasant Enclaves in Beijing*.

23 Lee, *From Organized Dependence to Disorganized Despotism*, p. 44.
24 Zou Lanchun also notes, among the advantages for the local population, 'an increasing availability of services' in the city (repair shop, small restaurant, housekeeping...) Zou Lanchun, *Beijing Liudong Renkou*, p. 102.
25 Solinger, *Contesting Citizenship*, pp. 178–82, points out how the export of labour became an economically relevant activity for some local bureaucrats.
26 Ibid., pp. 52–53.
27 Ma and Xiang, *Native Place, Migration and the Emergence of Peasant Enclaves in Beijing*.
28 Zhao Shukai, *Zongheng chengxiang*, pp. 168–169.
29 Ibid., p. 168
30 Ibid., p. 170
31 Zou Lanchun, *Beijing liudong renkou*; Ma and Xiang, *Native Place, Migration and the Emergence of Peasant Enclaves in Beijing*.
32 Yuan Yue, Wang Xin and Zhang Shouli, 'Beijing de wailai jianzhu baogong dui' (The Migrant Labour Construction Teams in Beijing), unpublished Horizon Research Group report, Beijing: 1996.
33 Victor Yuan and Xing Wong, 'Migrant Construction Teams in Beijing,' in Pieke and Mallee (eds.), *Native Place, Migration and Internal and International Migration: Chinese Perspectives*.
34 Estimates vary considerably but generally never exceed the monetary wages of formal workers (399 RMB in SOEs, 270 RMB in COEs, and 525 RMB in POEs, monthly in 1994), while requiring much longer working hours under worse conditions.
35 Zhao Shukai, *Zongheng chengxiang*, p. 13.
36 Huang Weiding, *Zhongguo de yinxing jingji*, 2nd edition, p. 2.
37 Wang Xin, Yuan Yue and Zhang Shouli, 'Beijing wailai renkou zhong de quanwei.'
38 Yuan and Wong, 'Migrant Construction Teams in Beijing,' p. 117.
39 Gong Wei, *Laodong li waichu jiuye yu nongcun shehui bianqian* (Migrant Labourers and Social Changes in Rural Areas). Beijing: Wenwu chubanshe, 1999.
40 Solinger, *Contesting Citizenship*, p. 211.
41 Huang Weiding, *Zhongguo de yinxing jingji*, pp. 68–70.
42 Zhao Shukai, *Zongheng chengxiang*, p. 13.
43 Solinger, *Contesting Citizenship*, p. 214.
44 Zhao Shukai, Zongheng chengxiang, cit. p. 171
45 *CLSYB-95*, p. 502.
46 Yuan Yue, Wang Xin and Zhang Shouli, *Beijing de wailai jianzhu baogong dui*, p. 3.
47 Huang Weiding, *Zhongguo de yinxing jingji*, 2nd ed., pp. 69–70.
48 Yuan Yue, Wang Xin and Zhang Shouli, *Beijing de wailai jianzhu baogongdui*.
49 The single largest collection of information on Zhejiang Village is the result of a project run by the Sociology Department of Beijing University; several authors, however, have pointed out the specificity of this experience. Migration from Zhejiang was one of the foci of a European Science Foundation-sponsored conference held in

July 1996 in Oxford, entitled 'European Chinese and Chinese Domestic Migrants.' Proceedings are published in Pieke and Mallee (eds.), *Internal and International Migration: Chinese Perspectives*. See also Ma and Xiang, *Native Place, Migration and the Emergence of Peasant Enclaves in Beijing*, and Solinger, *Contesting Citizenship*.

50 Ma and Xiang report a population of 96,000 non-hukou migrants and 14,000 urban residents. See their *Native Place, Migration and the Emergence of Peasant Enclaves in Beijing*, p. 570.

51 Xiang Biao, 'Beijing you ge 'Zhejiang cun' (shang bian)' (There's a Zhejiang Village in Beijing – first part), *Shehui xue yu shehui diaocha*, no. 3 (1993), pp. 68–74. This is the first of a series of three articles with the same title. The following two parts (*zhongbian* and *xiabian*) appeared in the two subsequent issues of the same journal.

52 Some Zhejiang businessmen active in Beijing markets claim they are not related to the overall structure of economic activities concentrated in Zhejiang Village, meaning that Zhejiang Village is probably not the only organised presence of Zhejiang economic interests in the city.

53 The official data for output value was about US$ 200 million per year in 1995, but it is hardly computable due to the nature of production, and is probably related also to the growing 'export' of *Zhejiang cun* products to northern Chinese markets. Xiang Biao, 'Beijing you ge Zhejiang cun.'

54 Dorothy J. Solinger, 'The Floating Population in the Cities: Chances for Assimilation?' in Deborah Davis, et al. (eds.), *Urban Spaces in Contemporary China: The Potential for Community in Post-Mao China*. New York: Cambridge University Press, 1995.

55 Xiang Biao, 'Beijing you ge Zhejiang cun, zhong bian.'

56 Ibid.

57 Local informants, June 1995.

58 Liu, 'Reform from Below.'

59 The term is by Zhang Lizhi. See Huang Weiding, *Zhongguo de yinxing jingji*, 2nd edition, p. 78.

60 Families pay around 200 RMB per month per child, for a full day kindergarten service.

61 Xiang Biao, 'Beijing you ge Zhejiang cun'; Ma and Xiang 'Native Place, Migration and the Emergence of Peasant Enclaves in Beijing,' p. 571.

62 A major police raid on Zhejiang Village occurred in anticipation of the U.N. Women Conference that was held in Beijing in September 1995. During this raid, many workshops were closed and some compounds were razed. This was widely publicized by the local government, and similar interventions followed in other areas. Field visits, 1996. Before the recent celebration of the fiftieh anniversary of the PRC (October 1999) almost two million migrants allegedly were driven out of the capital. See also, Xiang Biao, 'Liudong, chuantong wangluo shichang hua yu 'feiguojia kongjian' (Mobility, Marketisation of Traditional Networks, and the 'Nonstate Space,' in Zhang Jing (ed.) *Guojia yu shehui* (State and Society). Hangzhou: Zhejiang renmin chubanshe, 1998.

63 Ma and Xiang, 'Native Place, Migration and the Emergence of Peasant Enclaves in Beijing,' p. 576.

64 Ibid. See also Wang Xin, Yuan Yue and Zhang Shouli, 'Beijing wailai renkou zhong de quanwei.'

65 Yuan Yue, Wang Xin and Zhang Shouli, 'Luoren: Beijing liumin de zuzhi hua zhuangkuang yanjiu baogao' (Naked: Research Report on the Organisation of Beijing Migrants), unpublished Horizon Research Group report, Beijing, December 1995.

66 Field visits and interviews, 1995 and 1996.

67 Field visits, 1999.

68 Yuan Yue, Wang Xin and Zhang Shouli, 'Luoren: Beijing liumin de zuzhi hua zhuangkuang yanjiu baogao,' pp. 77–115.

69 Ibid., p. 91.

70 *CLSYB-95*, p. 8.

71 Wang, *From Family to Market*, pp. 247–51.

72 'Tianjin rencai shichang zanxing banfa' (Provisional Method for Tianjin Municipality's Talent Markets), 17 April 1992, in *Zhongguo rencai*, pp. 46–47.

73 Reportedly, similar regulations were promulgated in other cities and provinces: Shandong, Jiangsu, Zhejiang, Inner Mongolia, Guizhou, and Chengdu (Sichuan). Ibid., pp. 47–64.

74 'Beijing shi rencai fuwu zhongxin jianjie' (Brief Introduction to Beijing Talent Service Center), Leaflet, 1996.

75 Interview, June 1995.

76 Interview, June 1995. The gender composition has recently shown an increasing number of women (from 35 percent in 1992 to 44 percent in 1995).

77 CLSYB 1995, p. 8. We can consider this only as a trend, as the overall data still report that about 73.5 percent of total urban employment is in the state-owned sector in 1994, with a lower proportion in the provinces where the high tide of private business occurred earlier, such as Zhejiang (58.9 percent), Jiangsu (62.7 percent), Fujian (62.3 percent) and Guangdong (63.1 percent). Ibid., p. 16.

78 *LDFQS*, p. 120.

79 Ibid., p. 121.

80 Guoyou qiye gaige yu fuyu zhigong fenliu keti, 'Guanyu Tianjin shi laodong li shichang fayu zhuangkuang' (Development and the Situation of the Labour Force Market in Tianjin), Commission for the Restructuring of the Economic System (CRES), unpublished report, 1995, p. 3. I thank Professor Guo Shuqing and his work group at the 'Comprehensive Department of CRES' for allowing me to participate in the discussions of the group and for making available to me the final reports.

81 *LDFQS*, pp. 120–21.

82 Guoyou qiye gaige yu fuyu zhigong fenliu keti, 'Guanyu Tianjin shi laodong li shichang fayu zhuangkuang.'

83 The high level of informatisation in Yichang apparently is boosted by the large flow of workers from the countryside attracted by the construction of the 'Three Gorges Dam' on the Yangzi River just northwest of Yichang.

84 Kristen Parris, 'Local Initiative and National Reform: The Wenzhou Model of Development,' *The China Quarterly*, no. 134 (June 1993).
85 See footnote 3 in this chapter.
86 'Labour Market Survey,' and Zhu Jianfang, Dai Yuanchen and Chen Dongqi, 'Zhongguo laodong li shichang peiyu yu gongzi gaige.' p. 27.
87 This probably will be an increasing mobility factor in the future, due to the growing dismissals of military personnel.
88 The data collected in the survey are from 1992. As mentioned, the number and proportion of contract workers increased greatly since 1994–95.
89 'Labour Market Survey.'
90 Zhao and Nichols, 'Management Control of Labour in State Owned Enterprises: Cases from the Textile Industry.'
91 Ibid., p. 1.
92 That is, Sundays and national holidays. In 1995 after approval of the labour law, a short working week (Monday through Friday) for all workers was implemented.
93 Zhao and Nichols, 'Management Control of Labour in State Owned Enterprises: Cases from the Textile Industry,' p. 19.
94 Guoyou qiye gaige yu fuyu zhigong fenliu keti, 'Guoyou qiye fuyu renyuan: xianzhuang, chengyin yu chulu' (Redundant Personnel in State-Owned Enterprises: Present Situation, Main Causes and Solutions), Commission for the Restructuring of the Economic System, unpublished report, 1995.
95 Ibid., pp. 6–7.
96 *CLSYB-95*, p. 511.
97 Wang Chengying, *Zhongguo zai jiuye*, pp. 5–7.
98 Zhongguo kexueyuan guoqing fenxi yanjiu xiaozu, *Jiuye yu fazhan*, pp. 161–162.
99 Ibid., p. 161.
100 Andrew Walder focuses on this change as a feature of the new 'paternalistic' approach of work-unit labour management as opposed to the earlier maoist 'ascetism' based on political struggle. Walder, *Communist Neo-traditionalism*, pp. 222–41.
101 'Labour Market Survey.'
102 Wang Chengying, *Zhongguo zai jiuye*, p. 10.
103 I refer to official statistics including only 'Staff and Worker' households, that is, those having at least one member working in SOEs or COEs.
104 *CLSYB-95*.
105 Walder, *Communist Neo-Traditionalism*, p. 43.
106 'Labour Market Survey.'
107 'Labour Market Survey.'
108 Min Zhou and John R. Logan, 'Market Transtition and the Commodification of Housing in Urban China,' *International Journal of Urban and Regional Research*, vol. 22, no. 3 (1996), p. 402.
109 Ibid., p. 403.
110 Bian Yanjie, John R. Logan, Lu Hanlong, Yunkang Pang, Ying Guan, 'Work-units and Housing Reform in Two Chinese Cities,' in Lü and Perry (eds.), *Danwei*.

111 Zhou and Logan, *Market Transtition and the Commodification of Housing in Urban China*, p. 416.
112 For example, houses can be sold by the state to the unit at a certain discount rate, and then further discounted once the unit offers it to the worker.
113 Anita Chan, 'Chinese Enterprises Reform: Convergence with the Japanese Model?,' in Barrett L. McCormick and Jonathan Unger (eds.), *China After Socialism: In the Footsteps of Eastern Europe or East Asia?* Armonk, N.Y.: M.E. Sharpe, 1996.
114 Guoyou qiye gaige yu fuyu zhigong fenliu keti, *Guanyu Tianjin shi laodong li shichang fayu zhuangkuang*, p. 4.
115 Wang Chengying, *Zhongguo zai jiuye*, pp. 5–7.
116 Ibid., p. 6.
117 Ibid., p. 10.
118 Ibid. p. 17.
119 Guoyou qiye gaige yu fuyu zhigong fenliu keti, 'Guanyu Tianjin shi laodong li shichang fayu zhuangkuang.'
120 Doug Guthrie, *Dragon in a Three-Piece Suit: The Emergence of Capitalism in China*, Princeton, Princeton University Press, 1999.
121 This was the estimate in a recent article in the official *Jingji Ribao* (Economic Daily), 7 July 1997.
122 Wu Jinglian, quoted in *South China Morning Post*, 27 August 1997.
123 See, for example, *Jingji ribao* (Economic Daily), 24 August 1997.
124 World Bank, *China Labour Market Development Project*, Staff Appraisal Report, November 1995.

BIBLIOGRAPHY

Adam, Jan ed. 1982. *Employment Policy in the Soviet Union and Eastern Europe*. London: Macmillan Press.

Aubert, Claude ed. 1986. *La societé chinoise après Mao: entre autorité et modernité*. Paris: Fayard.

Bakken, Børge, ed. 1997. *Migration in China*. Copenhagen: Nordic Institute of Asian Studies.

Bao, Jianbing and Zhu Cong. 1995. 'Gongbao hetongzhi shi banhao gongyouzhi qiye de youxiao zhidu' (The Collective Contract is the Method to Positively Solve the Issue of SOEs), *Gonghui lilun yu shixian* (Theory and Practice of Trade Unions), no. 1.

Barnett, Clough. 1986. *Modernizing China*. Boulder, CO: Westview Press.

Bauer J.,Wang F., Riley N.E., Zhao X.H. 1992. 'Gender Inequality in Urban China: Education and Employment,' *Modern China*, July, no.3.

Beijing daxue zhongguo jingji yanjiu zhongxin (Research Center on the Chinese Economy at Beijing University). 1995. *Jingji xue yu Zhongguo jingji gaige* (Economics and Economic Reform in China). Shanghai: Shanghai renmin chubanshe.

Beijing Jeep Plant Trade Union. 1985. 'No Change in Position of Staff Members and Workers Being Masters in their own House in Joint Venture Enterprises'. *Gongren ribao* [Worker's Daily]. October 23 (JPRS-CEA 86–074).

Bian, Yanjie. 1987. 'A Preliminary Analysis of the Basic Features of the Life-style of China's single-child Families,' *Social Sciences in China*. N. 3

— 1994. 'Guanxi and the Allocation of Urban Jobs in China,' *The China Quarterly*, n. 140.

— 1994b. *Work and Inequality in Urban China*. New York: New York University Press.

Blecher, Marc. 1991. 'The Contradictions of Grass-root Participation and Undemocratic Statism in Maoist China and their Fate.' In Brantly Womack, ed. *Contemporary Chinese Politics in Historical Perspective*. Cambridge: Cambridge University Press.

Blecher, Marc and Gordon White. 1979. *Micropolitics in Contemporary China*. White Plains: M.E. Sharpe.

Braverman, Harry. 1974. *Labor and Monopoly Capital: The Degradation of Work in the Twentieth Century*. New York: Monthly review press.

Burawoy, Michael. 1978. 'Toward a Marxist Theory of the Labour Process: Braverman and Beyond,' *Politics and Society*, vol. 8, n.3–4.

— 1985. *The Politics of Production*. London: Verso.

— 1992. 'A View from Production: the Hungarian Transition from Socialism to Capitalism'. In Smith and Thompson, eds., *Labour in Transition*.

Burawoy, Michael and Janos Lukacs. 1989. 'What is Socialist about Socialist Production? Authority and Control in a Hungarian Steel Mill'. In Wood, S., ed. *The Transformation of Work?* London: Unwin.

Burawoy, Michael and Janos Lukacs. 1992. *The Radiant Past: Ideology and Reality in Hungary's Road to Capitalism*. Chicago, Ill.: University of Chicago Press.

Cao, Shengde and Wang Yuejin. 1987. 'Shixing laodong hetongzhi haochu henduo, wenti bu shao' (There are many Merits and Problems in Implementing the Labor Contract System), *Jingji guanli* (Economic Management), no. 12 (5 December).

Ceng, Bizhong. 1984. 'Lun laodong fuwu gongsi zai laodong jiuye gongzuo zhong de zuoyong' (On the Role of Labour Service Companies in Employment Work), *Jingji wenti tansuo* (Economic Survey), no. 7.

Ceng, Nanjie. 1987. 'Shehui zhuyi laodong li shangpin xingzhi de biran xing ji qi lilun de shijian yiyi' (The Real Theoretical Meaning of the Commodity Nature of Labour), *Jingji wenti tansuo* (Economic Survey), no. 3.

Chan, Anita. 1993. 'Revolution or Corporatism: Workers and Trade Unions in Post Mao China,' *Australian Journal of Chinese Affairs*, no. 29.

— 1996. 'The Changing Ruling Elite and Political Opposition in China,' in Rodan, ed., *Political Opposition in Industrialising Asia*.

— 1997. 'Chinese Danwei Reforms: Convergence with the Japanese Model?,' in Lü and Perry, eds. *Danwei*.

— 1998. 'Labour Relations in Foreign Funded Ventures, Chinese Trade Unions and the Prospects for Collective Bargaining,' in O'Leary, ed., *Adjusting to Capitalism: China's Workers and the State*.

Chan, Anita and Irene Norlund. 1998. 'Vietnamese and Chinese Labour Regimes: on the Road to Divergence,' *The China Journal*, no. 40 (July).

Chan, Cecilia L.W. 1993. *The Myth of Neighborhood Mutual Help: The Contemporary Chinese Community Based Welfare System in Guangzhou.* Hong Kong: Hong Kong University Press.

Chan, Kam Wing. 1999. 'Internal Migration in China: A Dualistic Approach'. In Pieke and Mallee, eds., *Internal and International Migration: Chinese Perspectives.*

Che, Shuquan. 1985. 'A Nationwide Employment Network'. *Ban yue-tan* (Semi-monthly Talks), September 25, translated in JPRS-CEA 86–050.

Cheek, Timothy and Tony Saich, eds. 1997. *New Perspectives on State Socialism in China.* Armonk, N.Y.: M.E. Sharpe.

Chen, Dongqi. 1995. 'Zhongguo de fei gongzi shouru' (Non Wage Income in China), unpublished paper presented at the Beijing Labour Market Conference, August.

Chen, Xiuhua. 1987. 'Laodong li shangpin de jige zhuyao lilun wenti' (Some Major Theoretical Points on the Commodity Nature of Labour), *Jingji wenti tansuo* (Economic Survey), no. 5.

Chen, Zongsheng. 1995. 'Nongcun laodong li de kua quyu zhuangyi' (Cross-regional migration of agricultural labour force). Paper presented at the Beijing Labour Market Conference, August.

Cheng, Tiejun and Mark Selden. 1994. 'The Origins and Social Consequences of China's *Hukou* System,' *The China Quarterly*, no. 139.

Cheng, Xuan. 1990. 'Problems of Urbanization under China's Traditional Economic System,' in: Kwok Parish, Yeh A., Xu, eds., *Chinese Urban Reform: What Model now?*

Chevrier, Yves. 1990. 'Micropolitics and the Factory Director Responsibility System,' in: Davis and Vogel, eds. *Chinese Society on the Eve of Tiananmen.*

Chiang, Chen-Chang [Jiang Zhenzhang]. 1990. 'The Role of Trade Unions in Mainland China,' *Issues and Studies*, no. 2.

Christiansen, Flemming. 1990. 'Social Division and Peasant Mobility in Mainland China: The Implications of the *Hu-k'ou* System,' *Issues and Studies*, no.4.

— 1992. 'Market Transition in China: the Case of Jiangsu Labour Market.' *Modern China*, no. 1 (January).

— 1993. 'The Legacy of the Mock Dual Economy: Chinese Labour in Transition'. *Economy and Society*, no. 4 (November).

— 1996. 'Chinese Labour in Transition 1978–1991: A Case of Institutional Evolution,' in Rodgers, Foti, Lauridsen eds., *The Institutional Approach to Labour and Development.*

Christiansen, Flemming and Klara Foti. 1996. 'Transitions from the Public to the Private: Different Strategies for the Labour Market in Transforming Chinese and Hungarian Economies,' in Rodgers, Foti, Lauridsen eds. *The Institutional Approach to Labour and Development.*

Cook, Sarah and Margaret Maurer-Fazio, eds. 1999. *The Worker's State Meets the Market: Labour in China's Transition*. London: Frank Cass.

Croll, Elizabeth J. 1984. 'Marriage Choice and Status Group in Contemporary China,' in J.L.Watson ed., *Class and Social Stratification in Post Revolutionary China*. Cambridge, Cambridge University Press.

Croll, Elizabeth J. and Huang Ping. 1997. 'Migration For and Against Agriculture in Eight Chinese Villages.' *The China Quarterly*, no. 149 (March).

Dai, Yuanchen. 1994. *Zhongguo laodong li shichang peiyu yu gongzi gaige* (The Growth of a Labour Market and the Reform of Salaries in China). Beijing. Zhongguo Laodong chubanshe.

Dai, Yuanchen and Li Hanming. 1995. 'Zhongguo laodong ziyuan peizhi fangshi de fazhan bianhua' (The Changes and Development of the Modes of Allocation of the Labour Factor in China), unpublished paper presented at the Beijing Labour Market Conference, August.

Davis, Deborah. 1988. 'Unequal Chances, Unequal Outcomes: Pension Reform and Urban Inequalities,' *The China Quarterly*, no. 114.

— 1990. 'Urban Job Mobility,' in Davis and Vogel, eds. *Chinese Society on the Eve of Tiananmen*.

— 1999. 'Self Employment in Shanghai: A Research Note'. *The China Quarterly*, no. 157.

Davis, Deborah, Richard Kraus, Barry Naughton and Elizabeth J.Perry, eds. 1995. *Urban Spaces in Contemporary China*. Melbourne: Woodrow Wilson Center and Cambridge University Press.

Davis, Deborah and Ezra Vogel, eds. 1990. *Chinese Society on the Eve of Tiananmen*. Cambridge, Mass: Harvard University Press.

Day, Lincoln H. and Ma Xia. 1994. *Migration and Urbanization in China*. Armonk, N.Y.: M.E. Sharpe.

Deng, Youping. 1984. 'Laodong li zhi lun' (On Labour Force), *Jingji wenti tansuo* (Economic Survey), no. 2.

Du, Haiyan. 1993. 'Guoyou qiye de jiuye zhidu gaige de lilun sikao,' (Theoretical Thoughts on the Reform of the Employment System in State-Owned Enterprises), *Jingji Yanjiu* (Economic Survey), no. 1 (January).

Emerson, John Philip. 1983. 'Urban School-leavers and Unemployment in China,' *The China Quarterly*, no. 93.

Feng, Lanrui. 1981. *Laodong baochou yu laodong jiuye* (Wages and Employment). Beijing: Zhongguo zhanwang chubanshe.

— 1988. *Anlao fenpei, gongzi, jiuye* (Distribution According to Labour, Salary, Employment). Beijing: Jingji kexue chubanshe.

— 1988b. 'Le chomage chez les jeune en Chine'. *Revue Internationale des Sciences Sociales*, May, no. 116

— 1991. *Lun zhongguo de laodong li shichang* (On China's Labour Market). Beijing: Zhongguo chengshi chubanshe.

— 1991b. 'Comparaison entre les deus grandes vague de chomage en Chine pendant la dernière décennie,' *Revue Internationale des Sciences Sociales*, no. 127.

Feng, Lanrui and Gu Liuzhen. 1987. 'Labor Force Mobility and the Mechanism for Regulating it,' *Renmin ribao* (People's Daily), 2 January, translated in JPRS-CEA 87–015.

Feng, Lanrui and Jiang Weiyu. 1988. *Shehui zhuyi chuji jieduan laodong jiuye wenti yanjiu* (Research on the Question of Employment in the Initial Stage of Socialism). Changsha: Hunan Renmin chubanshe.

Feng, Lanrui and Jiang Weiyu. 1988. 'A Comparative Study of the Modes of Transfer of Surplus Labour in China's Countryside,' *Social Sciences in China*, no. 3.

Feng, Lanrui and Zhao Lükuan. 1981. 'Urban Unemployment in China,' *Selected Writings on Studies of Marxism*, no. 20.

Feng, Lanrui, Zhou Beilong and Su Chongde. 1983. 'On the Relationship Between Employment and Economic Growth,' *Selected Writings on Studies of Marxism*, no. 4.

Feng, Lanrui, Su Shaozhi, Yan Honglin and Wu Jinglian, eds. 1978. *Lun anlao fenpei* (On 'Distribution According to Labour'). Beijing: Beijing renmin chubanshe.

Feng, Tongqing. 1994. *Zhihua zhishou yu jizeng gonghui zhuxi tantan xin* (Speak Without Reservations: Heart to Heart Talks with Grassroots Trade Union Leaders). Beijing: Jingji guanli chubanshe.

Feng, Tongqing and Zhao Minghua, eds. 1996. 'Workers and Trade Unions under the Market Economy: Perspectives from Grassroots Union Cadres,' *Chinese Sociology and Anthropology*, vol. 28, no. 3.

Field, Robert Michael. 1984. 'Changes in Chinese Industry since 1978.' *The China Quarterly*, no. 100.

Gao, Wenhan and Gao Mianhou. 1987. 'Do Labor Markets Exist under Conditions of Socialism? Summary of Recent Discussions'. *Jingjixue zhoubao* (Economics Weekly), 8 March, translated in JPRS-CEA 87–026.

Gipouloux, Francois. 1986. *Les cent fleurs à l'usine: agitation ouvrières et crise du model sovietique en Chine 1956–1957*. Paris: L'École des Haute Etudes.

Gold, Thomas B. 1990. 'Urban Private Business and Social Change,' in Deborah Davis and Ezra Vogel, eds. *Chinese Society on the Eve of Tiananmen*. Cambridge, Mass: Harvard University Press.

Gong, Wei. 1999. *Laodongli waichu jiuye yu nongcun shehui bianqian* (Migrant Labourers and Social Changes in Rural Areas). Beijing: Wenwu chubanshe.

Goodman, Roger, Gordon White and Huck-ju Kwon eds. 1998. *The East Asian Welfare Model: Welfare Orientalism and the State*. London: Routledge.

Granick, David. 1991. 'Multiple Labour Markets in the Industrial State Enterprise Sector,' *The China Quarterly*, no. 126.

Gu, Shengzu. 1991. *Feinong hua yu chengzhen hua yanjiu* (Research on De-Ruralisation and Urbanisation). Hangzhou: Zhejiang renmin chubanshe.

Guo, Daofu. 1986. 'Jichou laodong – shehuizhuyi jiben jingji fanchou' (Labour Remunaration, a Basic Category of Socialist Economy), *Jingji Yanjiu* (Economic Research), no. 6.

Guo, Jun and Li Wenhua. 1994. *Laodong fa yu laodong zhengyi shiyong shouce* (Handbook of Labour Law and Labour Disputes). Beijing: Zhongguo jiancha chubanshe.

Guo, Yuanxi. 1997. *Zhongguo dier zhiye* (China's Second Jobs). Chengdu: Xinan caijing daxue chubanshe.

Guojia jingji tizhi gaige weiyuanhui (State Commission for the Restructuring of the Economic System). 1995. 'Guoyou qiye gaige yu fuyu zhigong fenliu keti diaoyan baogao' (Report of the Research Team on 'Reform of State Enterprises and Surplus Labour Distribution'), unpublished CRES report.

Guojia renshibu liudong diaopei si (Department of Mobility Control of the Department of Personnel).1993. *Zhongguo rencai liudong zhengce fagui daquan* (Collection of Policy Documents on Talent Exchange in China). Beijing: Jingji guanli chubanshe.

Guthrie, Doug. 1999. *Dragon in a Three-Piece Suit: The Emergence of Capitalism in China*. Princeton. Princeton University Press.

Harastzi, Miklos. 1977. *Worker in a Workers' State*. London: Penguin Books.

He, Ganqiang. 1986. 'A Brief Discussion of the Causes and Forms of the Flow of Labor Force,' *Guangming ribao* (Enlightenment Daily), 20 September, translated in JPRS-CEA 86–116.

Hebel, Jutta. 1990. 'Der Betrieb als kleine Gesellschaft: Die Bedeutung des chinesischen Betriebstyps für den Prozess der Reform des Arbeitssystems,' *Soziale Welt*, no. 2.

— 1996. 'Institutional Change in an Enterprise-Based Society and its Impact on Labour: The Case of the People's Republic of China,' In Rodgers, Foti, Lauridsen, eds. *The Institutional Approach to Labour and Development*.

Hebel, Jutta and Günther Schucher. 1991. 'From Unit to Enterprise. The Chinese Tan'wei in the Process of Reform,' *Issues and Studies*, no. 27.

Hebel, Jutta, Günther Schucher. 1992. 'Die Reform der drei Eisernen: Strukturwandel im chinesischen Arbeitssystem'. *Berichte des Bundesinstitut für Ostwissenschaftliche und Internationale Studien*, no. 44.

Henderson, Gail E. and Myron C. Cohen. 1984. *The Chinese Hospital: A Socialist Work Unit*. New Haven: Yale University Press.

Honig, Emily. 1992. *Creating Chinese Ethnicity: Subei People in Shanghai. 1850–1980*. New Haven, Yale University Press.

Honig, Emily. 1996. 'Regional Identity, Labor and Ethnicity in Contemporary China,' in Perry, ed., *Putting Class in its Place: Worker Identities in East Asia.*

Howard, Pat. 1991. 'Rice Bowls and Job Security,' *Australian Journal of Chinese Affairs,* no. 25 (January).

Howard, Pat and Roger Howard. 1995. 'The Campaign to Eliminate Job Security in China,' *Journal of Contemporary Asia,* vol. 25, no. 3.

Howell, Jude. 1990. 'The Impact of China's Open Policy on Labour,' *Labour, Capital and Society,* vol. 23, no. 2 (November).

Hsu, Robert C. 1989. 'Changing Conceptions of the Socialist Enterprise in China, 1979–1988,' *Modern China,* vol. 15, no. 4.

Hu, Qili. 1986. 'Zhengque renshi laodong zhidu de gaige' (Thoroughly Understand the Reform of the Labour System), *Hongqi* (Red Flag), no. 19.

Hu, Zuliu. 1994. 'Social Protection, Labor Market Rigidity, and Enterprise Restructuring in China,' IMF Papers on Policy Analysis and Assessment, 94/22.

Huang, Weiding. 1992 (2nd edition, 1996). *Zhongguo de yinxing jingji* (China's Shadow Economy). Beijing: Zhongguo shangye chubanshe.

Jefferson, Gary H. and Thomas G. Rawsky. 1992. 'Unemployment, Underemployment and Employment Policies in China's Cities,' *Modern China,* no. 1.

Jia, Guancai and Zhou Lijin. 1986. 'Establishing Labor Markets, Improving Labor Management. Meeting held in Beijing to discuss Labor Market Issues,' *Jingjixue zhoubao* (Economics Weekly), 19 January, translated in JPRS-CEA 86–047.

Jiang, Changyun. 1995. *Nongmin jiuye moshi de fenhua yu jingji xingwei* (Differentiation and Economic Behaviour in Peasants' Employment Patterns). Paper presented at the CASS Beijing Labour Market Conference, August.

Jiang, Chenglong. 1987. 'Shehui zhuyi jingji zhong cunzai laodong li chengwei shangpin de tiaojian' (In the Socialist Economy Conditions still Exist for Labour to Become a Commodity), *Zhongguo shehui kexue,* no. 1.

Jin, Bu. 1984. *Laodong li liudong tansuo* (A Survey on Labour Mobility), *Jingji wenti tansuo* (Economic Survey), no. 5

Kahan, Arcadius and Blair A. Ruble. 1979. *Industrial Labour in the USSR.* New York: Pergamon.

Kang, Yonghe. 1987. 'New Understanding of the Question of Wages,' *Jingji ribao* (Economic Daily), 2 June, translated in JPRS-CEA 87–021.

Kaple, Deborah A. 1994. *Dream of a Red Factory: The Legacy of High Stalinism in China.* London: Oxford University Press.

Kornai, Janos. 1980. *Economics of Shortage.* Amsterdam: New Holland.

— 1989. 'The Hungarian Reform Process: Vision, Hopes, and Reality,' in: Nee and Stark, eds. *Remaking the Economic Institutions of socialism: China and Eastern Europe.*

— 1992. *The Socialist system: The Political Economy of Communism,* London: Oxford University Press.

Korzec, Michael. 1992. *Labour and the Failure of Reform in China.* New York: St. Martin Press.

Kwok, R.Yin-Wang, W.L. Parish, Gar-On Yeh and Xu Xueqiang, eds., 1990. *Chinese Urban Reform: What Model now?.* Armonk, N.Y.: M.E. Sharpe.

Laodong bu zhengce fagui si (Policy and Law Department of the Ministry of Labour).1994. *Laodongbu guanyu laodong tizhi gaige zongti shexiang yu jin zhongqi buzhu* (Labour Ministry's General Plan for the Reform of Labour System and Disposition for the Short and Middle Term). Beijing: Zhongguo Laodong Chubanshe.

Laodong bu zhengce fagui si (Policy and Law Department of the Ministry of Labour). 1991. *Zongguo dier zhiye wenti* (The Problem of Double Employment in China). Beijing: Zongguo Laodong chubanshe.

Lardy, Nicholas R. 1989. 'Dilemmas in the Pattern of Resource Allocation in China, 1978–1985,' in Victor Nee and David Stark, eds., *Remaking the Economic Institutions of Socialism: China and Eastern Europe.* Stanford: Stanford University Press.

Lary, Diana. 1997. 'Recycled Labor Systems: Personal Connections in the Recruitment of Labor in China,' in Timothy Brook and Hy V. Luong, eds., *Culture and Economy: The Shaping of Capitalism in Eastern Asia.* Ann Arbor: The University of Michigan Press.

Lee, Ching-Kwan. 1995 'Engendering the World of Labour,' *American Sociological Review,* vol. 60, no. 3 (June).

— 1998. *Gender and the South China Miracle: Two Worlds of Factory Women.* Berkeley: University of California Press.

— 1999. 'From Organized Dependence to Disorganized Despotism: Changing Labour Regimes in Chinese Factories,' *The China Quarterly,* no. 157 (March).

— 2000. 'Pathways of Labour Insurgency,' in Perry and Selden, eds., *Chinese Society: Change, Conflict, and Resistance.*

Lee, Lai To. 1986. *Trade Unions in China, 1949 to the Present.* Singapore: Singapore University Press.

Lee, Peter. 1986. 'Enterprise Autonomy Policy in Post Mao China: A Case Study of Policy Making, 1978–1983,' *The China Quarterly,* no. 105.

— 1991. 'The Chinese Industrial State in Historical Perspective: From Totalitarianism to Corporatism,' in Womack, ed., *Contemporary Chinese Politics in Historical Perspective.*

Lew, Roland. 1986. 'La Chine: un état ouvrier?,' in Claude Aubert, ed. *La societé chinoise après Mao: entre autorité e modernité.* Paris: Fayard.

Li, Baiyong and Yuan Shouqi, eds. 1995. *Laodong fa quanshu* (A Comprehensive Book on Labour Law). Beijing: Yuhang chubanshe.

Li, Hanlin and Wang Qi. 1996. *Research on the Chinese Work-Unit Society*. Frankfurt: Peter Lang Verlag

Li, Hanming. 1995. 'Economic Reform and the Chinese Urban Labor Market: Evidence from a Labour Market Survey,' unpublished paper presented at the Beijing Labour Market Conference, August.

Li, Honglin. 1977. 'Anlao fenpei shi shehui zuyi yuanze haishi ziben zhuyi yuanze?' (Is DATL a Socialist or a Capitalist Principle?), *Renmin ribao* (People's Daily), 27 September.

Li, Jingwen. 1995. *Zou ershiyi shiji de Zhongguo jingji* (The Chinese Economy Towards Tenty-first Century). Beijing: Jingji guanli chubanshe.

Li, Ke. 1987. 'Shilun shehuizhuyi tiaojian xia laodong li cengwei shangpin de biran xing,' (On the Need to Consider Labour as a Commodity under Socialism), *Jingji wenti tansuo* (Economic Survey), no. 4.

Li, Qiang. 1993. *Dangdai Zhongguo shehui fenceng yu liudong* (Stratification and Mobility in Contemporary China). Beijing: Zhongguo jingji chubanshe.

Li, Xiaojiang, Zhu Hong, and Dong Xiuyu.1994. *Xingbie yu zhongguo* (Gender in China). Beijing: Sanlian shudian.

Lin, Nan and Bian Yanjie. 1991. 'Getting Ahead in Urban China,' *American Journal of Sociology*, vol. 97, n.3.

Lin, Nan and Xie Wen. 1988. 'Occupational Prestige in Urban China,' *American Journal of Sociology*, vol. 93, no. 4.

Liu, Alan. 1992. 'The Wenzhou Model of Development and China's Modernization,' *Asian Survey*, vol. 32, no. 8.

Liu, Kejian. 1979. 'Lun anlao fenpei guilü' (On the Law of 'Distribution According to Labour'), in Yu Guangyuan et al., ed., *Guanyu anlao fenpei wenti* (1979).

Liu, Qintang. 1984. 'Laodong zhidu gaige wenti tantao' (On the Problems of Labour System Reform), *Jingji wenti tansuo* (Economic Survey), no. 8.

Liu, Tongde. 1984. 'Qieshi jiejue laodong jiuye zhong de xin wenti' (Thoroughly Solve the New Employment Problems), *Jingji wenti tansuo* (Economic Survey), no. 7.

Liu, Yia-ling. 1992. 'Reform From Below: The Private Economy and Local Politics in the Rural Industrialization of Wenzhou,' *The China Quarterly*, no. 130.

Long, Xianying. 1986. 'Floating of Total Wages in Accordance with Economic Results,' *Jingji guanli* (Economic Management), 5 May, no. 5, translated in JPRS-CEA 86–098.

Lü Xiaobo, Elizabeth Perry, eds. 1997. *Danwei: The Changing Chinese Workplace in Historical and Comparative Perspective*. Armonk, N.Y.: M.E. Sharpe.

Luo, Shouchu. 1986. 'Laodong li liudong he laodong zhidu gaige chuyi' (Initial Analysis of Labour Mobility and the Reform of Labour System), *Zhongguo shehui kexue* (Social Sciences in China), no.5.

Ma, Bin. 1985. 'Ye tan anlao fenpei de lao' (Again on the Meaning of 'Labour' in 'Distribution According to Labour'), *Hongqi* (Red Flag), no. 10.

Ma, Conglin. 1987. 'Dui laodong li shangpin lun ruogan lundian de zhiyi' (Some Theoretical Points on the Theory of Commodity Nature of Labour), *Zhongguo shehui kexue*, no.1.

Ma, Laurence J. C. and Xiang Biao. 1997. 'Native Place, Migration and the Emergence of Peasant Enclaves in Beijing,' *The China Quarterly*, no. 157 (March).

Mallee, Hein. 1995. 'China's Household Registration System under Reform'. *Development and Change*, no. 26.

McCormick, Barrett L. and Jonathan Unger, eds. 1996. *China After Socialism: in the Footsteps of Eastern Europe or East Asia?* Armonk, N.Y.: M.E. Sharpe.

Mao, Lei. 1986. 'All China Federation of Trade Unions Calls for Grasping Firmly the Work of Formulating a New Trade Union Law,' *Renmin ribao* (People's Daily), 14 November, translated in JPRS-CEA 86–126.

Mickler, Otfried. 1992. 'Innovation and the Division of Labour in State-Socialist and Capitalist Enterprise,' in Smith and Thompson, eds., *Labour in Transition: The Labour Process in Eastern Europe and China*.

Morris, Richard. 1985. 'Trade Unions in Contemporary China,' *The Australian Journal of Chinese Affairs*, no.13.

Naughton, Barry. 1995. 'Cities in the Chinese Economic System: Changing Roles and Conditions for Autonomy,' in Davis, et al., eds., *Urban Spaces in Contemporary China*.

— 1995b. *Growing Out of the Plan: Chinese Economic Reform 1978–1983*. Cambridge, Cambridge University Press.

— 1997. 'Danwei: the Economic Foundations of a Unique Institution,' in Lü and Perry, eds. *Danwei*.

Nee, Victor and David Stark eds. 1989. *Remaking the Economic Institutions of Socialism: China and Eastern Europe*. Stanford: Stanford University Press.

Ng, Sek-Hong and Malcolm Warner. 1998. *China's Trade Unions and Management*. London: Macmillan Press.

Ngai, Pun. 1999. 'Becoming 'Dagongmei' (Working Girls): The Politics of Identity and Difference in Reform China,' *The China Journal*, no. 42 (July).

O'Leary, Greg ed. 1998. *Adjusting to Capitalism: China's Workers and the State*. Armonk N.Y.: M.E. Sharpe.

Oded, Shenkar, ed. 1991. *Organization and Management in China, 1979–1990.* Armonk N.Y: M.E. Sharpe.

Oi, Jean C. 1992. 'Rethinking Internal Labour Markets,'. *World Politics,* no. 36.

— 1999. *Rural China Takes Off: Institutional Foundations of Economic Reform.* Berkeley: University of California Press.

Parish, William L. 1981. 'Egalitarianism in Chinese Society,' *Problems of Communism,* no. 30.

Parris, Kristen. 1993. 'Local Initiative and National Reform: the Wenzhou Model of Development,' *The China Quarterly,* no. 134.

Perry, Elizabeth J. 1993. *Shanghai on Strike: The politics of Chinese Labour.* Stanford: Stanford University Press.

— 1994. 'Shanghai's Strike Wave of 1957,' *The China Quarterly,* no. 137.

— 1995. 'Labor's Battle for Political Space: The Role of Worker Associations in Contemporary China,' in Davis, et al., eds. *Urban Spaces in Contemporary China.*

— ed. 1996. *Putting Class in its Place: Worker Identities in East Asia.* Berkeley: University of California, Institute of East Asian Studies.

— 1997. 'From Native Place to Workplace: Labor Origins and Outcomes of China's Danwei System,' in Lü and Perry, eds. *Danwei: the Changing Chinese Workplace in Historical and Comparative Perspective.*

Perry, Elizabeth J. and Mark Selden, eds. 2000. *Chinese Society: Change, Conflict and Resistance.* London: Routledge.

Pieke, Frank and Hein Mallee, eds. 1999. *Internal and International Migration: Chinese Perspectives.* London: Curzon Press.

Pyke, Frank, Giacomo Becattini, and Werner Sengenberger. 1990. *Industrial Districts and Inter-firm Co-operation in Italy.* Geneva: International Institute for Labour Studies.

Qian, Jin. 1994. *Laodong lun* (On Labour). Beijing: Qiye guanli chuban-she.

Qian, Shiming. 1986. 'Discussion of the Pros and Cons of the Enterprise Wage Reform' *Jingjixue zhoubao* (Economics Weekly), 15 December, translated in JPRS-CEA 86–66.

Renmin ribao teyue pinglun yuan (People's Daily Special Commentator). 1978. 'Guanche zhixing anlao fenpei de shehui zhuyi yuanze' (Carry on the Socialist Principle of Distribution According to Labor), *Renmin ribao* (People's Daily), 5 May.

Rodan, Garry, ed. 1996 *Political Opposition in Industrialising Asia.* London: Routledge.

Rodgers, Gerry, Klara Foti, and Laurids Lauridsen, eds. 1996. *The Institutional Approach to Labour and Development.* London: Frank Cass.

Ruan, D.Q. 1993. 'Interpersonal Networks and Workplace Control in Urban China,' *Australian Journal of Chinese Affairs,* no. 29.

Sabin, Lora. 1994. 'New Bosses in the Workers' State: The Growth of Non-State Sector Employment in China,' *The China Quarterly*, n. 140.

— 1995. *The development of Urban Labor Markets in China*. Ann Arbor, University Microforms International.

Saich, Tony. 1990. 'The Rise and Fall of Beijing People's Movement,' *Australian Journal of Chinese Affairs*, no. 24 (July).

— 2000. 'Negotiating the State: The Development of Social Organizations in China,' *The China Quarterly*, no. 161 (March).

Sargeson, Sally. 1999. *Reworking China's Proletariat*. London: Macmillan Press.

Scharping, Thomas. 1997. *Floating Population and Migration in China*. Hamburg: Institut für Asienkunde.

Sha, Jicai. 1994. *Gaige kaifang zhong de renkou wenti yanjiu* (On Population Problems During the Reform and Open-Door Policy Period). Beijing: Beijing daxue chubanshe.

Shang, Dewen. 1993. *Zhongguo shehui zhuyi shichang jingji tixi* (The Chinese Socialist Market Economy). Jinan: Shandong renmin chubanshe.

Sheehan, Jackie. 1998. *Chinese Workers: A New History*. London: Routledge.

Shen, Qinqin. 1995. 'Lun jiuye zhidao dui shengchan li fazhan de zujin zuoyong' (On the Positive Effects of Guided Employment on the Development of Productive Forces), *Gonghui lilun yu shixian*, no. 1.

Siu, Helen F. 1990. 'The Politics of Migration in a Market Town,' in Davis and Vogel, eds., *Chinese Society on the Eve of Tiananmen*.

Smith, Chris and Paul Thompson. 1992. *Labour in Transition: The Labour Process in Eastern Europe and China*. London: Routledge.

Solinger, Dorothy J. 1985. "Temporary Residence Certificate' Regulations in Wuhan, May 1983'. *The China Quarterly*, n. 101

— 1995. 'The Floating Population in the Cities: Chances for Assimilation?'. In Davis, et al., eds., *Urban Spaces in Contemporary China*.

— 1997. 'The Impact of the Floating Population on the Danwei: Shifts in Patterns of Labor Mobility Control and Entitlement Provision,' in Lü, and Perry, eds. *Danwei: The Changing Chinese Workplace in Historical and Comparative Perspective*.

— 1999. *Contesting Citizenship in Urban China: Peasant Migrants, the State and the Logic of the Market*. Berkeley: University of California Press.

Stark, David. 1986. 'Rethinking Internal Labour Markets: New Insights from a Comparative Perspective'. *American Sociological Review*, n. 51, August.

— 1992. 'Bending the Bars of the Iron Cage: Bureaucratisation and Informalisation in Capitalism and Socialism,' in Smith and Thompson, eds. *Labour in Transition: The Labour Process in Eastern Europe and China*.

Stark, David and Victor Nee. 1989. 'Toward an Institutional Analysis of State Socialism,' in Stark and Nee, eds., *Remaking the Economic Institutions of Socialism: China and Eastern Europe*.

Su, Linyou and Lincoln H. Day. 1994. 'The Economic Adjustment of Migrants in Urban Areas,' in Day and Ma Xia eds. *Migration and Urbanization in China*.

Su, Shaozhi. 1977. 'Anlao fenpei shi you liangzhong shehui zhuyi gongyou zhi jueding de ma?' (Is Distribution According to Labor Decided by a System of Double Socialist Ownership?), *Guangming ribao* (Enlightenment Daily), 20 June.

Su Shaozhi and Feng Lanrui. 1977. 'Bo Yao Wenyuan anlao fenpei chansheng zichan jieji de miulun'. (Confute the Wrong Assumption of Yao Wenyuan that 'Distribution According to Labor' Gives Birth to a Bourgeois Class), *Renmin ribao* (People's Daily), 9 August.

Sun, Xiaoli. 1992. *Laodong gaizao xing lun* (On Reform Through Labour). Beijing: Zhongguo renmin gong'an daxue chubanshe.

Takahara, Akio. 1992. *The Politics of Wage Policy in Post-revolutionary China*. London: Macmillan Press.

Tan, Shen. 1994. 'Dangdai zhongguo zhiye funu: you zhengfu anzhi gongzuo huo jinru laodong li shichang' (Women Workers in Contemporary China: Accept Assignment by the State or Enter the Labour Market], in Li Xiaojiang, Zhu Hong and Dong Xiuyu, eds., *Xingbie yu zhongguo* (Gender and China). Beijing: Sanlian shudian.

Thompson, Paul. 1992. 'Disorganized Socialism: State and Enterprise in *Modern China*,' in Smith and Thompson, eds. *Labour in Transition: The Labour Process in Eastern Europe and China*.

— 1989. *The Nature of Work: an Introduction to Debates on the Labour Process*. London: Macmillan Press.

Thompson, Paul and Chris Smith. 1992. 'Socialism and the Labour Process in Theory and Practice,' in Smith and Thompson, eds., *Labour in Transition: The Labour Process in Eastern Europe and China*.

Tilly, Charles. 1978. *From Mobilization to Revolution*. Reading, Mass.: Addison Wesley.

Tomba, Luigi. 1994. 'Operai in un paese di contadini: un caso di conflittualità operaia nella Cina contemporanea,' *Società e storia*, no 63.

— 1999. 'Exporting the Wenzhou Model to Beijing and Florence: Labour and Economic Organisation in Two Migrant Communities,' in Pieke and Mallee, eds. *Internal and International Migration: Chinese Perspectives*.

— 1999. 'La riforma del mercato del lavoro nella Cina Contemporanea: nuova legislazione e 'Informalizzazione,'' *Rivista Italiana di diritto del lavoro*, vol. 18, no. 1.

Walder, Andrew G. 1979. 'Industrial Organization and Socialist Development in China,' *Modern China*, no. 2.

— 1983. 'Organized Dependency and Cultures of Authority in Chinese Industry,' *Journal of Asian Studies*, vol. 43, no. 1.

— 1984. 'The Remaking of the Chinese Working Class, 1949–1981,' *Modern China*, vol. 10, no. 1.

— 1986. *Communist Neo-Traditionalism: Work and Authority in Chinese Industry*. Berkeley: University of California Press.

— 1987. 'Wage Reform and the Web of Factory Interests,' *The China Quarterly*, no. 109.

— 1989. 'Factory and Manager in an Era of Reform,' *The China Quarterly*, no. 118.

— 1989b. 'Social Change in Post-Revolution China,' *Annual Review of Sociology* vol. 15.

— 1989c. 'The Political Sociology of the Beijing Upheaval of 1989,' *Problems of Communism*, vol. 38, no. 5 (September–October).

— 1991. 'Workers, Managers, and the State: The Reform Era and the Political Crisis of 1989.' *The China Quarterly*, no. 127.

— 1992. 'Property Rights and Stratification in Socialist Redistributive Economies,'. *American Sociological Review*, August, vol. 57, no. 4.

— 1992b. *Popular Protest in the 1989 Democracy Movement*. Hong Kong: Institute of Asia Pacific, USC Seminar Series, no. 8.

— 1996. 'The Chinese Cultural Revolution in the Factory: Party-State Structures and the Pattern of Conflict,' in Perry, ed., *Putting Class in its Place: Workers Identities in East Asia*.

Walder, Andrew. G. and Gong Xiaoxia. 1993. 'Workers in the Tian'anmen Protest,' *Australian Journal of Chinese Affairs*, no. 29.

Wan, Guanghua. 1995. 'Peasant Flood in China: Internal Migration and its Policy Determinants,' *Third World Quarterly*, vol. 16, no. 2.

Wang, Chengying. 1998. *Zhongguo zai jiuye* (Re-employment in China). Chengdu: Sichuan daxue chubanshe.

Wang, Dahai. 1998. *Shiye de zhongguo* (China Unemployed). Beijing: *Jingji ribao* chubanshe.

Wang, Fei-Ling. 1998. *From Family to Market: Labor Allocation in Contemporary China*. Lanham: Rowman and Littlefield.

Wang, Haibo, Zhou Shulian, and Wu Jinglian. 1978. 'Anlao fenpei bu shi chansheng zichan jieji de jingji jichu' ('Distribution According to Labour' is not the Economic Foundation for the Creation of a Bourgeoisie), *Jingji Yanjiu* (Economic Research), no. 1.

Wang, Jue and Xiao Xin. 1986. 'More on the Labor Resources Market. A Reply to Comrade Han Zhiguo,' *Guangming ribao* (Enlightenment daily), 26 November, translated in JPRS-CEA 87–005.

Wang, Xi and Tu En [James A. Dorn], eds. 1994. *Zhongguo jingji gaige: wenti yu qianjing* (Economic Reform in China: Problems and Prospects). Shanghai: Fudan daxue chubanshe.

Wang, Yiying et al., eds. 1994. *Zhongguo laodong fa shiwu* (The Interpretation of China's Labour Law). Beijing: Jinri Zhongguo chubanshe.

Wei, Ming. 1987. *Woguo xian jieduan bixu rang laodong li caiqu shangpin de xingshi heli liudong* (At the Present Stage China Should Allow

Labour to Float as a Commodity), *Jingji wenti tansuo*, (Economic Survey), no. 3.

Wei, Xinghua. 1986. 'A Brief Comment on the Theory that Socialist Labor is a Commodity,' *Guangming ribao* (Enlightenment Daily), 27 September, translated in JPRS-CEA 86–118.

— 1987. 'Shehui zhuyi laodong li shangpin lun bu neng chengli' (The Theory of the Commodity Nature of Labour is Groundless), *Zhongguo shehui kexue* (Social Sciences in China), no. 1.

White, Gordon. 1987. 'The Politics of Economic Reform in Chinese Industry: the Introduction of the Labour Contract System,' *The China Quarterly*, no. 111.

— 1987b. 'The Changing Role of the Chinese State in Labour Allocation: Towards the Market,' *Journal of Communist Studies*, vol. 3, no. 2.

— 1988. 'State and Market in China's Labour Reform,' *The Journal of Development Studies*, no. 4

— 1993. 'Prospects for a Civil Society in China: a Case Study of Xiaoshan City,' *Australian Journal of Chinese Affairs*, no. 29.

— 1998. 'Social Security Reform in China: Toward an East asian Model?,' in Goodman, White, and Kwon, eds., *The East Asian Welfare Model: Welfare Orientalism and the State.*

Whyte, Martin King. 1989. 'Who Hates Bureaucracy? A Chinese Puzzle,' in Nee and Stark, eds., *Remaking the Economic Institutions of socialism: China and Eastern Europe.*

Whyte, Martin King and William Parish. 1984. *Urban Life in contemporary China.* Chicago: University of Chicago Press.

Womack, Brantly, ed. 1991. *Contemporary Chinese Politics in Historical Perspective.* Cambridge: Cambridge University Press.

Wu, Xiaoying Harry. 1994. 'Rural to Urban Migration in the People's Republic of China,' *The China Quarterly*, no. 139.

Xia, Jizhi and Zhu Hong. 1995. *Woguo jiuye wenti yanjiu* (On China's Employment Problem), unpublished paper presented at the Beijing Labour Market Conference, August.

Xiang, Biao. 1993. 'Beijing you ge 'zhejiang cun" (There is a Zhejiang Village in Beijing). *Shehui xue yu shehui diaocha* (Sociology and Social Surveys), no. 3–4–5.

— 1996 'Liudong, chuantong wanluo shichanghua yu 'fei guojia kongjian' (Mobility, Marketisation of Traditional Networks, and the 'Nonstate Space'), in Zhang Jing, *Guojia yu shehui.*

— 1999. 'Zhejiang Village in Beijing: Creating a Visible Nonstate Space through Migration and Marketized Networks,' in Pieke and Mallee, eds., *Internal and International Migration: Chinese Perspectives.*

Xiao, Yin. 1986. 'How to Implement Reform in the Labor System,' *Jingji Daobao* (Economic Herald), 1 October, translated in JPRS-CEA 86–124.

Xu, Haibo. 1987. 'Popularization of the Labour Contract System not Advisable,' *Zhong qingnian jingji luntan* (Forum of Young Economists), 10 January, translated in JPRS-CEA 87–27.

Xu, Xiaoju, ed. 1986. 'Combine Wage System Reform with the Perfection of the Economic Responsibility System,' *Jingji guanli* (Economic Management), 5 May, no.5, translated in JPRS-CEA 86–097.

Yang, Shaomin and Zhou Yihu. 1999. *Zhongguo danwei zhidu* (China's Work-unit System). Beijing: Zhongguo jingji chubanshe.

Yang, Yunyan. 1994. *Zhongguo renkou qianyi yu fazhan de changqi zhanlüe* (Internal Migration and Long Term Development Strategy in China). Wuhan: Wuhan chubanshe.

Yi, Shijie, et al. 1979. 'Anlao fenpei guilü de zhuyao tedian he yaoqiu' (Main Features and Needs for the Principle of DATL), in Yu Guangyuan et al., *Guanyu anlao fenpei wenti* (1979).

Yu, Guangyuan. 1998. *Zhongguo shehuizhuyi chuji jieduan de Jingji* (The Economy at the Initial Phase of Socialism in China). Guangzhou: Guangdong Jingji Chubanshe.

Yu, Guangyuan, et al. 1979. *Guanyu anlao fenpei wenti* (1979) (On the Principle of 'Distribution according to labour'). Beijing: Sanlian shudian.

Yuan, Victor [Yuan Yue] and Xin Wong [Wang Xin]. 1999. 'Migrant Construction Teams in Beijing,' in Pieke and Mallee, eds. *Internal and International Migration: Chinese Perspectives.*

Yuan, Yue, Wang Xin and Zhang Shouli. 1996. 'Luoren: Beijing liumin de zuzhihua zhuangkuang yanjiu baogao' (Naked: A Research Report on the Organisation of Beijing Migrants). Beijing: Horizon Research Group, Unpublished paper.

— 1996b. 'Beijing wailai renkou zhong de quanwei' (The Leadership Among Migrants in Beijing). Beijing: Horizon Research Group, unpublished paper.

— 1996c. 'Beijing de wailai jianzhu baogongdui' (The Migrant Labour Construction Teams in Beijing]. Beijing: Horizon Research Group, unpublished paper.

Zafanolli, Wojtek. 1986. 'De la main visible a la main fantôme: la réforme chinoise a l'épreuve de l'economie parallele,' *Revue Tièrs Monde*, vol. 27, no. 108 (October–December).

Zhan, Su. 1993. 'Essai sur les causes de l'"informalisation' des pétites activités marchandise en Chine,' *Revue Tièrs Monde*, vol. 34, no. 135 (July–September).

Zhang, Huzun et al. 1979. 'Nuli chuanzao tiaojian wei anlao fenpei guilü kaipi guangkuo de zuoyong changsuo' (Actively Build the Conditions for the Application of 'Distribution According To Labour'), in Yu Guangyuan, et al. *Guanyu anlao fenpei wenti* (1979).

Zhang, Jing, ed. 1998. *Guojia yu shehui* (State and Society). Hangzhou: Zhejiang Renmin chubanshe.

Zhang, Yide. 1986. 'Kaifang laodong li shichang yu laodong li guanli tizhi gaige' (The Opening Up of a Labour Force Market and the Reform of Labour Force Management), *Jingji wenti tansuo* (Economic Survey), n. 1.

Zhao, Lükuan. 1985. 'Paper Views Functions of Wages in Socialism,' *Jingjixue zhoubao* (Economics Weekly), 15 December, translated in JPRS-CEA 86–046.

Zhao, Lükuan and Yang Tiren. 1986. 'Is it a Labor Force Market or an Animate Labor Market?,' *Guangming ribao* (Enlightenment Daily), 23 August, translated in JPRS-CEA 86–046.

Zhao, Minghua and Theo Nichols. 1996. 'Management Control of Labour in State Owned Enterprises: Cases from the Textile Industry,' *The China Journal*, no. 3 (July).

Zhao, Shukai. 1998. *Zongheng Chengxiang: nongmin liudong de guancha yu yanjiu* (Between City and Countryside: Observation and Research on the Peasant Floating Population). Beijing: Zhongguo nongye chubanshe.

Zheng, Li. 1982. 'Zhongguo laodong xuehui shoujie nianhui taolun qingkuang jianjie' (The Yearly Meeting of the Labour Research Association Discusses the Present Situation), *Jingji Yanjiu*, no. 5.

Zhong, Jiyin. 1995. *Zhongguo zhigong de zaizhi shiye yu dier zhiye xingwei: yizhong guodu jingji zhong de zhiye tizhi xianxiang fenxi* (On-the-job Unemployment and Second Jobs: An Analysis of the Employment System in the Transitional Economy), unpublished paper presented at the Beijing Labour Market Conference, August.

Zhongguo kexueyuan guoqing fenxi yanjiu xiaozu (Chinese Academy of Science, Research Group on National Analysis). 1998. *Jiuye yu fazhan: zhongguo jiuye wenti yu jiuye zhanlüe* (Employment and Development: China's Employment Problem and Employment Strategies). Shenyang: Liaoning renmin chubanshe.

Zhongguo zhengzhi jingjixue shehui zhuyi bufen yanjiuhui xueshu zu (Study Group on Socialism, Society for the Study of Political Economy). 1984. *Guanyu anlao fenpei wenti* (1984) (On the Principle of 'Distribution according to labour' 1984). Beijing: Renmin chubanshe.

Zhou, Min and John R. Logan. 1996. 'Market Transition and the Commodification of Housing in Urban China,' *International Journal of Urban and Regional Research*, vol. 22, no. 3.

Zhou, Wenfu. 1987. 'Guanyu chuantong de shehui zhuyi laodong li fei shangpin lun de lilun fansi,' (Against the Traditional Theory that Socialist Labour is not a Commodity), *Jingji wenti tansuo* (Economic Survey), no. 2.

Zhou, Xiao Kate. 1996. *How Farmers Changed China. The Power of the People*. Boulder, Co.: Westview Press.

Zhu, Bin. 1985, 'On the Macro-Control and Adjustment of Wages,' *Jingjixue zhoubao* (Economics Weekly), 15 December, translated in JPRS-CEA 86–66.

Zhu, Jianfang, et al. 1995. *Zhongguo laodong li shichang peiyu yu gongzi gaige (tongji baogao)* (Labour Force Market and Wage Reform – Statistical Report) Paper presented at the Beijing Labour Market Conference, August.

Zhu, Wenzhou and Wang Faxing. 1999. *Laodong hetong zhizuo ji wenben fanshi* (The System of Labour Contract and Model Forms). Beijing, Falü Chubanshe.

Zhu, Xuemu, ed. 1993. *Zhongguo da chengshi laodong jiuye yu chengshi fazhan* (Employment in Chinese Large Cities and Urban Development). Beijing: Zhongguo laodong chubanshe.

Zhuang, Qidong and Sun Keliang. 1984. 'Gongye jiuye yu gongye jigou' (Industrial Employment and Industrial Plants), *Jingji wenti tansuo* (Economic Survey), n.11.

Zou, Lanchun. 1996. *Beijing de liudong renkou* (Beijing's Floating Population). Beijing: Zhongguo Renkou Chubanshe.

Zuigao renmin fayuan (The Highest People's Court). 1994. *Laodong zhengyi shenpang shouce* (A Handbook of Labour Disputes). Beijing: Falü chubanshe.

INDEX

239